BIG MEDIA, LITTLE MEDIA

PEOPLE AND COMMUNICATION

Series Editors: **F. GERALD KLINE** *Department of Journalism*
PETER CLARKE *University of Michigan*

Volumes in this series:

Volume 1: How Children Learn to Buy: The Development of Consumer Information-Processing Skills
SCOTT WARD, DANIEL B. WACKMAN, ELLEN WARTELLA

Volume 2: Big Media, Little Media: Tools and Technologies for Instruction
WILBUR SCHRAMM

Volume 3: The Costs of Educational Media: Guidelines for Planning and Evaluation
DEAN JAMISON, STEVEN J. KLEES, STUART J. WELLS

big media media
little media

Tools and Technologies for Instruction

WILBUR SCHRAMM

 SAGE Publications   Beverly Hills   London

Copyright © 1977 by Sage Publications, Inc.

For information address:

SAGE PUBLICATIONS, INC.
275 South Beverly Drive
Beverly Hills, California 90212

SAGE PUBLICATIONS LTD
St George's House / 44 Hatton Garden
London EC1N 8ER

Printed in the United States of America

Library of Congress Cataloging in Publication Data

Schramm, Wilbur Lang, 1907-
    Big media, little media.

    (People and communication; 2)
    Bibliography: p. 279
    Includes index.
    1. Educational technology. 2. Media programs
(Education) I. Title.
LB1028.3.S37   371.3'078   76-30522
ISBN 0-8039-0740-0
ISBN 0-8039-0745-1 pbk.

FIRST PRINTING

CONTENTS

Acknowledgments   9

1. Agenda   11

2. The Experimental Evidence   25

3. The Pedagogical Evidence   59

4. The Economic Evidence   105

5. Evidence from the Field:National Educational Reform Projects   141

6. Evidence from the Field: Media to Supplement the School   175

7. Evidence from the Field: Extending the School   197

8. Evidence from the Field: Nonformal Education   225

9. Some Conclusions   261

Bibliography   279

Subject Index   297

Name Index   307

About the Author   315

BIG MEDIA, LITTLE MEDIA

ACKNOWLEDGMENTS

Many people have helped with this book—so many that I cannot possibly name them. High on the list, however, would be my colleagues and students at Stanford and the East-West Center, and the scholars and educational organizations throughout the world who have generously shared with me their advice, their findings, and their experience.

For permission to reproduce or to quote I must specially thank Dr. Sidney B. Tickton, of the Academy for Educational Development, who allowed us to reproduce material from the report of the Commission on Educational Developement, which he edited; The Rand Corporation, of Santa Monica, and Educational Technology Publications, for permitting us to reproduce the charts by Rudy Bretz; Dr. David Hawkridge, of the Open University of Great Britain, for letting us quote sections from his landmark report on programmed learning in Africa; Drs. John Tiffin and Peter Combes, of the Multinational Project on Educational Technology, in Recife, Brazil, and Mexico City, respectively; and the Silver Burdett Company for consenting to our reproduction of the charts originally made by the General Learning Corporation.

The U.S. Agency for International Development provided me the opportunity to write a first version of this volume three years ago, and the Ford Foundation made me the most precious gift a scholar can receive— the gift of free time to think and write—resulting, among other things, in this manuscript. To what is good and useful in the following pages, these people and organizations have contributed greatly. For what is less good and less useful than it could be, I am alone responsible, although I have been abetted by a long line of scholars who (like me) have neglected to work upon some of the problems that, it is now clear, need to be studied. Ten years from now, I am confident, a much better book can be written on this topic. Meanwhile, I hope that what we have to say in 1977 will be useful.

—W.S.

CHAPTER 1

AGENDA

[The goal is to make it possible] for the teacher to teach less and the learner to learn more.

Sir Eric Lord Ashby
Master of Clare College,
Cambridge

This book is about the media of instruction.

By these we mean simply the media of communication used for teaching and learning. Only the *use* is different. Instructional television comes out of the same box that provides family entertainment and professional football; instructional radio, from the same sound system that offers news bulletins, talk shows, and popular music; instructional films, from the same photographic process that makes and projects theatre and home movies. The computers used for computer-assisted instruction are the same kind that set our type, keep our bank statements, and plot the paths of our space ships. And these uses of the media tend to merge. A good teacher, on or off media, includes some entertainment with his or her instruction. A school child learns a great deal at home from entertainment media, whether intended or not. Therefore, when we speak of *instructional* or *educational* media, we merely give notice that for the moment we are working on the educational end of the media spectrum which extends from entertainment through information to instruction.

The origin of media of instruction is lost in the haze of pre-history. So far as we know, there has always been instructional technology. The cave dwellers had stone edges for demonstrating and practicing the skills of cutting and shaping, bone needles for demonstrating and practicing the skill of sewing, small bows and arrows for demonstrating and practicing the skills of hunting. Even today, in some countries, we can see a patch of sand used, as sand must have been used millennia ago, for practicing drawing and counting. And the ancient technology of the slate still exists in our schools in the form of chalkboards.

The first instructional medium of modern times was print. It did the scribe's job, but multiplied his pen. Print shared the ideas of great thinkers and the strategies of teachers. Without it, no country would have dared contemplate the possibilities either of trying to achieve a literate population or of universal public education. The textbook, reference book, and workbook have been so fully accepted as part of education that they are neither questioned nor often made the subject of research—which is a pity, because they could be improved. But print at least demonstrates that the mass media *can* contribute to instruction, they *can* bring learning opportunities to far more people and at a far higher level than would be otherwise possible, and they can do that without unacceptably challenging vested interests.

Print, therefore, we take for granted. The "instructional media" we talk most about today are the electronic and photographic media that came into use in the nineteenth and twentieth centuries: photographs, slides, films, recordings, radio, television, computers. Like print these are not specially designed for instruction; they are simply information-carrying technologies that *can be used* for instruction. They have always held out, in their different ways, the bright hope of delivering educational information and experiences widely, quickly, vividly, with a realism and immediacy that print could hardly match. They can bring experience without clothing it in the abstractions of printed language; as McLuhan said, words can describe a bucket, but it is very hard to tell anyone exactly what a bucket looks like without a picture.

The media of instruction, consequently, are extensions of the teacher. A teacher writes the textbook. A teacher programs the computer for instruction, or at least specifies how it should be programmed. Behind an educational television program or a teaching film there may be a whole team of teachers, producers, camera operators, and the like. The "teacher" is not necessarily a member of the staff in a school, college, or university. The first teachers most children meet are their parents. A teacher may be a field worker in an economic and social development program. He may be a professional film maker or television producer who, through experience and insight, has learned how to make programs for learners. Whoever the teacher, he makes some use of media to extend learning opportunities.

The instructional media have bulked larger in the educational process in recent decades. During the last twenty years, in the United States alone (where the size of the educational system has been relatively stable compared to education in many developing countries), the number of textbooks commercially available to schools has increased by 200 percent, the number of 16mm films by 600 percent, discs by 700 percent, and filmstrips by 800 percent (for these figures, see Komoski, 1974). In the early 1950s it was very difficult for schools to buy audiotapes and cassettes, videotapes and videocassettes, overhead projected transparencies, 8mm filmloops, and educational games and simulations. Currently, to illustrate what has happened, there are in the United States more than 200 commercial producers and distributors each of overhead transparencies and 8mm films, more than 100 of videotapes and cassettes, and nearly 300 of audiotapes and cassettes.

We must not forget that almost all teaching is *multimedia*. The name is new and fashionable, but the practice is ancient. The caveman teaching his son to hunt, used not only words but also demonstration and practice. Even in the most isolated, impoverished school, the teacher will seek an additional medium of instruction beside what he or she can say to the students: a slate or (in our own time) a picture from a magazine. Comenius wrote the first illustrated printed textbook about 325 years ago, as Piaget pointed out in his brilliant introduction to the UNESCO commemorative volume on Comenius, and it is even more fascinating to reflect that there were already printed textbooks three centuries ago; in the intervening time they have spread through all the schools of the world and become a part of almost all formal learning. When we compare "media" teaching today with "face-to-face" teaching we are actually, in most cases, comparing one medium with multimedia—that is, with an active teacher plus textbook plus much more.

The problem of how to combine media in the art of teaching has therefore been with us for a very long time. The difference today is that media are so much more readily available than they previously were for instructional use, and many of them are expensive and elaborate tools over which the classroom teacher has less control than over a slate or a chalkboard or a picture clipped from a magazine.

During the last few decades we have frittered away an enormous amount of research time asking relatively useless questions about the media of instruction. *Can the media teach?* has been asked over and over again, and over and over again the answer has come back: *of course,* students can learn effectively from the media, from *any* medium. *Can they teach as well as a teacher?* The answer: what they can do, they can do as well as a classroom teacher, sometimes better. It depends on the performance of the teacher, the content of the media, what is being taught, and to whom. *Is one medium any more effective than others?* For some purposes, probably yes, but overall there is no superlative medium of instruction, any more than there is one simple algorithm for selecting one medium over others. We have come to realize in recent decades that learning from the media is not an area that lends itself to simple answers. It is an extremely complex multivariate process that challenges us, if we are to understand it, not to ask the simple questions, but rather to concern ourselves with the conditions for selecting one medium over another, for combining and for using media.

"Sometime in the 1960s," David Hawkridge wrote recently (Hawkridge, n.d.), "people writing about the systems approach to education and what an ideal educational system would look like began to insert in their flow-diagrams a box that said 'Select media' or something equivalent." David Hawkridge has a special reason to be concerned with the choice of media for teaching because he is director of an institute of educational technology at one of the leading multimedia teaching institutions of the world, the British Open University. He noted that he himself was among the writers who had inserted the box, "Select media," in the flow of specifying objectives, acts of learning, and so forth. Ruefully he admitted: "I am not suggesting that we were all wrong, but I do think we underestimated the contents of that box!"

This has proved painfully true. Not only is existing theory inadequate to "Select media," but even if it were more nearly adequate it would still have to operate in a most complicated situation. Suppose we were now able, on the basis of research and analysis, to dissect learning tasks into activities that were matchable to media, and could confidently say what medium would be most helpful for each: still it might well be beyond the practical capabilities of any teacher, school, or classroom to assemble these media when needed and to change from one to another. We shall discuss some of these practical problems in Chapter 2. But other considerations also must be loaded into the decision. One of these is cost: what will it cost to buy the learning effectiveness we want? For example, even if sound film were clearly the best choice at a given point in a class period, but a handful of slides, at perhaps one-fiftieth the cost of the film, were also a possibility, how much would be lost by using the less expensive medium? What is the relative cost-effectiveness of the two media for the intended purpose?

Thus the process of selection is a complex and difficult one asking for better theory than we actually have, for a gathering and analysis of experience, and for an examination of the economic and administrative aspects of the choice. The corner where the media intersect education is a location where every informed passerby moves cautiously. And it should be described less as a streetcorner than as a point on the ocean directly above one of the deeps. In years to come, let us hope, more sophisticated research will tell us what lies below, but for the time being it behooves any educator or media expert to be humble about putting forth elaborate guidelines.

This is where we now are in the study of the media of instruction. Instead of continuing to ask grand and no longer very useful questions (Can media teach? What is the best medium?) we should be well advised to ask the smaller, sharper questions (*How* can we best use a given medium for a given act of instruction? In a given situation what medium is more cost-effective than another? How do the symbolic coding systems of a given medium relate to what a student learns from it?). And at the present time in particular, if we want to make a practical contribution with media research, we can well try to illuminate the dark, confused area in which the selection of media for instruction takes place.

WHY IS IT SO IMPORTANT TO UNDERSTAND MEDIA SELECTION?

This is a priority topic. Perhaps we can make the reasons clear by returning to the title of this volume, *Big Media, Little Media.* Some Big

Media, of course, are considerably bigger than others, and some of the Little ones much smaller than others. By the Big Media, we mean the complex, expensive media like television, sound films, and computer-assisted instruction. By the Little Media, we mean the simpler ones, which stretch all the way from slides, slide films, and projected transparencies to radio and programmed texts. The unit cost of radio is in the neighborhood of one-fifth that of television, and the decision to introduce television into a school system or a developing area is therefore of a considerably different order from the decision to introduce radio. The complexity of sound films is of an entirely different order from that of slides. The unit costs of computer-assisted instruction are presently even higher than those of television, and the decision to use it therefore requires special considerations that are not present when one decides to make some transparencies for illustrating a lecture or to use radio to supplement one's own teaching. This is all we have in mind in distinguishing "Big" from "Little" along a scale that is obviously continuous rather than dichotomous.

The Big Media have been the glamor boys of the field. They have chiefly attracted the attention of non-educators to instructional media. Instructional films were the first of these media to offer audiovisual experiences of high excellence to classrooms and itinerant teachers. Television, when it became available, proved able to deliver comparable audiovisual experience to many classrooms simultaneously, with an ease that films could not match. Instructional television could not only transport a gifted teacher to learners, but could also bring with that teacher more elaborate illustrative materials than any classroom teacher could possibly have at hand. Computer-assisted instruction could program a machine to perform like a teacher—a teacher that never showed the effects of a headache, never became impatient, and was always ready to provide tutorial experiences when a student needed them. Therefore, teaching machines aroused the hopes that Sir Eric Ashby expressed (significantly in almost the words Comenius had used three centuries earlier): that as a result of the new pedagogy, "the work of the teacher will be lightened . . . all scholars will be taught and none neglected . . . scholars will attend better . . . [it will be necessary to] send children to school for as few hours as possible" (see Comenius, in UNESCO selections, 1957: 69). In other words, he expressed the hope that education will become more productive.

"Productive" is a magic word in our time, and education is constantly being challenged with it.

To a certain extent this has always been so. As long as education has been a wide public concern, taxpayers have asked why it costs so much, and parents have asked why their children do not learn more. But in the eighth decade of the twentieth century these questions have taken on an urgent and demanding quality they have never had before.

In relatively rich countries like the United States, higher education is coming close to being considered a right, rather than a privilege; ten million students are registered in American colleges and universities. Within a decade or two, lifelong education, or at least periodic retraining, is likely to be considered not only a right, but a necessity.

In the developing regions of the world, already more than a quarter of a billion students are in school, and this number represents far fewer than the felt needs of these countries. Already many developing countries are spending more than 25 percent of their budgets on education and are searching for relief. And today both the richer and the poorer countries are walking on the economic quicksand of the 1970s.

Therefore it is more than an *academic* question when critics ask how education can become more productive. It is more than an *economic* question to ask what investments in skills, facilities, equipment, and operation will produce a maximum output in learning for a maximum number of learners. The relation of educational input to output has to do with nation-building in the developing countries, with the creation of a viable postindustrial society in the countries that are farther along the path of development, and with improving the quality of life at all stages of economic and social development.

For the last two centuries the most successful formula for increasing productivity has been to combine new technology with technological skills. Thus, machines have made it possible to till the same acreage with fewer workers, and new strains of crops and techniques for enriching the soil have made it possible to produce more from the same land. New machines and highly trained workers can manufacture more goods in less time with the same investment. Technological replacements for the horse and mule have enormously increased the efficiency of transportation.

The question is, will the same thing work for education?

Can we find media that will *increase* learning, without proportionately increasing cost, so that the ratios of output to input will be higher? Can we find media that will bring learning opportunities to *more students* without a corresponding increase in learning or increase in cost? Can we find media that will do about the *same job* now being done but at substantially *lower cost?* These are the media an educator looks for when he seeks greater productivity.

The developing countries, in particular, have seen the "new media" as a way to raise the quality of instruction faster than it could be raised by increasing and upgrading the teacher corps, to supplement even good teaching with learning experiences impossible to create locally, and to extend the reach of education to areas where schools and teachers are not otherwise available. If new technology could raise the educational output without greatly increasing the budget for teaching (which is the largest part of educational cost) and without requiring too many more schools to be built, equipped, and staffed, then it would indeed offer great dividends in productivity.

It is not easy for a developing country to decide to allocate scarce resources to a nontraditional solution, and it is easier to use the smaller media. Thus Thailand decided to use low-cost radio to equalize some of the opportunities between metropolitan and small-town and village schools. Upper Volta and Niger decided to combine radio and slides in teaching agriculture and health. Colombia decided to teach functional literacy to its campesinos by means of radio broadcasts and by a special newspaper delivered to study groups in the villages. Yet three of these four countries are now also using television for teaching. In retrospect it seems rather remarkable that so many developing countries have been willing to make use of the more complex and expensive media. Part of the reason may be the introduction of television for public entertainment in the evenings, leaving daytime hours free for other uses. Part may be the availability of bilateral or international assistance. Thus, when the challenge was presented to transform quickly the educational opportunities in the Territory of American Samoa, the United States paid for television. Television was installed in Niger with large grants and technical assistance from France. When El Salvador and the Ivory Coast decided to make television a major element in their educational development policies, they were able to obtain large loans or grants from both individual countries and international agencies.

For the richer countries, the decision was easier. Australia had no difficulty, forty years ago, in deciding to use radio and correspondence study to teach hundreds of students in the remote parts of the country far from any school. The United States, Japan, Sweden, France, and others experimented with instructional television because they were accustomed to technology, believed in its potential, and were wealthy enough to shrug off a failure or two as "experimental."

More recently, two other factors have led the richer countries to become more interested in the Big Media. One has been the need to extend learning opportunities, especially to working adults, without indefinitely multiplying campuses and schools. From this kind of need have come institutions like the Telekolleg (technical preparatory school) in West Germany, built around television and weekend classes; and in Britain the

Open University, now the largest university in all Britain, teaching almost 50,000 students by a combination of television, radio, correspondence study, and tutorial opportunities.

A second reason to look harder at instructional Big Media has been the problems of countries that have universal public education and are trying to meet the educational needs of students from lower classes and minority groups. The United States is an example in which there has been growing uneasiness about how much the traditional school system is accomplishing with these nonelite students. The Coleman Report, *Equality of Educational Opportunity,* (Coleman et al., 1966) concluded that only a small fraction of the variation in student achievement in the traditional school could be traced to different conditions and practices in the schools; most of the difference came from the students' socioeconomic backgrounds. Other scholars tended to agree. For example, Averch and his colleagues decided flatly that "research has not identified a variant of the existing system that is consistently related to students' educational outcomes" (1972: x). The key word in that statement is *consistently.* Researchers have found numerous examples of educational practices that seemed to be related significantly to student learning. But the trouble is, as Averch said (1972: x-xi), that "other studies, similar in approach and method, find the same educational practices to be ineffective, and we have no clear idea why this discrepancy exists."

Ask a "good teacher" or a school administrator how to improve student learning, and he or she will probably recommend smaller classes. Unfortunately this is most expensive, requiring more teachers and more classrooms. But even teacher-student ratio, when studied by researchers, proved to have at best a weak and inconsistent relationship to student perfor- mance. Thus in the absence of clear guidance as to how changes in the traditional system might improve the product within acceptable financial constraints, attention has turned again to the potential of the media for increasing educational productivity, because—one hears the rueful complaint in many languages—"There must be a better way!"

THE ACT OF SELECTING MEDIA

The effort to select the most productive combination of media for instruction goes on continuously, in all parts of the world, at every level of education and investment, often under great pressure, without much really being known about how decisions are made.

At any moment some hundreds of thousands of teachers are deciding how to illustrate the classes they are about to teach—for example, whether to use a picture or a schematic drawing when explaining how a volcano works, and where to get it. Or whether to play for children who need the immediacy of it a few minutes of the voice of Churchill or Roosevelt in a class in recent history. Those decisions will have relatively little impact on the educational system as a whole although they may make a great difference in an individual class.

At this same time, however, a program committee of teachers, technologists, and producers may be meeting on the home campus of the British Open University deciding how many half-hours of television to request for a course just being designed. That is a much larger decision, because one period of television may cost them in the neighborhood of $20,000, and will be seen by thousands of university students and a very large audience watching, so to speak, over the students' shoulders.

Still another variant of this decision is facing institutions that have to buy instructional materials. For example, the University of Bath decided a few years ago to combine library and production facilities in order to make it easier for teachers to bring a variety of media experiences to their students. No such resource center could possibly stock everything that teachers would want. To what instructional media should the university have given priority in the new service it is creating? What investments in media would be most likely to pay off? Which media and what materials could be recommended most confidently to teachers who ask for advice and help?

If we think of the decision whether to use a picture of a volcano in a single class as a small act of selection, and the choice of equipment for a media resource center and specification of amount of television as medium-sized decisions, there are other acts of media selection that are very large indeed. Take the case of India. India has been using mostly what we should call Little Media—puppets, filmstrips, and radio—to reach its largely illiterate village people. But as this is written India has taken a giant step up the ladder of technology. For one year it has had available to it the most sophisticated communication satellite in the world, the ATS-6, with which to beam educational and development television into 2,400 of its remote villages. From puppets to direct satellite broadcasting is 5,000 years in time, millions of dollars in cost. India is betting on its ability to leap over the intervening steps in technology and reach its villages with instructional television half a century before it otherwise could. If the experiment works well, India hopes to continue it, using its own satellite, launched perhaps by the Soviet Union. If this is indeed confirmed, it will involve tens of millions of dollars, and the intellectual and economic growth of hundreds of millions of people.

Facing decisions of comparable magnitude are countries like Iran, which is determined to extend educational advantages nationwide and is planning a national system of educational television, with or without a satellite; Indonesia decided to install a national satellite in 1976; and Korea, which is embarked upon a revision of its national curriculum, making major use of programmed instruction and of instructional television relayed from captive balloons moored two miles above the earth.

Between the classroom teacher's decision and the India-Iran-Indonesia-Korea decisions, there are many other levels of media decisions. For example, Tanzania considered and resolutely refused to introduce television, for what seemed to President Nyerere and his advisors good and sufficient reason. They felt that television cost too much for their capabilities, that they would be better off depending on teacher-training and radio.

In the United States, a number of universities have decided upon the use of media to extend their teaching beyond their campuses. For example, Stanford University uses low-cost high-frequency transmission to televise a number of its engineering classes to employees in nearby industries and laboratories. Each receiving group has a VHF radio link by means of which to "talk back" and ask questions of the classroom teacher. The University of Illinois has programmed a large number of self-instructional courses on its huge computer, in order to offer the opportunity to people in some hundreds of cities throughout Illinois and elsewhere of studying such courses. This is the "Plato" system, so named for the Socratic dialogues between Plato and his master; the system is intended to permit dialogue and practice between students and the computer programs. The University of Nebraska is endeavoring to build an Open University, somewhat on the British model, and like that model depending on correspondence study and broadcasts.

We have already mentioned the ETV system in American Samoa. Now, after more than ten years of experience with the new system, Samoa has decided to cut back its television. Partly this is because of financial stringency; partly because of the level of teacher proficiency in the classrooms has risen.

All such decisions as these require assumptions about the effect and cost of one instructional medium vs. another, for one purpose or another. It would be reassuring to believe that all such decisions are made judiciously and rationally, and that all media are chosen in light of full information concerning their potential and effect. It would be reassuring to know that a decision maker at any level relies upon a set of principles from instructional technology concerning the desirable uses of given media; that he reviews the pertinent research concerning the effectiveness of one medium vs. another; that he is familiar with (or takes pains to familiarize himself with) the experiences of using different media in projects like his own; and that if estimated cost is an element he considers it, in human and technical as well as financial resources, measured against the resources available and against competing needs.

Unfortunately this is probably not the case. Such anecdotal evidence as exists suggests that the decision may as often be impulsive as judicial. The classroom teacher is likely to select what is easily available; the nation entering upon a massive use of instructional media may as often decide for political as for educational reasons. In some countries the decision to introduce a Big Medium has been only ostensibly for educational advantages; the real reasons have been prestige or social control. Often the decision to introduce costly instructional technology has been influenced by the interest of an outside country which has been willing to provide money. And when such a decision is taken to introduce a Big Medium, that decision tends to control all later ones. For example, when a government has made a large investment in television, it is difficult, if not politically impossible, to go any other educational road. So much is committed that one cannot afford to admit failure, and once the hardware is available, it is easier to make use of it than to change.

We are not implying that major investment in the media of instruction is necessarily wrong or that the motives of donor countries are other than honorable. The concept of "leapfrogging" over intermediate technologies to sophisticated ones is appealing. Why should a developing country have to follow the long, painful path of the older countries from agricultural toward industrial society? Why should they not jump directly from the oxcart to the airplane, from the drum and town crier to television? Why should they not make full use of the experience of Japan and the West, instead of learning everything by trial and error? This is doubtless the viewpoint that led many of the highly developed countries to offer money and their own advanced instructional technologies. Yet the whole concept of "leapfrogging" over certain stages of development needs to be reexamined.

As Carpenter writes:

> There is a strong tendency for highly industrialized countries like the United States or West Germany to try to accomplish, in developing countries and with overly complex equipment, what they have *not* succeeded in doing at home. Spain is advised to go all-out for computer-assisted instruction and micro-videotape teacher training before radio or simpler, more adaptive sound slide, sound tape, and motion picture technologies have been explored. Satellite relays of educational television programs are recommended for India by advanced industrial countries before All-India Radio and very

feasible expansions of audio radio facilities have been committed and applied for educational purposes. The pressures and goals for industrial growth and foreign markets, and perhaps as well, the frustrations of fully applying proved but less glamorous technologies In education often lead to "leap frogging" over the proved and practical to high-risk adventure with the largest great complex technological system [Carpenter, 1972].

On the other hand, Carpenter readily admits that the cheap and the small may not always be the best or most efficient. Underscaling may be as inefficient as overscaling. This, too, is an especially important matter for the less developed countries because they cannot afford *not* to take advantage of appropriate help from new technology. They have the same delicate problem in determining scale of size and complexity with instructional technology as in all other technology that relates to their national growth.

We have been talking mostly about the developing countries, because they can less readily afford a mistake in the choice of media, and the full impact of the act of decision is more easily seen. But, as we have tried to indicate, decisions on the media of instruction have to be made everywhere, in economically advanced as well as economically developing countries. They involve, in total, a substantial part of any national budget and affect any nation's chief wealth—the supply of knowledge and trained persons. And our impression is that such decisions are made casually and conveniently as often as they are made judicially, and they seldom are made with a great deal of information.

AGENDA FOR THIS VOLUME

Our purpose in this volume is to assemble and review the existing information that bears on the choice of media for instruction, and especially on the choice between Big and Little Media, so that the state of the art can be known to the teacher or planner who wants to understand as much as possible about the decision he or she has to make.

What do the laboratory experiments say about the effectiveness of different media for instruction? We shall review those findings in Chapter 2. What guidelines are available from pedagogy and instructional technology? Those are discussed in Chapter 3. In Chapter 4 we shall try to summarize present knowledge of relative media costs. What has been found out from field projects that have used the instructional media in an important way, and have recorded cost-effectiveness data or insights from administrative and educational experience? We shall review a number of these projects in Chapters 5 through 8. And finally, we shall try to put these various lines of information together into a few guidelines that represent the state of the art, at the present time, in the choice of media for instruction.

Do not expect too much.

Ideally, we should like to find in the research and theoretical literature the same precise kind of guidance that is available on the engineering side of communication: to launch a satellite of w weight requires a rocket with t thrust ... given a transmitter of p power, we can expect to deliver a signal of s field strength at m miles, and so forth. That is, we should like to be able to say that to teach mathematics in the third grade to a given number of students, television is a better investment than radio or programmed instruction or something else. That kind of guidance does not exist in any reliable form. Rather, the research evidence requires us to consider the situation and conditions of learning, and even then gives us relatively little specific guidance. As Smith and Smith said in their study of cybernetic learning, no audiovisual device or medium of nonverbal communication "has relatively invariant properties as an aid to verbal learning which can be studied and assessed independently of the operational situation" (Smith and Smith, 1966).

Therefore, the act of selecting a medium or media of instruction is not like looking in an engineering handbook for a field strength formula, nor in a road atlas for the most direct route. To the extent that selection is a rational act, the decision maker is likely to have to consider a skein of complex information. His search for that information will lead him *within* the media to the *message*. It will lead him to consider carefully the needs and abilities of the students he wants to teach, the precise nature of the learning events he wants to bring about, and the media coding system most likely to bring them about. If he is concerned with a large system, it will force him to consider costs, availability of personal and technical resources, and the relation of the proposed investment to the larger needs and resources of the system. And if the medium or combination of media has been used in a comparable situation for a comparable purpose, he will certainly want to ascertain and weigh that field experience.

This kind of procedure, rather than a cookbook of recipes—use television for this, use filmstrips for that, use CAI for this other—is the kind of guidance we can expect from existing literature at this time. But if research findings and field experience will throw light on the procedure of selection, which is complex and difficult at best, then they are worth reviewing, as we shall try to do in the following chapters.

CHAPTER 2

THE EXPERIMENTAL EVIDENCE

One of the questions I am frequently asked by visitors to the Open University is, "How do you choose which media to use for different parts of your multi-media courses?"

I feel that I am expected, in answer, to point to a beautifully constructed algorithm and explain how a carefully balanced analysis of pedagogical factors leads to the best choice. In fact, I have to admit that no such algorithm or analysis exists, and that the University's selections of media are controlled by logistical, financial and internal political factors rather than by soundly based and clearly specified psychological and pedagogical considerations.

I don't like admitting this: it seems as though it is not to the credit of the University, a leader in the multi-media field. But I don't feel too defensive about it. The fact is that instructional researchers and designers have not provided even the foundations for constructing strong practical procedures for selecting media appropriate to given learning tasks. If there has been British work in this area, I have been unable to discover it. In West Germany, the Deutsches Institut für Fernstudien has recently turned its attention to the problem. . . . In the United States, over 2,000 media studies have not yielded the answers we need.

David Hawkridge
(Media Taxonomies
and Media Selection, n.d., p. 1)

There is no shortage of research on instructional media, only a shortage of the kind of research that would be most helpful to us. Of the several thousand media studies Hawkridge mentions, about half are readily available *experimental* studies of instructional media—that is, investigations in which an attempt has been made to approximate laboratory conditions, control the essential variables, and test the results with appropriate statistics. The largest proportion of these deal with instructional television, the next largest with programmed instruction and film. Relatively few are concerned with radio, very few with the simplest media such as filmstrips, slides, or audiotape, and almost none with textbooks. Textbooks have become a large commercial industry, and publishers at this stage care more about expert opinion and market studies than about research on the amount of learning from their products. Television has been the most studied both because it requires the largest investment of any of the newer media, and also because it came into wide use at a time when media research was being supported by generous grants from Title VII of the Defense Education Act (see Filep and Schramm, 1970).

Research on programmed instruction also was generously supported in the late 1950s and early 1960s both because it was recognized as a new process among the old ones and because the Fund for Advancement of Education and the U.S. Office of Education had resources with which to contract for such research. Film has long been a popular subject for research because of its promise for use in teaching and because investigators find it easy to work with: it can be presented easily and repeated or reviewed as necessary. Thus we have had the slightly ironic situation that at the very time research on film became less fashionable as compared to the study of television, the treatment variable on "television" was being simulated by film or presented on videotape. As for radio, it came too early to take advantage of federal support for media research, and educators showed surprisingly little interest in what it could contribute to their classes. The really small media were taken for granted, as were textbooks—the latter because they had become a classroom fixture, the former because educators were not greatly worried about investment in a few slides, a picture, or even a projector. Consequently such experimental evidence as exists is most plentiful on television, very scant on the smaller and older media.

These nearly 1,000 experiments are the ones we are going to sample in this chapter. In general, we shall find them somewhat less illuminating than they could be. But let us first see what they say about learning from the media, and then we will talk about the experiments themselves.

The Experiments on Instructional Television

Most of these studies compare television instruction with classroom instruction. And the finding is clear: the more carefully such comparisons are designed and controlled, the more likely they are to show no significant difference in learning from the two sources.

In 1963, in the course of earning an Ed.D. at Pennsylvania State University, D. W. Stickell reviewed 250 experimental comparisons of this kind for the scientific acceptability of their design (see Stickell, 1963). He found only ten studies that he was willing to call fully interpretable, meaning that they had met every requirement of a rather demanding standard. All ten had been done at Penn State in the 1950s. These are listed, with some details and with a brief indication of the standard of excellence they were required to meet, in Table 2.1 (tables can be found beginning on page 44).

Perhaps to soften this rather harsh commentary on non-Penn State research, Stickell identified twenty-three other studies, some of which were done elsewhere than at Penn State. He called these "partly interpretable," meaning that they had some flaw in their design but not sufficient to cancel out their usefulness. In a number of instances the flaw was related to the assignment of experimental subjects. For example, in some cases the subjects were matched in pairs before assignment, or they may have been permitted to volunteer before random assignment rather than being selected from an entire population. Of all these thirty-three studies, which Stickell felt constituted the cream of the experimental comparisons, only three—none from the "interpretable ten"—showed a statistically significant difference, in favor of the television group.

Of the 217 studies Stickell discarded from his original 250—the 217 that did not meet his requirements—only 59 showed a difference between experimental and control groups, about evenly divided between results favoring television or favoring classroom teaching (Stickell, 1963: 65).

This finding is in agreement with the tabulation of Chu and Schramm of 421 television-classroom comparisons (1967: 7ff.), of which 308 showed no significant difference, 63 came out in favor of television, 50 in favor of classroom teaching. Dubin and Hedley (1969) examined 381 such studies, including many of those in the Chu-Schramm list, and found 191 showing no difference, 102 in favor of television, 89 in favor of classroom instruction. Not all these differences were statistically significant. Where possible, Dubin and Hedley computed standardized scores from reported data and combined them. Working with 192 comparisons, they found ITV *without* talkback significantly superior to ITV *with* talkback but not significantly different from conventional instruction, so far as learning was concerned. The studies in neither of these two reports were subjected to the close examination given by Stickell.

The last finding above is worth thinking about. Why should instructional television with a telephone or radio connection, permitting students to ask questions or make comments, be less effective than television without such an opportunity for the students to participate? Is it that the need of one student or of one classroom to ask or speak is an annoyance to other students or other classrooms? Is it that the best use of television is not to duplicate classroom teaching as closely as possible, but rather to teach in another way? Is it that discussion, questioning, and teacher-student interchange are better restricted to a small group where everyone knows each other and no one is inhibited by an unknown audience and the demands of a formal presentation? Until about ten years ago ITV produced by educators followed the assumption that teaching on television was mostly a matter of putting a good teacher in front of a microphone and letting him or her do as nearly as possible what would be done in a classroom. The slogan was "sharing the teacher" or sharing the "master teacher." "Sesame Street," "The Electric Company," and much other recent instructional television, however, have assumed that television puts quite different requirements on a teacher than does classroom teaching, and requires a different understanding of how the medium is best used. The Niger instructional TV programs, made by a skillful French team, assumed that the best TV would be, not a teacher on camera, but rather "shows for kids."

We conclude from the evidence that, overall, there is no basis in the research for saying that students learn more or less from television than from classroom teaching. This does not mean that under some conditions of teaching some students do not learn more of certain subject matter or skills from one medium or channel of teaching than from the other. But the results of the broad comparisons say that there is, in general, *no significant difference.*

Not all the ITV media experiments, of course, are comparisons with conventional teaching. Some other measures of learning—standardized tests, criterion reference tests, and others—have also been used. A few of these experiments are listed in Table 2.2, which demonstrates clearly that students of widely different kinds can, and usually do, learn a variety of subject matters efficiently when taught by television.

Recently children's learning from "Sesame Street" has been measured in the United States, Israel, and Latin America, among other places. This is of interest not because it compares learning from television with a known standard such as ordinary classroom teaching or standardized tests, but because "Sesame Street" was shown on open-circuit television, for home

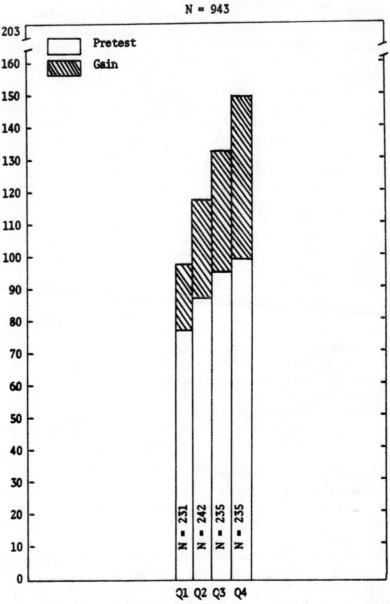

FIGURE 2.1

Learning from "Sesame Street." Pretest
and total test score for all children (by viewing quartiles).

(From Ball and Bogatz, 1970)

viewing by preschool-age children, without any teacher supervision, and with an entertainment format. The general results of the United States studies are shown in Figure 2.1. The students were tested, before and after the program series, on how much they knew of the skills the program was expected to teach—counting, the alphabet, and so forth. Their parents were asked how often the children viewed the program, and the children were divided into quartiles according to how often they had viewed. Figure 2.1 shows quite clearly that learning increased steadily with amount of viewing, from Quartile 1 (where the children viewed least) to Quartile 4 (where they viewed most). Thus the effectiveness of television as a teacher extends beyond the classroom and beyond the ordinary formats of instruction.

The Experiments on Instructional Film

It is generally assumed by educational technologists that what can be said about learning from film is much the same as what can be said about television. As a matter of fact, many of the experiments on instructional "television" have actually used a film for projection through the television system. Experimental comparisons of film with direct teaching have about the same results as television-classroom experiments. And it is generally agreed that the differences between television and film relate chiefly to the different ways of delivering the two media: the fact that television can be presented live, if desired, and the greater amount of control that a teacher has over the use of a film when he or she shows it in the classroom.

Rather than making a full review of instructional film research, therefore, we have illustrated in Table 2.3 some experiments that note the amount of learning from films. Here, also, the evidence leaves us no reason to doubt that students can learn efficiently from instructional films.

CAI and Programmed Instruction

What is the evidence on computer-assisted instruction, which we must call a Big Medium, and programmed instruction, which is a relatively Little Medium? CAI, especially, still in the experimental stage and in the hands of university developers, has had rather careful research. Programmed instruction is made in such a way, by careful statement of objectives and repeated pretesting and revision, that it is usually not released until it proves that it can bring about learning. And Tables 2.4 and 2.5 demonstrate that the results are as expected. Students learn from both media. The ability of CAI, in particular, to provide interactive drill and to save time over direct teaching has proved noteworthy. One study worth special attention is the Suppes and Morningstar report of teaching Russian language by computer. Seventy-eight per cent of the CAI students, only 32 percent of classroom students, finished the year, indicating some advantage for students being able to practice on their own time and with a carefully designed and interactive routine. Figure 2.2 reproduces another finding of this same study: CAI students were likely to make fewer errors than classroom students, regardless of rank on the examination.

CAI and programmed instruction are really methods of instruction rather than media. They use, respectively, the computer and print as media of transmission. This method can be efficiently applied to other media also. For example, Gropper and Lumsdaine (1961) have effectively "programmed" a televised lesson; Carpenter, a film (1968). One of the more

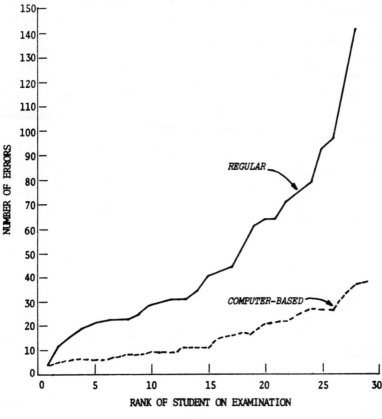

FIGURE 2.2

**Student performance for the portion of the fall
quarter final examination in first-year Russian that
was common to the computer-based and regular sections.**

(Suppes, 1971)

spectacular results of making instructional material by the methods of programmed instruction was reported by Markle (1967), who was able by empirical pretesting and revision to reduce the time for completion of a course in first aid by 25 percent, and to increase the final test score from 145 for a traditionally taught group to 270 for a group taught by his new materials. Furthermore, he was able to reduce the standard deviation for the experimental group from 42 to 9, indicating that programmed methods tended to equalize performance even while improving it. Actually, the worst performer in the experimental group scored 44 more points than the best students in the conventionally taught group.

Thus there is little doubt that a pupil can learn effectively either from CAI, using a computer, or from a printed program. The choice between them, or the choice between either of them and other methods of instruction, depends on other considerations which we shall explore later. One of these considerations is cost, which is much higher for CAI. Another is that whereas a student can *practice* with a printed program, he can *interact* with a programmed computer. Thus the computer can be programmed to take account of the kind of errors a student is making and of the material he or she seems to have learned well, and to provide more practice on the one, less on the other. The decision whether to expose a student to programmed practice rather than other learning experiences depends on questions both of availability and of strategy. The research we have been reviewing gives us little help on those matters. But, like the research on television and on film, it leaves us in no doubt that students of many kinds can learn diverse subject matter efficiently from *either* CAI or printed programmed instruction.

Research on Instructional Radio and Smaller Media

There is less research on the less expensive, less complex media, and especially on the older and better accepted media, in part because the need to evaluate them has seemed less urgent. In the case of instructional radio, a number of the studies were made before the great outpouring of media research in the 1950s, but without some of the careful attention to design which we come to ask of media research. The last extensive summary of research on radio as a tool of teaching appeared in the *Encyclopedia for Educational Research* in 1950. Since then, research has concentrated on the newer media.

Nevertheless, there is evidence, as Table 2.6 shows that students do learn from radio instruction. Some of the studies are carefully controlled; more of them are from the field and less well controlled.

Research on the "smaller" media—tapes, filmstrips, slides, transparencies, photographs, inexpensive mock-ups, and so forth—has been scant. The research evidence, as illustrated in Table 2.7, is favorable.

Do Students Learn More from the Big Media?

Concerning this question we are far from confident. For one thing, the picture is not complete. Very few of the combinations of media, subject matter, and learners have been tested in comparative studies. As we have just noted, there is almost a complete lack of studies intended to ascertain *under what conditions* and *for what purposes* one medium may be superior to another. And a high proportion of all the experiments that do address themselves to the problem are deficient in some way, either in design or in realism. We can therefore look only for a trend, rather than a conclusion, in the existing literature.

There has long been a belief among educators that two sensory channels used for instruction make for more learning than one. This belief was responsible in part for the rush to use instructional television and film. The early research literature, summed up by Day and Beach (1950), came to the same conclusion: the audiovisual mode makes for more learning than either the audio or the visual mode alone. But unfortunately, these early studies almost invariably were made without the aid either of satisfactory experimental design or of significance tests. And more recent evidence has cast doubt upon them.

Broadbent's theory of perception (1958) and Travers' adoption of that theory and his research on it (1964, 1966) have built upon the assumption that there is only a single channel to the higher centers of the brain. Although information may be received simultaneously from two senses, one of these inputs must be stored for a fraction of a second in a short-term memory. Inasmuch as perhaps only one percent of the input from the ear, and perhaps only one part in 100,000 of the larger input from the eye can be utilized by the brain, interference may well occur between two inputs. Therefore, any possible superiority of two channels to one depends both on the rate at which information is presented to the two senses and the relation of the information in the two channels. Travers' own research supports the hypothesis that in numerous conditions the use of two channels may be less productive than one. Hartman's independent approach to the question (1960) is rather inconclusive, although it seems to lean toward audiovisual superiority.

This is an important line of research to media planners because the two most-used Big Media (television and sound film) are audiovisual. Most of the Little Media (e.g., radio and slides) serve one sense only—one reason why they are less expensive and less complex.

Travers and Hartman both used nonsense syllables as the subject matter for their experiments. In Table 2.8 we have listed some of the experiments that use meaningful material in comparing Big with Little Media.

Bearing in mind the incompleteness of the evidence available, we are in no position to say that either the Big or the Little Media make for more learning than the other category. But this, at least, we can say: there is nothing in Table 2.8 to indicate any broad and general superiority for the Big Media.

Do Students Learn More from a Combination of Media than from a Simple Medium?

We have pointed out that almost all teaching is multimedia, and that "teacher instruction" as measured in most experiments and compared with "media instruction" is usually teacher plus textbook plus chalkboard and often plus more. We have thousands of years of educational history to tell us that teachers themselves believe multimedia instruction is more effective than a single medium.

What the question really asks is whether adding one or more of the audiovisual or programmed media will improve instruction, when the time of instruction is held constant. This latter qualification is important. For example, Schramm and Oberholtzer (1960) accomplished impressive learning gains by adding ITV to classroom instruction in Spanish, still more by adding programmed instruction, and even more by enlisting the aid of parents to practice with students at home. However, these learning experiences could not be added without also adding time, and the result was that students who studied Spanish one fifty-minute period a day in school and thirty minutes at home were being compared with students who spent 25 percent more time on it.

Nevertheless, such research as there is on this question almost invariably indicates that the addition of one or more supplementary or complementary channels of instruction makes a difference. In Table 2.9 we have summarized some of these studies.

More impressive than most of this research, however, is the example of some of the more sophisticated instructional programs, like the Swedish educational systems and the British Open University. These try to use whatever "media mix" a particular course and particular classes seem to require. The result of this strategy is to form different combinations of television, radio, textbooks, workbooks, filmstrips, kits, recorded material, charts, and anything else the learning task calls for. Such matching requires a discrimination among subject-media combinations which is scantily supported by research, but guided by expert experience and commonsense decisions.

WHAT THESE EXPERIMENTS SAY

If we now try to sum up what these experiments tell us, we can do it in relatively few words: students can learn a great deal from any of the media. Under most of the conditions tested, they could learn as much as from face-to-face teaching, about many subjects.

It seems hardly necessary to waste so many experiments underlining that conclusion. Both parents and teachers can testify that the ability of students to learn from any experience, under appropriate conditions, is truly phenomenal. They can learn what they are intended to learn and also what they are not intended to learn—for example, violent behavior. Authors and producers are repeatedly surprised by what people learn from their products. The contribution of television to the hula hoop craze in the 1960s was hardly anticipated; nor was it expected, as Monsivais noted with some amusement (1975: 13) that from reading the comic strip millions of people in many countries would learn to say "gulp!" A propaganda film made some years ago to show that American working classes were down-trodden and oppressed was reliably reported to have been a sensation in some of the socialist countries, not because of its success in teaching what it was supposed to teach, but because the working-class audiences noted that all the oppressed American workers wore very good shoes!

The question was most often asked in the form: can the media teach? (Or can television teach?) We should not be scornful about this, because, at least in the years of instructional technology's greatest growth it was necessary to establish the legitimacy of the new tools. There were gaudy claims from designers, manufacturers, and salesmen. There was adminis-trative suspicion and teacher resistance. Although research scholars had no doubt that students learned from the media, still they had to establish some sort of baseline for the amount, and later, the kind, of learning. Seeking such a measure, researchers turned to a comparison which, in retrospect, seems almost as unessential as the question of whether the media can teach. They designed experiment after experiment comparing learning from media with learning from the kind of face-to-face instruction that schools had depended on for centuries. Meaningless as this might have been, inasmuch as there was no serious thought of replacing teachers, still to many persons twenty years ago it seemed the most practical measure that could be made. That is, if a student could learn at least as much from exposure to media as to live teachers on a given topic, then the medium would deserve the attention of administrators and school boards—not to replace teachers, but to take over some of their instructional time and thus relieve them for other responsibilities.

Proving that students could learn *in general* from the media was a first step. When experiments began to show nonsignificant differences, the experimenters turned to questions of subject matter: could the media teach some things better than others? If students could learn algebra from television, could they also learn physics or government? Then the process passed to different educational levels: was television as effective with primary schools as with secondary schools as with college classes as with adults, in a given subject? Was it as effective with third grades as with sixth grades? With brighter as with slower learners?

The concentration of media research on television reflected in part a search for the super-medium. Television, of all the media, seemed to have most of the characteristics of a live lecturer, but with a glamor that few teachers could match. In contrast to films it was live and could change swiftly with time requirements. There were relatively few cross-media experiments, compared to the number of studies that measured media against live teaching, partly because of the difficulty of designing a really good cross-media experiment. But the wastefulness of this search for a super-medium was that investigators were looking for the medium that was best in general, best for every kind of teaching, whereas all our experience tells us that there is no such thing.

As a matter of fact, perhaps the most regrettable characteristic of the long line of instructional media experiments has been their *macro* quality. They have tended to prove repeatedly that students could learn well from a given medium, thus treating the medium as a whole, and, by studying an entire class period or school term, lumping together all the kinds of teaching that might be done on the particular medium. It would have been more useful to have a larger number of micro studies—trying to identify the unique strengths and weaknesses of a given medium for a given purpose, trying to maximize the learning from a particular medium and thus considering *how* it is used and how it can be used *best*.

Thus when we ask whether a given medium can do a given instructional task, or whether one medium can do a given task better than another medium, the existing research is hardly helpful. It gives us a macro answer: television can teach algebra, geometry, government, art, and almost any other subject. The same goes for film, radio, CAI, and other media which have been tested. But this represents an average over many tasks. Few media experiments have taken in less than a class period of instruction; many have included a term or a whole year. Thus the results are an average of performance, under many different conditions, over many kinds of instructional task—knowledge learning; concept, skill, and rule learning; problem-solving; affect and value learning. It would be useful to know how a given medium can be best used to do a given task—this is the level of study in which research can now shed the greatest light on practice.

SOME PROBLEMS OF QUALITY CONTROL

One reason then, why media research has given us less help than it might is that it has frittered away much energy on less than essential questions. Another reason is that it presents certain very difficult problems of design.

A great many of the experimental studies on instructional media leave something to be desired in scientific quality. We are not talking, now, about field studies, which are notoriously difficult to control. We are talking about studies that were done under quasi-experimental conditions, usually in a cooperating school or in a laboratory, where the researchers used small experimental groups over which they had some control. They made an effort to equate the experimental with the control treatment, most often the content of the television teaching with that of the face-to-face teaching. In some cases it was possible to assign subjects randomly in order to allow for unmeasured differences in learning groups. But even under the best conditions or a teacher-media study or a media-comparison study presents special difficulties for the experimenter.

Realism tends to conflict with science. Consider an example. Say that television is being compared with conventional classroom teaching. Experimental and control groups can be randomly assigned and then further tested for similarities; the same teacher can be used for both groups, or teachers can change places at intervals during the course; and if the experimenter has control of this kind, he may be able to achieve a quite orthodox experimental design.

But nagging doubts remain. Suppose the same teacher is used for both media (say, television) and face-to-face groups; will his teaching be identical in the two situations? If it is, we might doubt that he is making best use of either the classroom or television. Experimenters sometimes try to equate the treatments by using a studio class as the control group and televising the teaching to students in another classroom, who form the experimental group. This seems to ensure that both groups will have the same teacher and the same teaching. But does the studio group, surrounded by cameras, lights, microphones, and technicians, really represent typical classroom teaching? The teacher must decide how much he teaches to the class in front of him, how much to the camera. If he teaches to the studio class, he is likely to do the things a good teacher would do in a classroom situation—ask or answer questions, respond to individual questions or cues, perhaps encourage discussion. This is unlikely to be the best teaching for the television class. On the other hand, if he teaches to the camera, he is probably cheating the studio class out of some of the advantages they might expect from face-to-face instruction. One solution to this problem is to have the teacher give an uninterrupted lecture, as he might do in a very large face-to-face class. But to compare a lecture on television with a lecture face-to-face is to use only a small part of the capabilities of either type of teaching.

Or take the problem of equating the treatments when two media—say, radio and television—are being compared. Here the most common method used by experimenters to equate the stimuli is to let the sound track of the television represent radio; one group both sees and hears the program, while the other group hears the sound track. It is obvious that the television sound track is not very likely to equate with a skillful radio broadcast. Such a comparison, despite its scientific quality, is of limited practical usefulness. A more realistic solution would be to assemble two teams from among the most capable radio and television producers and performers, give them common subject matter, restrict them in expenditures and time, and then encourage them to do the best job they can with their medium. In fact, this is about what was done in the Westley and Barrow experiment (1959). But this solution, too, has certain drawbacks in experimental design. For example, are we sure that the two production groups are equally skillful? Or that the subject matter lends itself equally well to both media?

Another problem in designing both rigorous and practically useful research in this area is specifying what kind of learning effects will be measured. For some years now, teachers and future teachers have been taught that they should teach toward objectives that can be specified and measured in behavioral terms. For example, at the end of a period or a course unit, it is specified that a student should be able to spell correctly ten certain words, or solve an equation of a given kind in a given time, or name in order the Kings of England or the Presidents of the United States. But measuring the achievement of such objectives is hardly equivalent to measuring the total effects of exposure to a medium or a teacher. It is not even necessarily equivalent to measuring the most important effects.

We have good reason to believe that we are not measuring either the total effects or the most important ones. Is learning to spell 500 words or to recite the multiplication tables through 12 necessarily any more important than the models of social behavior or the attitudes toward future use of mathematics that a teacher conveys to students? The El Salvador result described in Chapter 5 suggests that some of the most significant results of using instructional television in schools may be those most experiments neglect to measure. Some of the assertions McLuhan has made about the differential effects of learning from print and pictures, difficult as they are to measure in the form he has stated them, are troubling, and challenge one of the most traditional assumptions of the makers of primary textbooks and teachers of reading: that pictures help a child learn to read. The implication of Samuels' (1970) study is that whereas pictures may be helpful in the short run, in the long run they may actually be found to be debilitating to that skill. In a sense, pictures may be *too* helpful in that they allow a child to guess the word from the picture without looking hard at the letters. Similarly, Salomon and Sieber (1970) showed certain results of a disorganized film that would not be measured in any ordinary study of effects. They compared a well-structured teaching film with the same film cut apart and randomly spliced together. Obviously, the intended content could be learned better from the systematic, well-organized treatment, but what if it were desirable to measure the effects of the film in teaching imaginative behavior, or creativity? When the students saw the film in its randomly spliced version, they were able to generate a much larger number of hypotheses about its meaning.

Much research is likely to be conducted in the next decades not only to learn how to maximize the usefulness of a given medium for a given purpose, but also to probe beyond the surface measures of learning objectives in search of other effects. By some scholars this would be referred to as a "humanistic" rather than a "scientific" approach. Be that as it may, it is good pedagogy and good communication psychology.

ANOTHER QUESTION, ANOTHER PROBLEM

Let us now pose another question that is of great practical interest to everyone teaching with media: are the different media equally effective in a given task with different kinds of learners?

Both common sense and experience tell us they probably are not. There is insufficient evidence as yet to let us conclude that some individuals are "print-minded," some "picture-minded," or some "audio-minded," and consequently better able to make use of a particular medium. Needless to say, if a person cannot see well he is likely to learn less from a visual medium than from an auditory one. If he is somewhat deaf he is likely to do better with pictures or print than with radio. But beyond these physical conditions, there is little reason to expect a differential media capability in individuals.

Mental ability is the personal variable that has been most studied, usually measured by one of the standard tests of school performance. The findings in general do not distinguish among the media, but rather show that abler students, other things being equal, tend to learn more *from any medium* than less able students.

The macro studies give us little help in selecting among media relative to ability levels, as Table 2.10 indicates. Most of the hints we have to guide us come from micro studies. Cronbach and Snow (quoted in Cronbach, 1975) conclude that the strength of the interaction between ability and learning, when ability is held constant, depends mostly on the instructional procedure. Cronbach suggests that one way to reduce the differential effect of general ability is to use pictures or diagrams. The presumed effect is to make it easier for less able students to transform the information in the lesson to a form in which it can be retained, and perhaps to slow up the abler student who is more accustomed to dealing with abstractions (1975: 119). Another way to reduce the difference in outcomes related to general ability is to make the lessons more didactic, less inductive. This supposedly favors the less able, lower-class students who do better with explicit requirements and close-coupled rewards. "Problem-oriented, ego-motivated, supportive methods of teaching, which educational theorists have long been advocating, seem to benefit only a middle-class clientele," wrote Cronbach. It should be noted, however, that this difference lies not within the media but with the method of teaching.

We have been quoting a remarkable article by Cronbach (from the *American Psychologist*, 1975: 116 ff.) which serves better than anything we could write here to point out an essential limitation in research of the kind we are talking about. The typical situation examined in a study of learning from media, according to Cronbach, is an interaction between treatment and ability (an ATI study, he calls it, for ability-treatment interaction). By treatment he means the form and content of the information presented by the media; by ability, any characteristic of the learner that affects his response to the treatment. Researchers typically handle this relationship in the usual matter of experimental design, by holding constant as many variables as possible and stating the results ceteris paribus—"other things being equal." The trouble is that it is a very dubious assumption that other things may be equal. There are many characteristics of the learner that interact and alter the effects for different individuals— more such characteristics than any experimenter is likely to be able to control, more than he is able to know about. "There *are* more things in heaven and earth than are dreamt of in our hypotheses," Cronbach (1975: 124) paraphrases. Beyond the interactions observed or thought to be controlled in the experimental design there are very likely to be higher-level interactions. This is one reason why experimenters obtain puzzling variations in results from experiments that use the same treatment and apparently "comparable" learners. To pin down all these interactions requires more data than an experimenter can ordinarily handle. Furthermore, the conditions that make for the interactions change with time. Thus the California F-scale is now obsolescent after only twenty-five years. Lewin's classic experimental results from the early 1940s are now thought to be both time-bound and sample-bound.

Cronbach is not contending that it is undesirable or useless to conduct ATI research: merely that we must be wary of expecting such studies to produce immutable laws. But in the present state of research on the selection of media, any reliable guidance, short- or long-term, is welcome.

THROUGH THE BACK DOOR

There is, of course, a considerable amount of research on methods of teaching with media which apply more often across media than to any one medium. Some of these results, however, will help in any given case to guide the *choice* of media.

For example, there is a long line of studies emphasizing the advantage of simplicity and clarity in media instruction. Most of these studies were done with film or television, but there is no reason to think they are not equally applicable to still pictures, audiotapes, or print. Some of these are cited in Schramm (1972) and Carpenter (1971). For example, VanderMeer (1953) compared a straight lecture film with a version of the same film he described as "jazzed up . . . with folk music in elaborate Hollywood style." The two versions were about equally effective, although the students liked the folk music version better. Carpenter and Greenhill (1958) found that using a blackboard on television was more effective than fancier visuals in teaching air science to college students, not significantly different in teaching psychology. Mercer (1952) tested special optical effects, such as dissolves, wipes, and fades in films designed to teach science to military trainees, resulting in no significant difference. Both Lumsdaine and Gladstone (1958) and McIntyre (1954) found plain versions of military training films more effective than consciously humorous ones. Studies on the use of animation—Vestal (1952), Fordham University (1953), Lumsdaine, Sulzer, and Kopstein (1953)—found conflicting results, the first two negative, the third positive.

The studies of animation suggest an explanation for times when "fancier" treatments are useful. Lumsdaine and his colleagues used animation to teach the use of the micrometer, where it could focus attention on the essentials to be taught; Vestal and Fordham used it in a more general, entertaining way. Neu (1951) found that attention-getting devices in visual treatments added nothing to learning unless they *introduced additional information.* Thus VanderMeer (1953) reported that one kind of embellishment frequently contributed to learning: attention-directing arrows focusing on the knowledge or process to be learned. The implication of these studies is that one should not select a medium for learning primarily because it can present the material with more embellishment or more attractively, but only if its mode of presentation and symbol system can make the intended learning task easier and more effective than another mode and symbol system. Chances are that a simpler medium or a simpler presentation can do a workmanlike job and accomplish as much learning, at less cost.

There has been a second long line of experiments emphasizing the importance of involvement and participation in all media teaching. As early as 1917 a pioneering study by Gates found that learning increased steadily in a classroom situation as the proportion of time spent in active recitation or practice was increased from zero to eighty percent. Media experiments have echoed this finding. Lumsdaine and Gladstone (1958) repeated the Hovland, Lumsdaine, Sheffield experiment of 1949 on learning the phonetic alphabet, and found that they could increase the performance of military trainees to near perfect by increasing the amount of active practice—which in that case consisted merely of saying the signs of the alphabet as they appeared on the screen. Kimble and Wulff (1961) concluded that the optimum time allocated to active student responses in a class built around visual media was probably from 50 to 75 percent. Lumsdaine, May, and Hadsell (1958) added four and one-half minutes of participation questions to a film that already ran eight and one-half minutes, and reported as much learning as could be accomplished by the showing of the film *twice* without participation. Even splicing questions into films has been found by these and other investigators to increase substantially the amount of learning from educational films.

Another effective way to increase the sense of participation and involvement was reported by Roshal (1949). He discovered that a "subjective" camera angle—i.e., taking a picture of hands tying a knot, from the same angle as a learner would see it—taught significantly more than an "objective" angle. Another device for involvement was demonstrated by Comenius in the seventeenth century: interrupting a story or an exposition to let the student finish it. The same device has been proved to work in the media of instruction. For example, Hoban and Van Ormer (1950) reported that the Scottish Film Council was making effective use of unclosed or uncompleted films, and Howell (in May and Lumsdaine, 1958) reported on devices to provoke and encourage discussion through "unclosed" treatments in films.

The general import of these two lines of research is the desirability of *simple* media and *active* students, as Schramm noted in *Quality in Instructional Television* (1972). The implication of the second kind of study is that one should look for the medium that will give the kind of practice or participation, and accomplish the kind of involvement, most needed for the learning task. This will often be one of the simpler media, although not necessarily. To take one example, continuously running film loops have proved very effective for student practice.

Some studies are more directly relatable to media selection. For example, we have already quoted Cronbach's assertion (listing results from Cronbach and Snow, 1976) that one way to reduce the differential effect of general ability is to introduce pictures or diagrams. Jenkins, Neale, and Deno (1967), and others also, have shown that recognition to be tested visually is superior when the first presentation is also by film. Salomon comments (1974: 389) that a picture, which employs a very dense symbol system, arouses more activity for the selection of cues, which are subsequently transformed into one or more verbal descriptions. A word, when presented, allows a far more restricted selection, while setting off, in many cases, a chain of private image-associations. The information extracted from pictures is consequently different from that extracted from words. No wonder, therefore, that in such studies, recognition of a picture, when the original presentation is a word, is inferior.

Cognitive style, however, in many cases interacts with general media rules like these. For example, Koran, Snow, and McDonald (1971) found that students who were less field-dependent benefited more from a lifelike visual presentation than did those who were more field-dependent. Salomon feels this is the case because field-dependent learners lack some of the necessary skill in decomposing and reencoding a complex situation. A visual presentation is indeed complex, whereas a verbal presentation provides a ready-made coding system that compensates for the learners' difficulty in doing the coding themselves.

It is out of studies like these that a usable research-based theory of media selection may ultimately emerge. But the difficulty of developing such a theory is illustrated by Carpenter's (1972: 200) comment:

> The central task is the precision matching of media and modes to instructional functions and objectives; to content characteristics; to target audience characteristics; to the logistics and strategies of designing and creating learning environments; and to providing for evaluations.

SUMMING UP

This is where we are with experimental research on learning from the media of instruction.

From the experimental studies we have plentiful evidence that people learn from the media, but very little evidence as to which medium, in a given situation, can bring about the *most* learning. We have hints that one medium may be more effective than another for a given learning task or a given kind of learner, but little systematic proof. Thus we can use the media with considerable confidence that students will learn from them, but, if we rely only on the experimental evidence, not with much discrimination.

The field has proved a difficult one. In research we have emphasized the macro elements—the delivery system rather than its contents, its "average" use rather than its use for specific learning tasks or specific kinds of learning. As a result we have fewer than we need of the insights and understandings that might come from micro studies. Even though studies of the kind cited in the last few pages give us some hope that a theory of media selection may emerge from research, still for the moment we must look elsewhere for help—to pedagogical theory, to the taxonomies of media, tasks, and learners that might help us straighten out the micro relationships, to field studies where the variables have been less well controlled but observation has been richer, and to economic and managerial knowledge that will necessarily contribute to media choices. This we shall do in the following chapters.

TABLE 2.1
Stickell's 10 "Interpretable" Studies of ITV

All these had (1) experimental and control groups of at least 25, (2) which had been randomly assigned from the same population, (3) were taught by the same instructor, either by two instructors exchanging classes in the middle of the term or by seating one group in the room from which the class was being televised to the other group, (4) measured by a testing instrument judged to be reliable and valid, (5) which was evaluated by acceptable statistical procedures.

Experimenter(s)	Course	Subjects Exp.	Subjects Con.	Instrument	Statistics	Result
Carpenter and Greenhill (1955)	Psychology college	152	75	Local test	F covariance	NSD
same	same	90	40	Local	F	NSD
Carpenter and Greenhill (1958)	Chemistry college	145	131	Local	F	NSD
same	same	153	159	Local	F covariance	NSD
same	Business Law college	45	42	Local	F	NSD
same	Sociology college	132	138	Local	F	NSD
same	Meterology college	49	54	Local	t test	NSD
same	Psychology college	97	42	Local	F covariance	NSD
same	Music Appreciation, college	45	29	Local (listening)	t test	NSD
same	same	45	29	Local (knowledge)	t test	NSD

TABLE 2.2
Examples of Learning from Instructional Television

Author	Study	Results
Ball and Bogatz (1970)	Measure of learning from *Sesame Street* by large sample of young children in four U.S. geographical areas.	The more that children watched the program, the more they learned of what it was intended to teach: numbers, forms, sorting, classification, etc.
Almstead and Graf (1960)	Study of 10th grade students taught geometry soley by television, and 4th and 6th grade students taught reading by television with access to a talkback when needed.	85 per cent of 10th graders passed the New York Regents Examination, 30 per cent with scores over 90. This record compares favorably with classroom students. The 4th and 6th graders gained an average of 10 months on a standardized test in 9 months of study.
Castle (1963)	Study of physicians and medical students viewing an evening extension course on diabetes mellitus, given by television.	Physicians gained over 25 per cent, pre to post course; students, about 33 per cent.
Herminghaus (1957)	High school students taught for a semester by television in English and general science.	Average gain on two standardized tests of language skills was 25 per cent; on two standardized tests of science, 60 per cent.
Peerson (1961)	173 Alabama adults, both blacks and whites, viewed a TV course in adult literacy, in supervised groups.	Average gain in 33 weeks was between one and one-half grades, as measured by a standardized test.
Corle (1967)	32 teachers assigned randomly to two types of groups, one of which viewed a televised course on teaching mathematics, the other did not.	Experimental groups made highly significant gains on standardized test of mathe mathematics, and showed significantly greater gains than controls on 2 of 8 measures of teaching performance; other six measures, n.s.d.

TABLE 2.3
Examples of Learning from Instructional Films

Author	Study	Results
Ash and Carlson (1961)	Military subjects assigned randomly to groups, one of which saw films on military topics, the other did not.	Exposure to the training films doubled the learning of experimental group as compared to controls.
Hovland, Lumsdaine, Sheffield (1949)	Very large samples of military subjects tested on learning from three films designed to implant attitudes and information about World War II.	Experimental groups averaged about 50 per cent higher, on post-tests, than controls who had not seen the films.
Neu (1951)	Very large sample of army recruits separated into experimental and control groups, the former being shown a training film.	Mean learning scores of experimental groups between between one and two standardized deviations higher than controls.
Wise (1939)	Motion pictures used as a supplement to high school course in American History for one class, not for another.	Adding the films raised learning scores of experimentals over that of controls by a critical ratio of 2.00.
VandeMeer (1945)	Some engine lathe operators taught with aid of films, others with aid of demonstrations.	Those who saw films able to complete jobs at significantly faster rate and had fewer products rejected.
Gagne and Gropper (1965)	Study of effectiveness of filmed review materials.	Filmed materials responsible for highly significant gains over no review.
Wittich et al. (1959)	Incidental information on teachers in 83 high school schools, in whose classes the Harvey White physics films were shown.	Teachers (as well as students) gained significant amount of additional information about physics from the films shown to their students.
Rulon (1933)	Samples of secondary students on learning of factual science items, and application of this know-	Mean scores of film-plus test group 14.8% superior in immediate learning of factual items, 24.1% in

TABLE 2.3 (cont.)

Author	Study	Results
	ledge to problems. One group used only test; other had science films integrated into course.	application. After three and one half months 33.4% and 41% superior to text-only group on same two criteria.
Wendt and Butts (1960)	Divided 315 10th grade students into two groups, one receiving usual history course for two semesters, other spending only one semester on same material but shown 54 history films as part of course.	Although spending only half as much time, film group learned 86% as much as other group, measured on standardized history achievement test.

TABLE 2.4
Examples of Learning from Computer-Assisted Instruction

Author	Study	Results
Atkinson (1968)	First grade students given 20 minutes tutorial daily in reading, on CAI terminal. Meanwhile, control group received similar tutorial in mathematics.	9 of 10 comparisons, on standardized post-test scores, significantly favorable to experimental group.
Suppes and Morningstar (1969)	Large samples of 1st through 6th grade students in Mississippi schools and 3rd through 6th grade students in California schools given 10 minutes of drill per day, on CAI terminal, in arithmetic;	7 of 7 comparisons in Mississippi significantly in favor of experimental over control groups. 3 of 7 in California significantly in favor of experimental groups, 1 in favor of controls, 2 n.s.d., one contaminated.
	control groups 5 hours of classroom weekly in comprehension of written and spoken Russian replaced by comparable time at CAI terminals. Control group has regular classroom instruction, and both groups had language laboratory and homework.	73 per cent of CAI students finished year course, 32 per cent of controls. Average number of errors was lower for experimental group on all three quarterly tests, but significantly so for only one quarter.

TABLE 2.4 (cont.)

Author	Study	Results
Hansen, Dick, and Lippert (1968)	Three groups of college physics students compared. Group (a) received bulk of instruction by CAI, (b) partly by CAI, partly in class, (c) classroom only.	Group (a) significantly higher on midterm and final tests. Other groups n.s.d.
Bitzer and Boudreaux (1969)	144 nursing students taught maternity nursing and pharmacology by CAI.	Significant saving in time. One group finished material in 50 hours or less that required 84 hours in classroom.
Homeyer (1970)	CAI class compared with face-to-face class in advanced computer programming.	CAI students completed course in average of 13.75 hours, as compared with average of 24 hours for classroom group, and no significant difference in scores on tests of learning.
Adams (1969)	One hour a week of CAI in reading and writing German compared with one hour a week of language laboratory as supplement to three classroom hours of college German.	CAI students performed significantly better than others in tests of reading and writing German, insignificantly more poorly in listening and speaking the language.
Cartwright, Cartwright, and Robin (1972)	114 college students in special education randomly divided into two groups, one receiving all instruction by CAI, others by lecture and discussion.	CAI group finished course in one third less time, scored 24% (.001) better on final 75-item criterion test.
Goodman (1964)	3000 airline ticket agents instructed on their jobs by CAI, and performance compared with that of other agents taught in usual airline classes.	CAI group did 5% better on criterion measures, and needed only half the training time.
Grubb and Selfridge (1964)	First half of beginning statistics course taught experimental group by CAI, Control group by lecture-discussion method.	CAI group spent mean of 5.8 hours on instruction and review, compared to 54.3 hours spent on control group in class, homework, and review. Mean scores on midterm test: 94.3% for CAI group, 58.4% for controls.

TABLE 2.4 (cont.)

Author	Study	Results
Schurdak (1965)	48 college students in one section of a Fortran programming course taught by CAI. Comparison groups, by text or programmed text.	CAI students scored about 10% better than either of comparison groups, required about 10% less time.

TABLE 2.5

Examples of Learning from Programmed Instruction

Author	Study	Results
Tanner (1966)	Groups of low achievers in 7th grade compared, with experimental group being taught arithmetic by programmed instruction, controls by classroom teacher.	n.s.d.
Bobier (1965)	12th grade students divided into experimental and control groups, to improve mathematical skills either by programmed instruction or classroom teaching.	n.s.d.
Doty and Doty (1964)	100 introductory psychology students studied program on physiological psychology for two weeks outside class and the subject was not discussed in class.	Learning on achievement test correlated highly with student's GPA.
Attiyen, Bach, and Lumsden (1969)	Over 400 students in 48 colleges and universities studied a programmed text on introductory economics. Divided into three groups: (a) studied program for period and attended no classes; (b) supplemented classroom teaching with programmed test; (c) classroom only.	Group (b) scored significantly higher than other groups. Group (a) lower but insignificantly so, than controls.
Ashford (1968)	Taught music theory by programmed text and compared with classroom teaching.	On recall test, three years later, students taught by programmed instruction did better than those taught in classroom.

TABLE 2.5 (cont.)

Author	Study	Results
Fincher and Fillmer (1965)	309 5th grade arithmetic students taught addition and subtraction in two groups — one with programmed textbooks, other with usual texts plus lecture and discussion.	Group with programmed texts performed better on criterion test (.05 level)
Hughes and McNamara (1961)	Class of IBM customer engineers divided into two groups to study 7070 system — one group with programmed text, other with lecture and discussion.	Programmed text group did significantly better on criterion test, and completed course in average of 8.8 hours as compared to 15 for conventionally taught group. Given a chance to experience both methods, 87% of engineers preferred programmed instruction.
Porter (1959)	Two groups of 6th graders studied spelling, one with programmed teaching machines other with conventional classroom methods.	Students taught by programmed instruction completed the unit in about one third the time, and did significantly better on criterion test.
Marsh and Pierce-Jones (1968)	295 college students in adolescent psychology divided into sections, incorporating programmed instruction into laboratories, others attending same laboratories but performing tasks other than programs.	Students using programmed materials scored significantly higher on 100-item final examination.

TABLE 2.6

Examples of Learning from Instructional Radio

Author	Study	Results
Constantine (1964)	Science taught by radio in elementary school.	Students gained on the average 14 months, in one school year, on standardized test of scientific information and 15 months on standardized test of work study skills.

TABLE 2.6 (cont.)

Author	Study	Results
Heron and Ziebarth (1946)	Learning from radio lectures compared with that from classroom lectures by the same teacher in college-level psychology. Groups changed places half-way through the course.	n.s.d.
NHK (1956)	Japan Broadcasting Corporation used radio to teach English and music in 3rd, 5th, 7th grades.	Reported learning gains in every case at or above level on conventionally taught classes.
Wisconsin Research Project in School Broadcasting (1942)	12 elementary school classes that received 25 minutes weekly of radio teaching of music plus 40 minutes of classroom practice compared with 8 classes taught same material for 75 minutes weekly in classroom.	Radio classes significantly better in tests of ability to recognize note values, read at sight, and recognize rhythms; n.s.d. on ability to take musical dictation.
Xoomsai and Ratanamangala (1962)	Very large sample study of teaching of social studies and music in 2nd and 3rd grades; English language in 6th and 7th grades, of rural Thai schools. Compared with control groups.	Experimental controls doubtful, but gains of radio groups reported as comparing very well with usual gains in those classes by conventionally taught students.
Lumley (1933)	High school students taught foreign languages with the aid of radio.	Pronunciation of students who heard radio lessons better than that of students who did not.

TABLE 2.7

Examples of Learning from "Smaller" Media

Author	Study	Results
Popham (1961)	Two sections of a graduate course in Education matched on aptitude and subject matter pretests; one section taught by lecture, the other by tape recordings of same lectures.	n.s.d.

TABLE 2.7 (cont.)

Author	Study	Results
Menne, Klingenschmidt, and Nord (1969)	Recorded lectures from introductory university psychology course, and provided students who so wished with their own tape recorders and printed chalkboard notes, to work at their own pace. 209 students chose to study from tapes, 408 from live lectures.	Overall, n.s.d. Lowest quartile (as divided by pretest) clear advantage for tape. Only 5 of 209 tape students dropped out of course, while 58 of 408 dropped out of lecture sections.
Elliot (1948)	Compared use of taped with live geography lessons in private secondary school.	Lower IQ students gained relatively more from tape.
Stein (1959)	Use of film loops as aid to learning typewriting.	Group with access to film loops learned to type significantly faster than group without access to loops.
Dworkin and Holden (1960)	Compared 60 graduate students who saw four filmstrips with tape recorded commentary on atomic bonding, with similar groups taught conventionally.	n.s.d.
Twyford 1960)	Reviews Air Force studies on training materials.	Inexpensive photo mockup of plane in many respects as effective as flight simulator. No appreciable difference in supplementary learning effect of cutaways, mockups, transparencies, and manual illustrations, although cost of providing them differed considerably.
Chance (1960)	Studied effect of adding 200 transparencies to college classes in engineering descriptive geometry.	Sections that saw transparencies did significantly better on final examination (.05) reported overwhelming preference for

TABLE 2.7 (cont.)

Author	Study	Results
		using transparencies, and saved average of 15 minutes teaching time per class period.
Kelley (1961)	Experimental groups of first graders learning to read had use of filmstrips, control groups did not but used same time for additional instruction by conventional classroom methods.	Experimental groups did significantly better on Gates test at end of term − .01 in word recognition, .05 in sentence reading.

TABLE 2.8

Results of Some of the Experiments on Big vs. Little Media as Vehicles of Learning

Author	Study	Results
Heidgerken (1948)	405 student nurses, randomly assigned to one of three groups, taught introduction to nursing arts respectively by films only, slides only, or films plus slides.	n.s.d.
Grosslight and McIntyre (1955) (1955)	947 college students taught Russian vocabulary by different means. Among their comparisons were:	
	films (motion Pictures) vs. slides	n.s.d.
	sound films vs. silent (this study also sums up Kale, 1953).	one n.s.d., one in favor of silent (sound interfered)
Vernon (1946)	732 Royal Navy trainees taught by films or filmstrips to take soundings. Groups equated on exams, and covariance used.	n.s.d.

TABLE 2.8 (cont.)

Author	Study	Results
Instructional Film Research Program (1954)	600 military police taught riot control by film, or filmstrips plus same soundtrack as film.	n.s.d.
Wells (1965)	594 college students randomly assigned to factorial design to test different treatments of a lesson in Introduction to Botany. Treatments were film (motion), slides, and sequential still pictures.	
	Conclusions: for concepts involving *time* concepts involving *motion* concepts involving *space*	films best n.s.d. slides and photographs best
Hovland, Lumsdaine, Sheffield (1949)	Very large sample of military trainees, assigned to instruction by sound films or filmstrips in map reading. Groups equated on Army GCT.	n.s.d. (filmstrips performed better by only 1.3 SE)
Westley and Barrow (1959)	228 6th grade students stratified on test of mental ability and assigned randomly to television or radio groups, for four 15-minute programs on current events. Programs used same news, but producers were told to use each medium in the best way possible.	TV "radio," on immediate test and after 8 months
Williams, Paul and Ogilvie (1957)	108 college sophomores stratified by grades, then randomly assigned to different groups including television vs. the television audio only (which they used to represent radio). Lecture on anthropology.	Silent film plus local commentary sound films

TABLE 2.8 (cont.)

Author	Study	Results
Craig (1956)	124 students, aged 9 through 15, compared with 136 matched on common entrance examination. First group had sound films on variety of informational subjects; second saw the visual track of the films, but heard commentary by their own classroom teachers.	Silent film plus local commentary sound films
Nelson (1951)	430 reserve officers randomly assigned to group to receive two lessons on theory and problems of flight with all possible combinations of sound and visual tracks in two films. Comparison thus resembled sound films vs. silent vs. radio.	Group that both saw and heard both films group that both saw and heard one film and *either* heard or saw the other other groups
Tannenbaum (1956)	406 practicing dentists in postgraduate extension course. One group (N=206) heard three weekly TV lectures, one hour each; group 2 (N=10) saw film strip with TV audio; group 3 (N=12) merely read the manual that other groups also had; group 4 (N=40) saw *in one day* kinescopes of all three TV programs.	Group 4 group 1 others
McIntyre (1966)	Randomly assigned college students (groups of 67 and 78 after absentees eliminated) taught economics by programmed instruction put together by usual method of trial, test, revision, or by a TV course revised several times in six years with guidance of expert judgement.	Program ITV

TABLE 2.8 (cont.)

Author	Study	Results
Spencer (1963)	43 11th and 12th grade students assigned to group that were taught a mathematics lesson either by programmed instruction on TV or on a teaching machine.	n.s.d.
Spector, Torres, Lichtenstein, Preston (1963)	Radio broadcasts, a combination of audiovisual media, and a combination of radio *and* the other audiovisual media compared in effort to persuade village mountaineers in Ecuador to adopt innovations.	Radio most effective in persuading people; films and other audiovisual media in conveying information.

TABLE 2.9

Some of the Studies on Multimedia Instruction

Author	Study	Results
Mathur and Neurath (1959)	Effectiveness of Radio Rural Forum (as contrasted with either farm radio or farmers' meetings alone) in 150 villages in India.	Combining discussion-and-decision group with radio broadcasts to feed the discussion brought about sensational increase in number of innovations accepted and rural improvements made.
VanderMeer (1950)	Comparison of groups of high school students taught respectively by films only, films and study guides, or conventional classroom instruction without either films or guides.	Combination of films and guides made for more learning than either of the other methods.
Whitted et.al. (1966)	Comparison of randomly assigned groups of Air Force trainees taught by automated multi-media self-study printed materials, or conventional classroom methods.	Both automated and classroom groups learned significantly more than home home study group. (We have pointed out that classroom teaching is usually multi-media anyway.)

TABLE 2.9 (cont.)

Author	Study	Results
Bryan (1961)	Chemistry and physics taught by variety of methods to students in remote Nebraska high schools too small to offer their own courses in science. Methods were (a) ITV plus correspondence, (b) ITV plus tutorial visits, (c) ITV plus correspondence plus visits.	Group (c) learned most.
Gillespie (1971)	Radio and a combination of audiovisual media compared, with Campbell's interrupted time series design, as devices to bring people to family planning clinic in Iran.	Both responsible for spectacular gains over control, but multi-media treatment accomplished significantly more.
Romano (1955)	Children in 5th, 6th, and 7th grades rotated between experimental and control groups. All groups had usual classroom teaching, including blackboards, bulletin boards, charts, models, flat pictures, and field trips. Only experimental groups had motion pictures plus projected still pictures. Measured on 50-item vocabulary tests derived from science textbooks used in the classes.	Experimental groups averaged between 26 and 63% higher scores on six units measured. Both teachers and students thought the use of projected materials enhances the learning situation.
Edwards, Williams, and Roderick (1968)	Beginning business college students taught introductory typing and first semester business machine operations in two groups, one with laboratory supervised by teacher, other using laboratory including programmed materials, sound tape loops, tape slide sets, and drill tapes.	Students using multi-media approach did significantly better than other (.05) on end-of-term performance examinations.

TABLE 2.10

**Examples of Effectiveness of Learning from Different Media
as Related to Mental Ability**

Author	Subject matter	Results
For high ability learners:		
Dreher and Beatty (1958)	Psychology	TV > conventional
Jacobs and Bollenbacher (1960)	Science	TV > conventional
Gordon, Nordquist, Engar (1959)	Slide rule	TV > conventional
Buckler (1958)	English	conventional > TV
Curry (1959)	Mathematics	conventional > TV
For low ability learners:		
Jacobs and Bollenbacher (1960)	Science	conventional > TV
Curry (1959)	Science	conventional > TV
Dreher and Beatty (1958)	Economics	TV > conventional
Wise (1939)	History	film > conventional
Porter (1961)	Spelling	program > conventional
Tanner (1966)	Mathematics	program, conventional, n.s.d.
Gropper and Lumsdaine (1961)	Science	conventional > program
For middle-ability learners:		
Wesley and Barrow (1959)	Current events	All ability groups *except* middle group, TV > radio

CHAPTER 3

THE PEDAGOGICAL EVIDENCE

First, no single medium is likely to have properties that make it best for all purposes. When effectiveness of one medium is compared with another for instruction in any given subject, it is rare for significant differences to be found. Lectures have been compared with reading, lectures with motion pictures, pictures with text, and many other kinds of comparison have been made without revealing clear superiority for any given medium. At any given time, a medium may enjoy unusual popularity, as has been the case, for example with television, teaching machines, and computerized instruction, at one period or another. Sometimes one medium is found by research to have an advantage for one subject matter only to be shown to have none for another subject matter. Over a period of years, researchers have learned to be skeptical of single instances of reported statistical superiority of one medium versus another.

Most instructional functions can be performed by most media. The oral presentation of a teacher can be used to gain and control attention, but so also can the use of paragraph headings in a textbook, or an animated sequence in an instructional motion picture. The learner can be informed of the expected outcomes of instruction by a printed text, by an oral communication, or in some instances by a picture or diagram. Recall of prerequisite learned capabilities can be done by oral communication, by means of a sentence or picture in a text, or by a movie or television pictorial sequence. Similar remarks could be made about every one of the functions of instruction. . . . It is possible, of course, that additional research of an analytic nature may yet reveal some important special properties of single media that make them peculiarly adapted to one instructional function or another. Up to now, however, the most reasonable generalization is that all media are capable of performing these functions.

In general, media have not been found to be differentially effective for different people. It is an old idea that some people may be "visual-minded," and therefore learn more readily from visual presentations, while others may be "auditory-minded," and therefore learn more readily from auditory presentations. While a number of studies have been conducted with the aim of matching media to human ability differences, it is difficult to find any investigations from which one can draw unequivocal conclusions. . . . If this idea has validity, it has not yet been demonstrated. A possible exception is this: several studies have shown that pictorial presentations may be more effective than printed texts for those who have reading difficulties or small vocabularies. This is hardly a surprising result, and it seems wise to refrain from over-generalizing its significance.

Robert Gagne
(*The Conditions of*
Learning, 1965, pp. 363-364)

Th
hese propositions from Gagne's notable book indicate how a
leading theorist of instructional technology reads the kind of
research we reviewed in the preceding chapters.

He concludes first that there is no one best medium, no super medium,
as we too decided in Chapter 2. Second, the media are very widely useful,
rather than narrowly restricted. He is not saying that, because any medium
seems able to contribute to almost any learning task, we should not try to
find the best medium—at least the *better media*—for that task. Indeed,
Gagne and his colleague Briggs have been deeply concerned with methods
of selecting media (for example, Briggs, 1970; Gagne and Briggs, 1974).
Nor is he saying that there is no need to try to relate media choice to
individual differences. His advice on this matter is quite restricted—merely
that he finds no evidence for the existence of "print learners," "picture
learners," or "audiovisual learners," except as some individuals are physi-
cally restricted from using one channel as efficiently as another or have
become accustomed to, and consequently more skilled in, using one
specific channel. He does not say that where a student stands on the ladder
of learning will make no difference in choice of media to meet his or her
needs at that point. He is not arguing that in a given situation for a given
learner one medium may not be more useful than others, or a combination
of media better than any one medium. And he is certainly not contending
that *one way of using* a given medium for a given learning task may not be
more effective.

In other words he is recognizing the limited usefulness of present
research in guiding the selection of media for instruction, and is prepared
to leaven those research findings, such as they are, with the practical
experience of pedagogy and the guidelines of pedagogical theory. Any
experienced teacher knows that at a certain point in a lesson on volcanoes
it helps to show students a photograph of a volcano, and at another point
to show them a diagram of the process that goes on inside that volcano. At
either time it would probably be less helpful to let them hear an audio
tape of a lecture. A teacher knows that a slow motion picture is more
effective than a still picture for showing students how an internal combustion engine works, and probably better than a diagram or a chart. A
map is better than a motion picture for showing someone where roads or
rivers are located. A teacher learns those discriminations by teaching, or
observing other teachers, and finds it hard to believe that there is little or
no base for them in research.

Some such doubts must have motivated the Council of Europe several
years ago when it commissioned Dr. Peggy Campeau to bring up to date

the literature review in Briggs, Campeau, Gagne, and May (1967), focusing on research that would guide the selection of media for teaching adults. Campeau published her painstaking report in *AV Communication Review* (1974), summing up her conclusions:

> In brief, an extensive literature search was made for research evidence relevant to selecting appropriate media for specified learning tasks. In particular, it was hoped that results of studies on the instructional effectiveness of media under a variety of learner and treatment conditions could be applied to the task of attempting to construct a media taxonomy. The disappointing result of the literature search was that little more than a dozen experimental studies were found to meet criteria that gave them some assurance that findings were interpretable.

> What is most impressive about this formidable body of literature surveyed for this review is that it shows that instructional media are being used extensively, under many diverse conditions, and that enormous amounts of money are being spent for the installation of very expensive equipment. All indications are that decisions as to which audiovisual devices to purchase, install, and use have been based on administrative and organizational requirements, and on considerations of cost, availability, and user preference, not on evidence of instructional effectiveness—and no wonder. To date, media research in post-school education has not provided decision makers with practical, valid, dependable guidelines for making these choices on the basis of instructional effectiveness [Campeau, 1974: 31].

Concerning research on the media of instruction, she writes:

> The question of which media to compare, or which learner and media characteristics to examine should be determined in the light of subject-matter and task characteristics. At present, an entire unit or course is programmed, or produced as a series of televised lessons, or filmed, or tape-recorded, or produced in multimedia format, without identifying specific instructional objectives to be met and without analyzing the types and conditions of learning required. Learners are assigned to these experimental treatments without regard for traits that might interact with media and task characteristics.

> The most illuminating evidence would come from research in which appropriate learner, media, task, and situational variables are specified for use in multivariate designs. . . . Interactions among variables might be found that could be used to enhance learning [Campeau, 1974: 33-34].

In other words, Dr. Campeau is saying: There should be less research that compares the outcome when sixth-grade arithmetic is taught by a classroom teacher to the outcome when it is taught by an instructional medium; more research that compares two or more ways of accomplishing a specified instructional task (one of the *many* instructional tasks within sixth-grade arithmetic) for a given kind of student in a given situation.

This requires, first, a detailed analysis of the kind of learning tasks and instructional events that make up teaching. It requires also a detailed analysis of the media of instruction, so that their characteristics and the ways of using them can be fitted to a design that includes also tasks, learners, and the situation in which learning takes place. Third, it requires a detailed analysis of relevant individual differences among learners, and a classification of situations whose differences may have an important bearing on the outcome of instruction. If taxonomies like these were available in a usable form they would guide not only research but also the thinking of teachers and educational planners.

When Campeau speaks of a "media taxonomy" and Saettler (1968) says that "an urgent need exists for a taxonomy of instructional media which can provide a systematic approach to the selection and uses of media for educational purposes," they are implying a very considerable intellectual effort. Important work has been done since Saettler wrote his 1968 review, but the need still remains.

TAXONOMIES OF LEARNING

The best-known taxonomy of learning is Bloom (et al., 1956), which is essentially a classification of the cognitive outcomes of education. The principal headings are knowledge, comprehension, application, analysis, synthesis, and evaluation. A brief version of this taxonomy will be found in Figure 3.1. Useful and comprehensive though this is, and even though many of the separate headings will suggest to a teacher the use of some media rather than others, the classification is still somewhat broad to be related to a particular act of media choice. The same may be said of Krathwohl's taxonomy of affective outcomes (in Krathwohl et al., 1965), which appears to be the only major attempt to classify the affective domain and, rather surprisingly in view of the importance generally ascribed to teaching values and attitudes, has had relatively little use.

There are also other varieties of learning typologies. For example, *developmental* psychologists like Piaget (1967) and Erickson (1963) have classified the stages in the development of a child's personality and intellect. It would stand to reason that some media must be better adapted than others for given purposes at different stages of development, but there is little hard evidence, even little theorizing, as to what they might be. *Personality* psychologists and psychoanalysts have classified learning outcomes in their own ways. Thus, Maslow (1962) deals with categories

FIGURE 3.1

Bloom's Taxonomy of the Cognitive Domain

1.00 Knowledge
    1.10 Knowledge of specifics
        1.11 Knowledge of terminology
            (Example: familiarity with a large number of words in their
              common range of meanings)
        1.12 Knowledge of specific facts
            (Example: the recall of major facts about particular cultures)
    1.20 Knowledge of ways and means of dealing with specifics
        1.21 Knowledge and conventions
            (Example: to make pupils conscious of correct forms and
              usage in speech and writing)
        1.22 Knowledge of trends and sequences
            (Example: understanding the continuity and development of
              American culture as exemplified in American life)
        1.23 Knowledge of classifications and categories
            (Example: becoming familiar with a range of types of literature)
        1.24 Knowledge of criteria
            (Example: knowledge of criteria for the evaluation of
              recreational activities)
        1.25 Knowledge of methodology
            (Example: knowledge of scientific methods for evaluating
              health concepts)
    1.30 Knowledge of the univerals and abstractions of a field
        1.31 Knowledge of principles and generalizations
            (Example: recall of major generalizations about particular
              cultures)
        1.32 Knowledge of theories and structures
            (Example: knowledge of a relatively complete formulation of
              the theory of evolution)

(Bloom characterizes the remaining five headings as "Intellectual Abilities and Skills"
as contrasted with "Knowledge")

2.00 Comprehension
    2.10 Translation
        (Example: skill in translating mathematical verbal material into symbolic
        statements and vice versa)
    2.10 Interpretation
        (Example: the ability to interpret various types of social data)
    2.30 Extrapolation
        (Example: skill in predicting continuation of trends)
3.00 Application
    (Example: application to the phenomena discussed in one paper of the
    scientific terms or concepts used in other papers)
4.00 Analysis
    4.10 Analysis of elements
        (Example: ability to recognize unstated assumptions)
    4.20 Analysis of relationships
        (Example: ability to check the consistency of hypotheses with given
        information and assumptions)

FIGURE 3.1 (cont.)

    4.30   Analysis of organizational principles
          (Example: ability to recognize the general techniques used in
          persuasive materials, such as advertising, propaganda, etc.)
5.00 Synthesis
    5.10   Production of a unique communication
          (Example: ability to tell a personal experience effectively)
    5.20   Production of a plan, or proposed set of operations
          (Example: ability to propose ways of testing hypotheses)
    5.30   Derivation of a set of abstract relations
          (Example: ability to make mathematical discoveries or generalizations)
6.00 Evaluation
    6.10   Judgments in terms of internal evidence
          (Example: ability to indicate logical fallacies in arguments)
    6.20   Judgments in terms of external criteria
          (Example: ability to compare a work with the highest known standards
          in its field — especially with other works of recognized excellence)

Source: Adapted from Krathwohl et al., 1965, II, 186 ff.; greater detail in Bloom, 1956)

like "self-actualization," Kelley (1962) with the "fully functioning self," Hollister and Bower (1966) with categories like "differentiation versus confusion." These are not of obvious assistance in matching needs to instruction.

It is not surprising that many of the most usable taxonomic bridges between theory and practices should be built by the so-called "training psychologists." These are scholars most of whom have studied under one or more of the great laboratory learning theorists—like Thorndike, Hull, Guthrie, Tolman, or Skinner—and then have worked for a time in the training programs of the military services or of industry, where they applied the principles of experimental psychology where it was necessary to produce practical results. I refer to men like Melton, Lumsdaine, Hawkridge, Glaser, Stolurow, Briggs, and Gagne, most of whom have now moved to university professorships, where they make major contributions to the scholarly literature but remain on the growing edge of the developing field of instructional technology.

Gagne's *The Conditions of Learning* (1965) led the way toward linking learning theory and the technology of instruction. Gagne's is the seminal volume for a series of useful books written by psychologists most of whom were or are associated with the American Institutes of Research. Among these are Briggs' detailed *Handbook of Procedures for the Design of Instruction* (1970 and earlier versions); Briggs, Campeau, Gagne, and May (1967) on instructional media; and Gagne and Briggs, *Principles of Instructional Design* (1974). We shall make extensive use of these volumes in the following pages.

Classifying the Types of Learning

Gagne's taxonomy of learning, in his own words, appears in Figure 3.2. It will be useful to say a few words about each of these kinds of learning, and some of their implications for instruction.

Signal learning does not ordinarily play a very large part in the design of, say, a pub ic school curriculum. Rather, it occurs when a child learns

FIGURE 3.2
Gagne's Taxonomy of Types of Learning

Type 1:   *Signal Learning.* The individual learns to make a general, diffuse response to a signal. This is the classical conditioned response of Pavlov (1927).

Type 2:   *Stimulus-Response Learning.* The learner acquires a precise response to a discriminated stimulus. What is learned is a connection (Thorndike, 1898), or a discriminated operant (Skinner, 1938), sometimes called an instrumental response (Kimble, 1961).

Type 3:   *Chaining.* What is acquired is a chain of two or more stimulus-response connections. The conditions for such learning have been described by Skinner (1938) and others, notably Gilbert (1962).

Type 4:   *Verbal Association.* Verbal association is the learning of chains that are verbal. Basically, the conditions resemble those for other (motor) chains. However, the presence of language in the human being makes this a special type because internal links may be selected from the individual's previously learned repertoire of language (see Underwood, 1964b).

Type 5:   *Discrimination Learning.* The individual learns to make *n* different identifying responses to as many different stimuli, which may resemble each other in physical appearance to a greater or lesser degree. Although the learning of each stimulus-response connection is a simple Type 2 occurrence, the connections tend to interfere with each other's retention (Postman, 1961).

Type 6:   *Concept Learning.* The learner acquires a capability of making a common response to a class of stimuli that may differ from each other widely in physical appearance. He is able to make a response that identifies an entire class of objects or events (see Kendler, 1964). Other concepts are acquired *by definition,* and consequently have the formal characteristics of rules.

Type 7:   *Rule Learning.* In simplest terms, a rule is a chain of two or more concepts. Its functions to control behavior in the manner suggested by a verbalized rule of the form, "If A, then B," where A and B are previously learned concepts. However, it must be carefully distinguished from the mere verbal sequence, "If A, then B," which, of course, may also be learned as Type 4.

Type 8:   *Problem Solving.* Problem solving is a kind of learning that requires the internal events usually called thinking. Two or more previously acquired rules are somehow combined to produce a new capability that can be shown to depend on a "higher-order" rule.

From Gagne, 1965: 63-64

that a reproving shout by a parent is likely to signal punishment, or that a siren signals danger. Guthrie (1935: 48) gave a delightful illustration of signal learning in a passage which Gagne also chose to quote:

> Two small country boys who lived before the day of the rural use of motor cars had their Friday afternoons made dreary by the regular visit of their pastor, whose horse they were supposed to unharness, groom, feed, and water, and then harness again on the departure. Their gloom was lightened finally by a course of action which one of them conceived. They took to spending the afternoon of the visit retraining the horse. One of them stood behind the horse with a hay-fork and periodically shouted "Whoa," and followed this with a sharp jab of the fork. Unfortunately, no exact records of this experiment were preserved save that the boys were quite satisfied with the results.

Stimulus-response learning is something that plays a large part in all educational experience, formal and informal. Whereas the outcome of signal learning is a relatively involuntary and emotional response, the outcome of S⟶R learning, as Gagne very properly points out, is a precise and controlled action. The child learns to say "mama" on demand, and the dog learns to "shake hands" as that has been demonstrated to him. The conditions for this kind of learning are (1) the stimulus ("say 'mama' " or "shake hands"), (2) some guidance in the response, and (3) some reward or reinforcement when the response is made. Whereas the horse probably responded without any guidance when he was stuck with the hay-fork, the dog is not likely to shake hands until he is shown how to do it and until his progressive improvements in the act are rewarded. This encouragement of an ever-nearer response to the intended outcome is what Skinner (1968) calls "shaping." It occurs when we listen to a foreign language practice tape and repeat what we hear until our pronunciation more nearly resembles that on the tape.

Chaining is a type of learning that can take place only when several stimulus-response connections have already been learned. Every parent has seen his or her child begin to use words in a new instrumental fashion. The child has learned that his mother brings to him warmth, security, and food, and he has learned to say the word "mama." One day he suddenly puts all this together and *calls for* the person who brings these rewards. In other words, he has made a chain. We learn complicated motor chains when we learn to tie a knot. The conditions for such learning are (1) the previous learning of the individual links in the chain, and (2) the occurrence of these events close together. The second step in the knot sequence must follow closely up the first, and so forth, until the knot itself appears.

Verbal association occurs when one learns the foreign equivalent of an English word. The conditions for this kind of learning are (1) the prior learning of an English word and its meaning, (2) the ability to say the foreign word, and (3) the presence of some "coding connection" that enables the learner to associate the two words. Studies of nonsense syllables (for example, Jenkins, 1963) have demonstrated that even paired associates can be most easily learned by finding a mediating term by which to connect them. Gagne gives the example of learning the French word *alumette,* meaning "match" in English. The learner must first associate the word "match" with the object "match," and he must also be able to say the French word *alumette.* If he can say it well enough to note the syllable *lum,* then he may have a built-in coding connection: *Lum* may make him think of the word "illuminate," or vice versa. And thus he can build an associative chain: Match calls up the picture of a burning match which illuminates the surrounding space; illuminate calls up the syllable lum; and this ties in the word *alumette,* which now is associated not only with the word "match" but also with the image of the burning match.

Discrimination learning goes on when one learns which of his or her keys fits the office door and which fits the front door at home; or when a child learns to distinguish a triangle from a square. Obviously this is a very important kind of learning. The conditions for accomplishing it are (1) prior learning of the chains that are to be discriminated (for example, we know the appearance and the name of a triangle), and then (2) sufficient practice in distinguishing one shape from the other to get rid of the "interference" that occurs in trying to remember a number of things that are only slightly different. In other words, the individual chains must be learned so well that the differences among them will be obvious.

Concept learning is classifying stimuli. We have to recognize the concept of "peopleness" in order to distinguish people from animals or trees, and the concept of "hotness" in order to classify certain stimuli as hot rather than cold or wet or expensive. We generalize upon individual occurrences, relate them to each other, and store them away for easier retrieval. Thus, the learning of concepts is one of the major keys to handling the complexity around us. The conditions for learning concepts are (1) a sufficient number of past discriminations to make it possible to recognize and respond to the particular attribute that is to be conceptualized; and (2) exposure to a variety of stimuli incorporating this attribute, so that discrimination is of the attribute rather than merely the stimuli themselves. This will ordinarily require practice with a number of different situations which include the attribute to be conceptualized. The amount of practice can be reduced, and the learning of concepts can be greatly speeded, if an individual has learned enough language to take a verbal shortcut. For example, he can learn the concept of "middle" by simply being told that it means "in between"—if he understands "in between."

Learning rules is learning a relation between concepts. For example, one learns that "round things roll," "spring follows winter," or "the square of the hypotenuse of a right triangle is equal to the sum of the squares of the other two sides." To learn a rule, it is necessary (1) to learn the concepts involved—e.g., the idea of roundness, and rolling, and things. Then (2) one can be presented a verbal chain that relates the concepts, and a chain is easily learned if it is not too complicated. The actual practice of learning rules usually involves demonstration and often the kind of investigation by the learner that some scholars call "discovery." To learn to state the rule is not always to "understand" it fully. But the importance of learning rules is that they make it possible to comprehend and often predict dynamic and hierarchical relationships in the world around one. They let us think in terms of "if . . . then. . . ." Needless to say, much of the learning that goes on in school is the learning of rules.

Problem solving is the use of learned rules to create new ones. It is the essence of "thinking something out," and, thus, it may be very complex or very simple. A person solves a problem when he calculates how many hours he will have for work if he arises at a certain time. Then he is in position to make his new rule: If I want to do so much work, I must get up at such-and-such a time. A student calculating how long it would take to go to Mars, given a certain rocket, is solving a more academic kind of problem. Einstein was following the same process when he combined sophisticated rules of mathematical physics into rules that became known as the Theory of Relativity.

What is this process? One must (1) have some idea of what kind of solution he is looking for; otherwise, he will waste effort. Then (2) he must recall the rules that are relevant to the problem. Finally, (3) he must combine those rules so that a new rule—which may either be the solution or a step toward the solution—emerges. Gagne and others are quick to admit that we know relatively little about the act of combining rules to make a new one, which is to say that we know little about the act of thinking through problems so that the solution emerges, usually in a "flash of insight." But this is a high order of thinking and perhaps the highest order of learning.

HIERARCHIES OF LEARNING

It can easily be seen that Gagne's taxonomy is hierarchical in nature. Thus:

Learning

stimulus-response connections (2)[1]

is prerequisite to learning

chains (3) and

verbal associations (4)

which are in turn prerequisite to learning

discriminations (5)

which must precede the learning of

concepts (6)

which are prerequisite to the learning of

rules (7)

which are required for

problem solving (8).

Most learning is hierarchical. One step must be taken before another can be successfully accomplished, and all the simpler types of learning are subsumed under the more complex forms. Instruction is designed that way. As an example, see Figure 3.3, which outlines a process for learning a basic reading skill—the ability to pronounce printed words.

Note that this begins with a relatively simple skill, the ability to reproduce the sounds of single letters. As a matter of fact, it begins wherever the learner is. If he cannot discriminate letters and sounds (for example, the f from the s sound, printed p from printed b), those skills must be mastered first. Then he can relate these sounds to the appropriate letters. Soon after that he must learn the hard news that some English letters have more than one sound (for example, i and c). Then he moves gradually to pronounce groups of letters and finally to reading whole words.

But note the right side of the chart: If the learner is already able to pronounce the sounds of printed syllables, he can skip over some of the activity represented by the left side of the chart. If he can already pronounce the sounds of groups of syllables, then he can skip further practice of that skill and go directly to the more advanced practice of reading aloud.

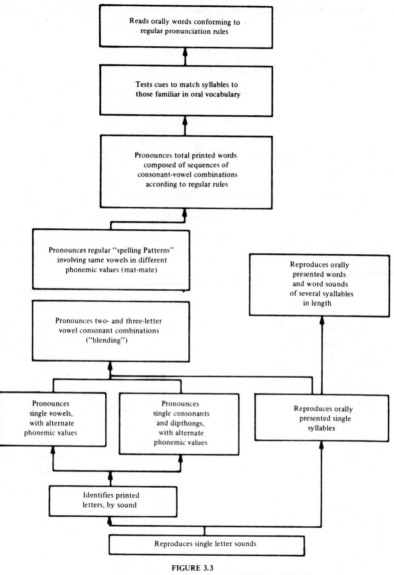

FIGURE 3.3
A Learning Hierarchy for the Skill of "Decoding" Printed Words
So As To Be Able To Read Them Aloud

(After Gagne, 1965, Figure 20, p. 271)

Thus, the design of instruction requires one to ask where the student is on a hierarchy of learned skills leading up to the objective of the lesson or the course. Incidentally, it presents a problem for media, except individualized media, because the media material must strike some balance between losing the students who are not ready for it and boring the students who are already beyond it.

IS THIS A BROAD ENOUGH VIEW OF LEARNING?

Before going any further it is necessary to ask whether this taxonomy includes all types of learning to which we might want to match media. Where, for instance, are motor skill learning and value learning? These are obviously *not* directly included in Gagne's (1965) taxonomy, and in his 1974 book (with Briggs), he looked at learning with a wider-angle lens. The eight categories we have listed were all included under the heading of *intellectual skills,* which were described as "the most basic and at the same time the most pervasive structure of formal education . . . the capabilities that make the human individual competent." But they were only one of five large types. The 1974 taxonomy, then, would include:

(a) Intellectual skills

(b) Cognitive strategies

(c) Verbal information

(d) Motor skills

(e) Attitudes

The five larger categories are not all completely and obviously separate. Motor skills and attitudes are learning objectives which are clearly different from the intellectual skills and probably require different media specification. "Cognitive strategies" are defined as the "capabilities that govern the individual's own learning, remembering, and thinking behavior" (Gagne and Briggs, 1974). In other words they are intellectual *management* skills. Bruner used the same name for them (et al., 1956); Rothkopf (1968) called them "mathemagenic behaviors"; Skinner (1968), "self-management behaviors." Gagne gives as an example learning the process of *inference* or *induction.* "Suppose," he says,

> that a student has become acquainted with magnetic attraction in a bar magnet—he has noted that a force is exerted by each pole of a magnet on certain kinds of metal objects. Now he is given some iron filings which he sprinkles on a piece of paper placed over the magnet. When the paper is tapped, the filings exhibit lines of force around each pole of the magnet. The student proceeds to verify his observation in other situations, perhaps using other magnets and

other kinds of metal objects. These observations, together with other knowledge, may lead him to induce the idea of a magnetic field of force surrounding each pole of the magnet. It is important to note, in this example, that the student has not been told of the magnetic field beforehand, nor has he been given instruction in 'how to induce.' But he does carry out this kind of mental operation [Gagne and Briggs, 1974: 27].

This is clearly a larger and less specific operation than is described by any of the "intellectual skills." It probably takes a fairly long period of time to develop. Once learned, it can be applied to many different situations and used to solve a great variety of problems.

The difference between what Gagne and Briggs call intellectual skills and what they call cognitive strategies may be illustrated by recalling that one of their most advanced intellectual skill categories is *learning a rule:* For example, that kilometers can be translated approximately into miles by multiplying the number of kilometers by 0.6. This is a useful tool for translating back and forth between two units of measure, but by itself it is not of general use for managing intellectual operations. Once one masters the process of induction, however, that spell can be applied almost without reference to subject matter. Intellectual skills, then, are the basic and most pervasive objectives of education. Cognitive strategies are the managerial skills which a person learns in order to manage most effectively his learning experiences and his intellectual baggage. How is "verbal information" distinguished from these two?

Verbal information, say Gagne and Briggs, is the packaged information we acquire (1974: 24):

> such as the names of months, days of the week, letters, numerals, towns, cities, states, countries, and so on. We also have a great store of more highly organized information such as many events of American history, the forms of government, the major achievements of science and technology, the components of the economy.

By verbal information, they mean the baggage we pick up that is translated into verbal form; by intellectual skills, they mean ways of learning it; by cognitive strategies, ways of managing it.

One nagging question intrudes: Is there no place in this taxonomy for visual or auditory information (such as the memory of a face, a house, or a mountain, or the sound of a theme from a symphony or of a familiar voice) which is not usually stored in verbal form? And are there any special skills for learning those?

But the Gagne type of taxonomy includes five large categories of learning, with eight subheads under the category of basic intellectual skills. It also includes an analysis of the actual events of instruction.

ANALYZING THE EVENTS OF INSTRUCTION

Thus far in our analysis we have not found any code that shows us how to fit a given medium to a given learning task. We have worked down through the basic intellectual skills to the idea of hierarchies of learning, then stepped back to see where the basic skills belong in a larger taxonomy of learning. But there is still another set of activities to be added into the Gagne-Briggs taxonomy before one decides how and to what to match the media of instruction.

These are what Gagne (1965) and Gagne and Briggs (1974) called the "events of instruction." They are represented in Figure 3.4.

The events of instruction are what the teacher has to work with, once he has clearly stated his objective and defined the beginning point for his students. They guide what the teacher does in the classroom, what appears on the television screen, what goes into the lesson plan. They are sequenced. Gagne points out that not all his eleven "events" occur in every

FIGURE 3.4
The Events of Instruction

1. *Gaining attention.* A stimulus is presented to appeal to the learner's interest or his curiosity. It may be a question, a challenge, a demonstration, a sharp change in the visual scene, or the like.

2. *Informing the learner of the objective.* The learner has to know how he will *know when* he has learned what is expected of him in the lesson.

3. *Stimulating recall of prerequisite learned capabilities.* For any except the most fundamental learning, the learner must have at hand certain knowledge and skills he has previously learned so that he can use them in the new task. The problem is to remind him of this necessary background.

4. *Presenting the stimulus material.* When the learner is ready, he or she must be shown the material to be learned or to be worked with.

5. *Providing "learning guidance".* The learner will need to be directed by prompts or hints or questions toward the objective.

6. *Eleciting the performance.* Having arrived at the objective the learner must now be challenged to show that he can "do it," perhaps by use of an example or a problem.

7. *Providing feedback.* The learner must be informed of the correctness of his performance – by words, by a smile or a nod, or by some other means.

8. *Assessing performance.* The teacher wants to make sure that the learner has indeed learned to accomplish the objective. One of the commonest ways to make sure of this is to ask for one or more repetitions.

9. *Enhancing retention and transfer.* This calls for practice, especially with varied tasks requiring the same skill that has been the objective of the lesson.

After Gagne, 1962: 304 ff., Gagne and Briggs, 1974: 123 ff.

lesson, nor do they always occur in exactly the given order, although, he says, the order he gives is the most probable. Most treatments of instructional technology make much of the importance of sequencing. Schalock (1970) is an example.

The events of instruction are perhaps the least distinctive part of the Gagne-Briggs taxonomy, for there are literally hundreds of such lists, short or long, all resembling in general the ones we have quoted.

Fitting Media to Tasks

What we need now is an algorithm for translating instructional events (backed up by the analysis of learning tasks and learning hierarchies) into

FIGURE 3.5
Summary of Briggs' Outline for Designing Instruction

1. *Define the boundary conditions.* Note any limiting conditions for both development and implementation in terms of time, costs, skills, and resources available.

2. *Decide between individual and group instruction.* This affects the media choices, as well as how the finished instructional materials are used. Two analyses of the same objectives and competencies could be made, one for individual, and one for group instruction. Or, different competencies could be planned for the two methods, for use with a single group of learners.

3. *Identify the characteristics of the learners.*

4. *Identify a competency to be analyzed.* Note carefully the significant verbs (behaviors) and objects (content reference).

5. *List the general instructional events to be used.*

6. *List the special instructional events* for the type of learning the competency represents.

7. *Arrange the entire list of events in the desired order,* and consider whether more than one application of each event is needed.

8. *List the type of stimuli for each event,* considering both learner and task characteristics.

9. *List the alternate media* from which a choice is to be made for each event.

10. *Make a tentative media selection* for each event from among the alternates recorded. Note a rationale of advantages and disadvantages for group or individual use.

11. *Review an entire series of tentative media choices,* seeking optimum, "packaging".

12. *Make final media choices for package units.*

13. *Write a prescription to the specialist for each package unit,* or one continuous, uninterrupted use of a medium

14. *Write a prescription for the teacher* for instructional events not provided by the other media.

From Hawkridge, n.d., after Briggs, 1970

the choice of media for instruction. This is where the theoretical literature begins to break down.

Perhaps the most direct attempt by either Gagne or Briggs to face up to this problem was by Briggs in his 1970 handbook. He suggested a procedure in fourteen steps, reproduced in Figure 3.5.

This is undoubtedly good advice for designing instruction. But what we need is some specific guidance for steps 9-12.

In his 1970 volume, Briggs gives some directions to the students who were trying out an early version of the book in their classes. The goal, he says, is to choose a medium of instruction to fit each instructional event. This requires that the necessary "competencies" to be learned should first be identified (Step 4, Figure 3.5). For each competency, a series of instructional events must be specified to accomplish the desired learning. These must be arranged in an optimum way, and for each the stimulus or stimuli most likely to be effective must be selected. Then the designer is to select the media by which to present the stimuli.

How? Briggs (1970) says:

> For each instructional event . . . you choose a medium of instruction and defend your choice on the basis of one or more of the following:
>
> (a) a systematic model for the design of instruction;
>
> (b) other theoretical or logical analysis models;
>
> (c) research findings in this subject-matter area;
>
> (d) other documented evidence (not intuition).

Briggs thus provides an admirably logical model but little research to guide the selection. Gagne and Briggs are quite candid about the lack of such research (1974: 151-152):

> Unfortunately, research has not yielded data permitting sweeping generalizations about media. Individual differences among learners and among teaching topics are too many and diverse to permit simple rules for decision-making. Consequently, *good judgment* must be used in planning just how to accomplish each instructional event for the lesson plan. In doing this, it may be found desirable to make a separate medium selection for each event; alternatively, it may be possible to use a single medium in such a way as to introduce all the events for a lesson.

At another point, Gagne says:

> One method for making media selections is to ask 'What type of stimuli would be needed for this instructional event?' If this can be decided, some media alternatives at once present themselves for

further consideration. At the same time, other media can at once be excluded. In this approach, one makes a tentative, separate medium choice for each instructional event, and then reviews the list of tentative media before making final media choices. By this method, the selection of media is based upon the instructional events *within* lessons, rather than at the level of the lesson, topic, or course.

Another aid to media selection is to consider Dale's (1969) 'Cone of Experience' [1974: 150-151].

Dale's "Cone of Experience" (Dale, 1969, and earlier editions of that much-used textbook) classified learning experiences beginning with "direct, purposeful experience" and leading upward through presumed levels of abstraction to "verbal symbols." Dale's book visualized this as a cone with the least abstract experience at the bottom, numbered 1, and the most abstract at the top, numbered 12. Figure 3.6 reproduces this list.

Anyone can argue against placing a *particular* film at number 8 on the scale as compared to a *particular* still picture at number 9. Anyone can object that the table is not unidimensional. But the table is at least a rough approximation of levels of abstraction in learning, and no one can quarrel with Dale's own rule, which is "Go as low on the scale as you need to in order to insure learning, but go as high as you can for the most efficient learning." Gagne and Briggs (1974) said it in their own way: "By considering the opposing factors of 'slow but sure' (time-consuming direct experience) and 'fast but risky' (typically occurring when learners are not skilled readers), one may decide just where on the scale is the best decision point for media selection."

FIGURE 3.6
Dale's "Cone of Experience"

12.	Verbal symbols
11.	Visual symbols (signs; stick figures)
10.	Radio and recordings
9.	Still pictures
8.	Motion pictures
7.	Educational television
6.	Exhibits
5.	Study trips
4.	Demonstrations
3.	Dramatized experiences (plays, puppets, role-playing)
2.	Contrived experiences (models, mock-ups, simulations)
1.	Direct, purposeful experience

"Good judgment" and "common sense" are beginning to bulk large as we seek guidance on how to translate this sophisticated taxonomy into media choice. For instance, here are Briggs, Campeau, Gagne, and May again:

Determining appropriateness of media ... is a complex decision which cannot be done in cookbook fashion. For example, if the introductory portion of a course in science requires the learning of a number of concepts . . . the need for pictures (or actual objects) may be frequent. In such a case, an instructional sequence emphasizing pictures might be an efficient way to present this part of the course. In practice, a sequence of slides or a film might be designed, and might be the medium of choice provided it could include the *other* modes of presentation required (accompanying oral and printed speech).

At the other end of the spectrum, there will be portions of a course which need pictures to only a limited degree. For example, if the student already knows the required concepts, a presentation of the principles . . . is simply not going to be helped by many pictures, if any.

When a series of analyses of objectives indicates need for a mixture of diagrams, still pictures, verbal descriptions, and decisions to be made by the student, a format like programmed instruction would be appropriate.

If movements of objects in space and time relationships are involved, as in understanding what causes night and day, a motion picture showing rotation of the earth and its revolution around the sun, accompanied by sound narration of the principles involved, would be relevant [Briggs et al., 1967: 34].

At this point in the analysis, another problem in media selection becomes evident. Even if a teacher goes through the painstaking analysis required to identify the competencies to be learned, the learning events needed to teach them, and the stimuli required by each of these learning events, and if by common sense or any other guides available the teacher selects a "best" medium by which to present each of those stimuli, it is unlikely that any school will be able or willing to provide all the media and the required software. It is also unlikely that any teacher is going to be skillful enough to change constantly from medium to medium through the lesson. What is almost sure to happen is one of two things: (a) *One or two* media will be chosen, preferably simple ones, to present *one or two* key points in the lesson; or (b) rather than using the optimum medium for each learning event, one medium will be chosen which is able to present stimuli for a large number of the required learning events. It may not be the best choice for *all* of them, but the stimuli will be packaged in that one medium for simplicity, at the cost of maximum effectiveness.

This is recognized by Briggs, Gagne, and their colleagues. After (1) identifying the required instructional events and (2) choosing the necessary stimuli, designers of instruction are advised to (3) "state the media options that would be acceptable." Then:

(4) Prepare a summary of the media options for a group of objectives making up a sequence of instruction, and scan these to identify *frequently occurring media options.*

(5) Assign the media in which the instruction should be packaged to achieve the best *trade-off* in respect to effective stimulus display, *convenience in changing from medium to medium,* and *economy* in terms of size of unit in which each sequence is to be prepared in the given media [Briggs, 1970: 28-29].

Thus, after all the brilliance of the analysis of instructional design summarized in this chapter, we find ourselves having to settle for something far less than brilliance in media choice. It is simply not practical to present all the stimuli encompassed in the learning events by means of the media best suited to do so (even if we had better evidence than common sense to tell us what those media are). It is not practical to switch back and forth between media as often as the analysis would require. We must therefore choose one or two points at which to use media, or "package" a number of stimuli in some medium which may be second or third best for a given presentation, but is most manageable for the total teaching situation. It is a little like practicing with surgeons' tools, and then having to work with an axe.

TOWARD A TAXONOMY OF MEDIA

Managerial Questions

To select the media that can best present the kinds of stimuli required by the learning task, we should like to have a taxonomy of media parallel to the five major areas of learning, the eight basic types of learning, and the eleven "events of instruction" (as we have presented them, drawing mostly on Gagne and Briggs), or some combination of these in one pattern. It is hardly necessary to say that no such taxonomy exists.

Most of the media taxonomies that have been attempted are on what might be called the "managerial" level. By this we mean the relatively superficial questions of selecting a medium for efficiency and availability when it has already been decided that "we need a picture" or we do not, we need words or we do not, and so forth. This part of a taxonomy can begin with fairly obvious things. Some media carry a picture to the eye; some, a series of sounds to the ear; some, both. Some of those that carry pictures can present them in rapid sequence so as to represent motion. Some are live; some, recorded, although almost any recorded information can also be transmitted over "live" media if desired. One medium—the computer used for instruction—permits a student to interact with a subtly

Telecommunication	Sound	Picture	Line Graphic	Print	Motion	Recording
Class I: Audio-Motion-Visual						
	X	X	X	X	X	Sound film
Television	X	X	X	X	X	Video tape
						Film TV recording
	X	X	X	X	X	Holographic recording
Picturephone	X	X	X	X	X	
Class II: Audio-Still Visual						
Slow-scan TV	X	X	X	X		Recorded still TV
Time-shared TV						
	X	X	X	X		Sound filmstrip
	X	X	X	X		Sound slide-set
	X	X	X	X		Sound-on-slide
	X	X	X	X		Sound page
	X	X	X	X		Talking book
Class III: Audio-Semimotion						
Telewriting	X		X	X	X	Recorded telewriting
Audio pointer	X		X	X	X	
Class IV: Motion-Visual						
		X	X	X	X	Silent film
Class V: Still-Visual						
Facsimile		X	X	X		Printed page
		X	X	X		Filmstrip
		X	X	X		Picture set
		X	X	X		Microform
		X	X	X		Video file
Class VI: Semimotion						
Telautograph			X	X	X	
Class VII: Audio						
Telephone	X					Audio disc
Radio						Audio tape
Class VIII: Print						
Teletype				X		Punched paper tape

FIGURE 3.7

Bretz's Taxonomy of Communication Media

(As revised and presented in Bretz, 1971, inside cover on 55-56) designed and recorded program so that the effect, within limits, is that of live communication. Bretz (1971) has shown a great deal of ingenuity in schematicizing the choice of media at this level. Three of his diagrams—a basic classification of media of instruction, a flow chart for distinguishing among media in terms of sensory requirements, and another flow chart for distinguishing between abstractness and concreteness of the stimuli required—are presented in Figures 3.7, 3.8, and 3.9.

Like most such lists, these do not include all the possible media of instruction. Bretz's taxonomies omit the computer, probably on the grounds that programmed instruction is a method rather a medium and can be presented by many media—print, television, tape loops, and others. However, when a computer is programmed so that a learner can *interact* with it, this is something qualitatively different from a printed program that tells a student whether his answers are correct, or an arithmetic text that prints the right answers in the back of the book. Be that as it may, Bretz's diagrams are highly usable on the level we have specified: e.g., does the learning require a picture? If so, does it require a *moving* picture to describe a process or an action? If a still picture is needed, there are at least twenty-one choices; if a moving picture, at least six. Does it require sound and picture together? If so, at least fourteen possibilities are available. If sound, picture, and motion are all required, there are six. If print is to be combined with picture, there are twenty-four possibilities. If print with sound, seventeen. This amounts, of course, to a suggestive catalogue of available technologies. It says nothing of the learning tasks each medium can perform, or which one it can perform better than other tasks or other technologies.

Educators take into account other characteristics of instructional media while working at the "managerial" level of selection. One of these is where different media can deliver the stimuli they are asked to deliver. Any of the media can be used individually, of course, at home or in a study room, although it is less expensive to do this with recorded than with live media—for example, with videotape rather than television—unless many individuals are to be using the media simultaneously. A few of the media have this ability to deliver a learning experience simultaneously to individuals or groups over a large area: radio and television, for example. Still other media are designed primarily for use by groups in classrooms or auditoriums—for example, films. Figure 3.10 catalogues some of the media in terms of the coverage for which they are primarily designed.

When an educator or an educational planner chooses between a very wide-range medium like television or radio, and a room-size medium like film or tape, it is necessary to consider how much control over the learning activity one wants to centralize and how much to leave with the local

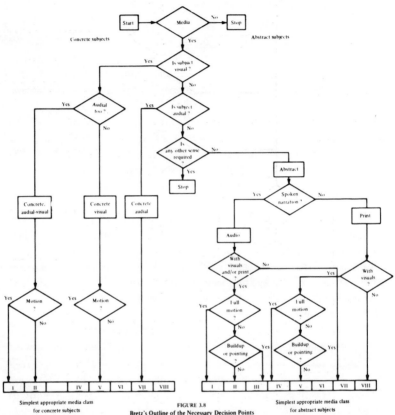

FIGURE 3.8
Bretz's Outline of the Necessary Decision Points
in Selecting Appropriate Media for a Given Instructional Need
(Bretz, 1971, p. 30)

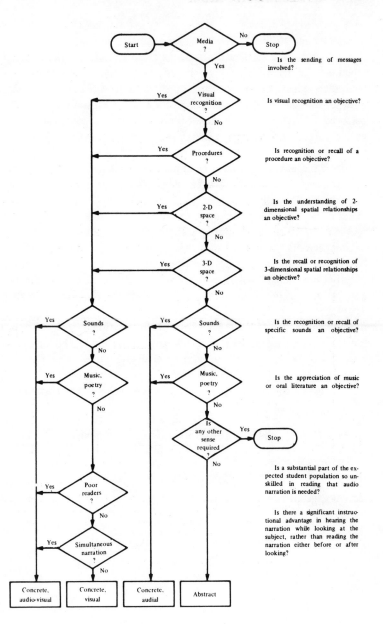

FIGURE 3.9
Bretz's Elaboration of the Decision Points for Distinguishing between
Concrete and Abstract Subject Matter, Specified in Figure 2
(Bretz, 1971, p. 32)

teacher or the student. Television, for example, is mostly out of the hands of local users. Unless they can record a broadcast on videotape, they must schedule the lesson when the broadcasting station schedules it. Once begun, no teacher or student can stop the broadcast (as they could do with a locally projected film) to ask a question, emphasize a point, or repeat a passage. Furthermore, the rate of presentation is controlled centrally, unlike a slide or filmstrip presentation which can be run as slow or as fast as users wish.

Thus, the quality resulting from central production and the economies in unit costs possible with a large wide-coverage medium must be weighed against the flexibility of a smaller medium, and the greater ease of matching such a "Little" medium to the needs of its users.

Figures 3.10 and 3.11 sum up some of these differences.

Another question asked more frequently is which media can be effectively combined. This is both a cost and an effectiveness question, not only because more media are now available to the classroom teacher, but also because an increasing amount of instruction goes on at long distance. Tiffin and Combes (1974) have prepared a chart of combinations, which is reproduced in Figure 3.12. They look at the decision as it would appear to the teacher and to the learner. They assume that the teacher as well as the learner will depend mostly on a "master medium" and then decide what other media can be used for complementary purposes. For example, a student of the British Open University would probably use books (the unit

FIGURE 3.10
Delivery Capabilities of Different Media

Simultaneous wide coverage
   Television (including slow-scan TV)
   Radio
   Facsimile

Room-size, or otherwise limited to a single place

Sound film	Slide
Silent film	Filmstrip
Videotape	Audiotape
Sound filmstrip	Audiodisc
Sound on slide	Photograph
Radiovision	Poster
	Chalkboard, slate

Individual
   Print
   Telephone
   Computer-assisted instruction (although a computer system can be
      "shared" by individuals in different places)

FIGURE 3.11
Extent of User Control of Instructional Media

Media	Can he carry it around?	Use at home?	Decide when to use?	Control flow (stop, start)	Use individually	Get a response from it
Television		X			X	
Radio	X	X			X	
Radiovision						
Film	films portable; projectors less so	not most homes	X	X	X	
Sound on slide, sound Filmstrip	projectors less easily	not most homes	X	X	X	
Slide	X	X	X	X	X	
Filmstrip	X	X	X	X	X	
Audiotape with cassette	X	X	X	X	X	
Audiodisc with phonograph	disc, yes; phonograph?	X	X	X	X	
Photographs	X	X	X	X	X	
Print	X	X	X	X	X	To a degree (with programmed instrution, dictionary, etc.)
Computer-assisted instruction			X	X	X	X

Compare the much more detailed list by Miller, 1973

texts) as a master medium. The chart says that practical materials—video cassettes and audio cassettes—would be the preferred complementary media. Actually, the Open University makes use of live radio and television for this purpose, but provides some cassettes and tapes for reference in the regional study centers. A classroom teacher who depends basically on face-to-face instruction has a large choice of complementary media, as the figure shows. You may not agree entirely with this chart, but it will at least suggest the importance of this element in selection.

Cost is another inevitable managerial question. We shall cover cost at greater length in Chapter 4. But here it may be useful to suggest some of the subquestions that will crop up. For any given medium, is the technology available, and, if not, how much will it cost to obtain or develop? Is the software available, and, if not, how much cost is involved? If trained persons are needed (for production, distribution, or use), are they available, and what cost items must be added? And for each of these questions, it is necessary to ask how much time it will take to make the technology or software available, or to train the necessary personnel. Both finances and time will thus enter into the total cost.

This is all common sense, and not very profound. If we want more sophisticated guidance, we must carry the taxonomy below the managerial level.

Strategic Level

Some readers of this chapter must have felt a bit uncomfortable when they saw in Figure 3.7 the printed page lumped with filmstrips and picture sets as "still-visual" media. The truth is that the "still-visual" media present to the eye profoundly different experiences because they use very different symbolic codes.

Salomon, in a provocative article (1974), offered a rule for the selection of media. "The better a symbol system conveys the *critical features* of an idea or event, the more appropriate it is," he wrote (p. 392). Thus, in choosing a medium of instruction, one analyzes what is to be taught, then looks for the symbolic coding system (e.g., iconic) and the method of presentation (e.g., motion or still, large or small size) that best fits the key features of the information to be conveyed. "If the simultaneous operation of valves in an engine is taken as the critical feature," he continues, "language would not be an appropriate medium to convey that sort of information. Moreover, if the knowledge to be extracted is supposed to be a mental representation of a simultaneously occurring set of events, a linear message would require additional re-encoding on the learner's part." This "fit" of the unique symbolic features of a medium to the unique features of a stimulus to be conveyed is most likely to produce unique cognitive effects. *Provided,* he cautions (p. 401), the "code is isomorphic in some way to the learner's symbolic mode of thinking." Thus there must be a "fit" to the learner as well as to the stimulus.

What Salomon is calling for is a media taxonomy in which most of the important distinctions are at the strategic and tactical levels. He calls it a "taxonomy of media attributes which is paralleled by a hierarchy of effects on cognition." All of us would like to have that, but must admit that it is not close at hand.

At the top of such a taxonomy, Salomon writes, one will find

> overriding media attributes unrelated to content. Their cognitive effects are quite universal, given a particular culture. They could be taken as the most fundamental categories of the major symbol systems . . . such as prearranged objects and events, iconic systems, analogue systems (e.g., movement in ballet), and digital symbolic systems (e.g., language and number systems).
>
> Further down on the taxonomy one would place basic coding elements such as dimensionality, iconicity, movement, simultaneity, and the like. Below that we might find features of the 'secondary coding system', such as ways of editing and juxtaposing, sequencing, and so on. Then, still further below, explicitness of information, complexity, redundancy, and ambiguity [p. 390].

This takes us from the strategic considerations into the tactical ones.

We have only the foggiest of ideas about this area that Salomon is opening up. McLuhan (1962, 1966) wrote about the difference in experience of receiving information from print or from visual codes. He pointed out that the experience of reading requires a linear input to the senses, as does also the experience of listening to language. Language flows consecutively, symbol after symbol, word after word, or word group after word group. One has to listen to all of a language unit before the total information emerges. Visual information, on the other hand, can be absorbed all at once, except as visual impressions are translated into words. What is transmitted to the right hemisphere of the brain (where nonverbal information is believed to be stored, verbal being stored in the left hemisphere) is undoubtedly associated with verbal information also, but the iconic impressions themselves are extremely vivid and resilient to loss. They can often be sharply recalled after many years.

The printed media, and all the language parts of media, use a digital code. (The name is borrowed from the computer.) Most computers are coded using only two digits—0 and 1, on and off—which are then combined into an infinite number of meanings. English print uses twenty-six letters and a number of typographical signs, like the period that follows this sentence, to represent all the agreed-upon meanings that English-speaking people have felt the need to have. Number is another digital code; in our system using ten digits in addition to signs like +, -, and =.

We know that the digital system, as contrasted with the iconic code of pictures and direct observation, is capable of passing on at great speed an enormous amount of prepackaged information. If one had a week to learn

FIGURE 3.12
Preferred Combinations of Media

Complementary Media	Master Media for Teaching					Master Media for Learning		
	TV	Radio	Corresp.	F/Face	Books	Audio Cass/Discs	Video Cass/Discs	P.I. Teaching Machines
Correspondence	Yes	Yes						
Face/Face	Yes	Yes	Yes					
Radio			Yes	Yes				
TV	Yes	Yes	Yes	Yes				Yes
Print (words and pictures)	Yes	Yes	Yes	Yes		Yes	Yes	Yes
Blackboard/Whiteboard				Yes				
Wall Visuals (Charts, posters, maps, etc.)		Yes	Yes	Yes				
Practical materials	Yes	Yes	Yes	Yes	Yes	Yes	Yes	Yes
Filmstrips/Slides		Yes	Yes	Yes		Yes		Yes
Film		Yes	Yes	Yes		Yes		Yes
Video Cassettes	Yes	Yes	Yes	Yes	Yes			Yes
Audio Cassettes	Yes	Yes	Yes	Yes	Yes			Yes
Telephone	Yes	Yes	Yes					

Tiffin and Coombes, 1974: 204

about the rise and fall of the Roman Empire, one would certainly read Gibbon's history rather than trying to watch films of 500 years of Roman history, even if those were available. But the history he reads in Gibbon has been passed through Gibbon's mind, and before that through the minds of other writers, and the language and interpretation are Gibbon's. If one could watch authentic films of ancient Rome for a week, one would hardly expect to extract from that experience the breadth of carefully interpreted information to be found in Gibbon. But one would doubtless learn things he couldn't get from Gibbon, and his interpretation of events Gibbon did include might differ considerably from Gibbon's. If *two* viewers were to watch these same films, their own interpretations would differ not only from Gibbon's but from each other. It is not proper to say they would learn more or less; certainly they would learn less of what historians think of as the history of Rome. But they would have been through a creative experience, making their own translation of experience, recording images of events.

The iconic symbol system is very dense. It is packed with possible visual experiences and possible meanings, much more than can be captured in a title. It offers many cues, in contrast to the digital symbol systems which offer only a few but in a large number of possible combinations. The digital symbol system requires the learner to focus on one linear experience; the iconic code invites the learner to wander around and pick out the cues of most interest to him. The iconic code is very concrete, but encourages a user to move from it to a set of meanings that can be abstracted and verbalized if necessary; the digital code is abstract, but encourages the user to move from abstraction to assigned meanings which permit the calling up of visual experiences if desired. Because the digital code is already abstract, the level of abstraction can be controlled only by controlling the vocabulary and the syntax; it serves only learners able to deal with that level of abstraction. The digital code, on the other hand, because it is concrete and densely packed, can offer something to everyone, regardless of his ability to deal with abstraction. Ask five people five different questions about a picture of people in a living room and you will see (Allander, 1974) five very different patterns in the eye camera, indicating that the same picture offered diverse experiences and called forth diverse behavior.

The analogue code (derived from the example of digital and analogue computers) is closer to the iconic code, but seldom representational. There are analogue elements in spoken language (voice quality, rhythm, tone, and the like), but these are less specific than the digital code of printed language. Music and movement in the dance are illustrations of analogic encoding. Music, for example, communicates its own enjoyment and its own emotions and often is used to provide an emotional background as a learning set for the other codes. Thus analogue encoding covers a broad range between representation and nonrepresentation. On the side of representation, for example, a flourish of trumpets has come to signal the arrival of an important person. And in Western society the Bridal Chorus from Wagner's Lohengrin has come to announce the beginning of a wedding ceremony.

To a greater or lesser extent, these codes have to be learned. Learning a language is perhaps a child's greatest accomplishment, and learning to read and to use a number system occupy much of the early years of schooling. No such effort is made to teach the iconic or the analogue coding systems, and yet they clearly have elements that must be learned. The teaching of "visual literacy" is a problem that has long concerned teachers and audiovisual specialists. We really know very little, in comparison to what is known of teaching reading and arithmetic, about how to teach visual skills. One of the most important things is probably acquiring some discrimination concerning what to "read" in a picture, learning to disregard some of the information in it. A child looking at a lampshade or picture of a lampshade may notice lines and shape and color. Later, because of the enormous amount of visual experience each of us has, he will simply call it a "lampshade" and disregard some of the iconic experience. But visual discrimination should not limit the creative experience of looking. For example, one child, looking at a lampshade called it "a skirt for the light." For that moment, the child was a poet, and nothing should be done to eliminate that order of experience.

As Wittich and Schuller say in their standard text on media, a person who is being given "visual literacy training" should not only have practice in "selecting and attending closely to visual phenomena of importance to him." He should also have "opportunities to interact in his own way with what he is looking at" (1972: 91). Third, they say, he should "have opportunities to create meaningful statements of his own," and should be encouraged to arrange ideas visually in the way he wants to arrange them." Thus, when a child spends a period of "drawing," he is not necessarily practicing to be an artist; he is becoming familiar with the iconic code. Every teacher knows also that certain special uses of the iconic code must be learned. One of these is the abstraction of reality into diagrams and charts. This is difficult for a young child or for primitive people unaccustomed to reading, but is one of the conventions necessary to learn.

Figure 3.13 illustrates some of the distribution of different coding systems among media.

On the level of theory and experience, we have made a beginning at understanding the use and combination of different coding systems. For

FIGURE 3.13
Symbolic Codes Used by Different Media

Digital, only
    Print, without illustrations
    CAI, except when audio or videotapes are combined with computer

Iconic, only
    Silent film, without subtitles or music
    Slides without print
    Filmstrip without print
    Photograph

Analogue, only
    Audiotape or audiodisc, without spoken language

Digital, Analogue
    Audiotape or audiodisc, without spoken language

Digital, Analogue
    Audiotape or audiodisc, with spoken language
    Radio
    Telephone

Digital, Iconic
    Silent film, with subtitles
    Slides, including print
    Filmstrip, including print
    Chalkboard
    Print, with illustrations

Iconic, Analogue
    Silent film, with music

Digital, Iconic, Analogue
    Television
    Sound film
    Videotape
    Radiovision
    Sound on slide or sound filmstrip

one thing, we have come to understand that combining different media in instruction is not merely combining different levels of experience; it is really combining different *kinds* of experience. McLuhan's insight concerning the difference in the same message when communicated through different media is what Cezanne was talking about when he said that the artist does not *copy* the world: he *recreates* it in the world of his own medium.

A remarkable article by Bruner and Olson (1973: 209-227) applies the concept to instruction. Bruner deals with the consequences of direct and mediated experiences, and within the latter class the differences between "observational learning" using what we have called the iconic coding systems of the media, and "symbolic learning" using what we have called the digital codes and the abstracted forms of graphic representation. His theme is that the choice of an instructional medium "must not depend solely on the effectiveness of the system for conveying and developing knowledge," but also "on the realization that the medium of instruction, the form of experience from which that knowledge is gleaned, has important consequences on the kinds of intellectual skills children develop" (Bruner and Olson, 1973: 226). Thus, he points out, the experience of kicking a ball teaches a child not only something about the ball but something about the act of kicking. The experience of looking at a face from various angles teaches one to see a picture of one angle of face as a representation of a whole face. The instructional effect of a model (by iconic media) or a demonstration (direct observation) are strengthened by a digital rule such as "Keep your weight on the downhill ski," but the lesson is probably never comprehended until one has had his first fall and says, "*That's* what he meant!"

The balance of knowledge and skills and the combination of experiences, including media experience, used to convey them, Bruner regards as the essential debate about education that has hardly started but is long overdue. What direct experience (including structured uses of the environment, laboratories, educational toys and games, etc.), what observational learning (observation and modeling, through demonstration or iconic media), and what symbolic learning (through print, oral explanation, diagrams, etc.) will best combine to achieve the goals of education?

This is precisely what we should like to be able to explain at this point. But, frankly, in reviewing the evidence from which we might draw such guidance, we find ourselves at the level of insight and supposition, rather than doctrine. We have no taxonomy that matches media experiences to cognitive results or to learning tasks. We have only begun to understand what goes on cognitively when a learner is given instructional experience in one symbolic code rather than another; and it is a great advance even to hear it said that "the *learner* needs this kind of experience," rather than "the lesson needs a picture." But this is about the best thing we can report from the pedagogic front: We are far from the specific guidance we should like.

A recent manual for selecting "instructional strategies and media" (Merrill and Goodman, 1971) illustrates this present state of the art. For each of a number of sample behavioral objectives, the manual takes its readers through basic questions about the audience to be taught and suggests an instructional strategy. Then it suggests media an experienced teacher might consider helpful. An example is what the manual does in handling the objective of being able to identify six propaganda objectives: "bandwagon," "card stacking," and so forth. The instructional strategy section can be sampled with this initial sentence:

> It might be very helpful to start the instructional sequence by presenting definitions of each of the seven techniques along with a number of examples illustrating each definition [p. 88].

Then what about the selection of media? Here is the section on Media Alternatives:

A. Written Verbal Material

> As much persuasive communication is carried on either by written or oral language, a good place to start is with the written word. One of the advantages of the written word is that the student can study the material as long as he needs to, obtain material from political organizations, advertising materials from newspapers and magazines and use written versions of radio commercials.

B. Pictures

> You'll find that magazine and newspaper advertisement will be a rich source for both written and visual examples of these seven propaganda techniques. For example, it wouldn't be too hard to find a "everybody's doing it" (the "bandwagon" technique) in the next magazine that you pick up.

C. Audio Recording

> Record radio commercials and sections of political speeches [pp. 88-89].

This is undoubtedly useful to a new teacher or one who is not accustomed to using media. It is practical. It is informed common sense. It is teachers speaking from the experience of teaching. It does not have the generality or the theoretical grounding we have been looking for in this chapter. The authors of the manual modestly subtitle it: "A Place to Begin."

Other Elements of a Taxonomy

Complex as these analyses of learning and media may seem to be, they are by no means the only elements that need to be added into a complete taxonomy.

One missing element is the learner. There is no taxonomy for all the attributes of a learner, but there are many scales. The principal one is *general ability*, usually measured by a standardized test. "Ability" is ordinarily defined as ability to learn skills or verbal knowledge. When such tests are correlated with learning, the most common finding is that higher ability goes with more learning. However, one of the oldest guidelines of teaching is, "If they are having trouble learning it, show them a picture." And earlier we quoted Cronbach's (1975: 119) statement that "one way to reduce the effect of general ability is to bring in pictures or diagrams." Supposedly this kind of pictorial presentation of appropriate subject matter makes learning easier for an individual with lower ability to decode verbal presentations. It is a fascinating question whether the use of pictures operates to reduce the learning gap between different ability levels, in part, by *slowing up* the individual who *can* process verbal material swiftly and efficiently.

Intelligence is often defined in the same terms as general ability and is just as multidimensional. Still other attributes sometimes used to distinguish learners are language ability (ability to learn in the language of instruction), age (used as an indicator of maturation or experience), sex (indicating learned behaviors and values), social status and home background (the latter two used to suggest the kind of experience an individual has had and the sort of values he has probably absorbed), motivation, learning goals, previous schooling, visual and auditory acuity, and a host of cognitive factors measurable with greater or lesser sharpness and many of them discussed in Cronbach and Snow (in press).

Still another element in the taxonomy would necessarily be the situation in which the learning takes place. Some of the subheads are: in-school versus out-of-school, formal versus informal education, individual versus group learning, supervised versus unsupervised learning, relationship between teacher and pupil, equipment available for instruction, physical surroundings of the school or other learning place, existing norms of the learning group, and so forth.

Any reader can think of other elements. As Salomon says, there is a growing body of evidence "to indicate that no media variable, minute or gross as it may be, affects all groups of learners in one and the same way." This fits with the experience of every teacher. And yet recall Cronbach's observations about the great number of "concealed interactions" between instructional treatment and facets of individual ability that often mask the main effects of an experiment and cast doubt on general statements about the treatment. As he writes, the study of higher-level interactions is a "hall of mirrors extending to infinity."

The number of such interactions is forcing psychologists to revise their hopes of being able to state general laws about the effect of instruction. Nevertheless, evidence piles up that the relationship among the instructional treatment, the attributes of the learner, and the learning situation are extremely important. For example, there is good reason to think (McKeachie, 1974, Brophy and Evertson, 1973, Cronbach, 1975) that a lower-class child tends to respond better to didactic teaching, in which the requirements are made explicit and the rewards are kept always in view. "Problem-oriented, ego-motivated, supportive" methods of teaching, which have recently been the vogue, appear to be useful chiefly to middle-class students. Domino (1968) and Majasan (1971) found that agreement between student and teacher as to their beliefs and approach to learning made a significant difference in the results. Certain qualities in a learner seem to predict success in working by himself; others predict the need of supervision.

McNeill (1962) has found that responding is especially conducive to more learning for low-IQ students of programmed instruction, not nearly so useful to students who have high IQs. Campeau (1965) found that girls with high anxiety learned significantly more with feedback—when the correct answers were given to them after they had worked a problem or replied to a question. On the other hand, girls whose anxiety was low worked more efficiently without such feedback. Dick and Latta (1970), comparing CAI and programmed instruction of students in mathematics, found that on the average the students receiving programmed instruction did better, due almost wholly to the poor performance of the less able students on a fairly difficult CAI program. And Monahan et al, (1966) found that whereas high-ability students performed equally well on two versions of a multimedia presentation, low-ability students did significantly better on a version made with their particular abilities in mind.

THE WISDOM OF EXPERIENCE

The practical wisdom derived from experience in teaching is usually kept as a teacher's private treasure, modified as experience is extended, and seldom summarized except around specific problems. However, there are such summaries, and we shall look at a few of them in the following pages.

In April 1975, a committee of the British Open University submitted a report to the National Committee on the Future of Broadcasting, which included the former committee's own estimate, based on such theory as seemed applicable and on the four-year experience of the Open University, on "The Pedagogic Value of Broadcasting." In Figure 3.14 we have set down the outline of what they regarded as the "particularly appropriate" uses of radio and television in the multimedia teaching of the Open University.

FIGURE 3.14

"Particular Appropriate Uses of Broadcasting" as Identified by a Committee of the British Open University

Television

1. To demonstrate experiments or experimental situations, particularly:
   (a) where equipment or phenomena to be observed are *large, expensive, inaccessible* or *difficult* to observe without special equipment;
   (b) where the experimental design is *complex;*
   (c) where the measurement of experimental behavior is not easily reduced to a single scale or dimension (e.g., human behaviour);
   (d) where the experimental behaviour may be influenced by *uncontrollable but observable variables.*

2. To bring to students *primary resources material,* i.e., film or video-recordings of actual situations, which, through careful editing and selection, can demonstrate principles covered in the units. This material may be used for a number of purposes, e.g.:
   (a) film of naturally occurring events, e.g., teaching situations, mental disorders, medical cases, to enable *recognition* of categories, symptoms, etc.;
   (b) film of naturally occurring events, to enable students to *analyse* situation, using principles of criteria established elsewhere in unit;
   (c) to provide student with a selection of *sources* of evidence to analyse. It may also include, besides contemporary material, archive film or historical material.

3. To *record specially* events, experiments, species, places, people, buildings, etc., which are crucial to the content of units, but may *be likely to disappear,* die or be destroyed in the near future.

4. To bring to students the views or knowledge of *eminent people,* who are often prepared to be televised or filmed, but not to write material specially for the institution. (This function might be able to be carried out however more economically through radio in most—but not all—instances).

5. To change *student attitudes;*
   (a) by presenting material in a novel manner, or from an unfamiliar viewpoint;
   (b) by presenting material in a *dramatised* form, enabling students to identify with the emotions and viewpoints of the main participants;
   (c) by allowing the students to *identify* closely with someone in the programme who overcomes problems or himself changes his attitudes as a result of evidence presented in the programme or televised exercise.

6. To explain or demonstrate *activities* that the students are to carry out (e.g., home experiments, survey interviewing).

7. To *feed back* to students 'mass' or total *results of activities or surveys* carried out by the students themselves, where the 'turn-round' time is too short for printed feedback.

8. To illustrate principles involving *dynamic change or movement.*

9. To illustrate abstract principles through the use of specially constructed *physical models.*

10. To illustrate principles involving *two-, three-, or n-dimensional* space.

11. To use *animated, slow-motion, or speeded-up* film or video-tape to demonstrate changes over time (including computer animation) . . . .

FIGURE 3.14 (continued)

12. To bring works of the performing arts (drama, music) into existence, by a performance, and to bring that performance into the students' own home. Without the essential affective experience of performance of the play or work, cognitive acitivyt has restricted value in the learning process. Although gramophone records (and radio) may put a performance into the students' own home, this gives sound only.

13. Through performance, to demonstrate methods or techniques of *dramatic production,* or different interpretations of dramatic works;

14. To demonstrate methods of playing instruments, and the relationship between music, musicians and their instruments.

15. To demonstrate *decision making processes*
    (a) by filming or observing the decision-making as it occurs;
    (b) by dramatisation;
    (c) by simulation or role-playing.

16. To *condense* or *synthesise* into a coherent whole a wide range of information which would require considerable length in print, and which in print would not provide the richness of background material necessary for students to appreciate fully the situation.

17. To demonstrate how basic principles have been *applied* in the real world, where visualisation of the application in its total environment is necessary to understand the way the principle has been applied, and the difficulties encountered.

18. To *test students' ability,* by requiring them to apply concepts or principles learned elsewhere in the course; by explaining or analysing 'real-life' situations presented through television.

19. To demonstrate the use of tools or equipment, or the effects of tools, or equipment.

20. To increase students' sense of *belonging; identification* of and with course designers; making the teaching *less impersonal;*

21. To *reduce the time* required by students to master content;

22. To *pace* students; to keep them working regularly; to break inertia of beginning to study in evening.

23. To *recruit or attract new students* (either to the University or to specific courses); to interest general viewers in subject matters.

24. To establish *academic credibility* of course to 'outside' world.

Radio

1. To provide *remedial tutorials,* or some other form of tutorial, based on feedback.

2. To provide *corrections,* alterations or up-dating of material, where print re-make budgets are limited, or where print cannot reach students quickly enough.

3. To bring to students *primary resource material,* i.e., recordings which, through careful editing and selection, can demonstrate principles covered in the units. This material may be used in a number of ways, for example
   (a) recordings of naturally occurring events, e.g., political speeches, children talking, concerts or performances, talks previously recorded for other than Open University purposes (e.g., Reith lectures), eye-witness interviews at historical events;
   (b) to provide students with a selection of *sources* of evidence to analyse.

FIGURE 3.14 (continued)

4. To bring to students the view or knowledge of *eminent people* who can condense in an interview, or be edited afterwards, to provide the essential points, which in written form may be more complex or lengthy.

5. To *record specially* the voices of people who have not been recorded before, but whose contribution to the course would provide a unique experience (e.g., famous poets reading their own work, civil servants talking—perhaps anonymously—about their role in decision making).

6. To change *student attitudes*
   (a) by presenting material in a *novel* manner, or from an unfamiliar viewpoint;
   (b) by presenting material in dramatised form, enabling students to identify with the emotions and viewpoints of the main participants.

7. To bring works of the performing arts into existence, by a performance direct into the students' own home; and to demonstrate methods or techniques of drama or music, through performance.

8. To provide the student with a *condensed argument,* in lecture form, which may
   (a) reinforce points made elsewhere in the course;
   (b) introduce new concepts not covered elsewhere in the course;
   (c) provide an alternative view to that presented in the correspondence text and/or television programmes;
   (d) analyse material contained elsewhere in the course, especially in specially written broadcast notes or television programmes;
   (e) summarise the main points of the block or course as far as it had gone, providing integration and orientation;
   (f) draw on quotation, recorded information, interviews, etc., as evidence in support of (or against) the argument.

9. To enable students to perceive that *different points of view* exist, and observe ideas being challenged, through discussions and interviews.

Source: Open University, 1975.

This is a long catalogue. Reading it, we must keep in mind that it applies to entire thirty-minute programs, and therefore will not correspond very closely to taxonomies of events of instruction or basic intellectual skills.

It is apparent that the committee put a high value on using television and radio to bring to students experiences from life that would otherwise probably not have been available to them. For example, such primary resource material as films or recordings of important events or observations hard to come by; the views, voices, and images of eminent people; events, places, species that are likely to disappear in the near future unless recorded; notable artistic performances (television 2, 3, 4, 12; radio 3, 4, 5). Mentioned just as frequently is the advantage of using the media for teaching that would otherwise be difficult or impossible to present: expensive and complex experiments; demonstrations and physical models of abstract principles; animation, slow-motion, or speeded-up film to show changes over time; condensations of information that would take much longer in print; illustrations from life of differing points of view (T 1, 9, 10, 11, R 8, 9). Another highly recommended use of these media is to demonstrate a process that requires special illustration or combined observation and explanation: principles of dynamic change or movement, the methods of the performing arts; decision-making processes either from life or from simulation; the use of tools and equipment (T 8, 13, 14, 15, 19; R 7). The committee feels that television can reduce the time needed to master the content of a course, supposedly by providing iconic material rather than print (T 21). They feel that television can be used to guide and pace the student through his individual studies (T 6, 22); that it can be used to test students' accomplishment by giving them a chance to apply or transfer what they have and to encourage transfer by showing how others have applied the principles taught in the course (T 17, 18). They envisage the usefulness of both media for feedback, radio especially for remedial tutorials, and to supply corrections or updates for the instructional materials, television to feed back the results of learning activities such as surveys conducted by the students themselves (T 7, R 1, 2). They feel that both television and radio can be used to have an effect on student attitudes—in the direction of desirable values, and to increase their sense of belonging and combat the impersonalness of an open university (T 5, 20; R 6). And finally they recognize the importance of using television for public relations—to recruit or attract new students, to impress "over-the-shoulder" viewers with the academic quality of the university (T 23, 24).

Four differences seem to be evident between their list for television and that for radio. For one thing, they see *more* uses for television. Second, they envisage a more *personal* use for radio—feedback in the form of remedial tutorials, for example, in which the broadcaster can talk directly to a group of students rather than impersonally to all students. Third, they seem to expect television to be more useful than radio for demonstrating processes (except those of the performing arts) and difficult and complex experiments, where they seem to feel that the iconic element is very important. And fourth, they rely on television rather than radio for their public relations needs. Probably this is because they expect television to attract a larger nonstudent audience.

Another example of summary wisdom is William H. Allen's chart of presumed effectiveness of different instructional modes for different learning objectives (see Figure 3.15). This chart, like the list we have just seen, is a product of common sense and good judgment, rather than detailed research. It has a special interest for us, however, because Dr. Allen is both a researcher and a user of instructional media. He himself has done a great deal of research on these media, has written several competent reviews of research in the field, and until recently was editor of the *AV Communication Review.* The fact that he is able to cite relatively little research in support of the media judgments in the chart is further confirmation of what we have found or, rather, failed to find.

Only seventeen of the fifty-four combinations in Allen's matrix are rated "low" (eight of them in the psychomotor area), eight "high," and twenty-nine "medium," suggesting that most instructional tasks can probably be performed by a number of different media. On the other hand, there is considerable variation in rating of different media for different goals, suggesting that some media can do certain tasks better than others. If one separates out the three kinds of direct experience that Allen considered (3-D objects, demonstrations, and oral presentation), then actually the six media come off better than the direct experience, thus:

	Low	Medium	High
3 kinds of direct experience	8	8	2
6 kinds of media experience	9	21	6

Finally, it is interesting to note what one of the great theorists in this field now suggests about the particular usefulness of some of the media. This comes from a personal communication of Robert Gagne to the author, and therefore I do not feel justified in quoting either directly or in detail. Dr. Gagne, however, addressed himself to the question of what television can do in the five great areas of learning—verbal knowledge, intellectual skills, motor skills, cognitive strategies, and attitudes and values. He believes that television can help substantially in each of these but in different ways. In the learning of verbal knowledge, he believes that its most significant contribution may be to provide a meaningful context so that new names and definitions can be retained and used. In the learning of intellectual skills, he feels that television can be especially helpful for recalling the necessary rules and concepts and the procedures for applying them. In motor skills, it promises to be very useful in recalling the necessary physical or motor routine. For example, one can hardly learn how to throw a curve with a baseball solely from looking at a television picture of the act, but the picture can illustrate the routine and thus make it easier to learn and recall the kinesic procedures one has to store away from actual physical practice. In the case of learning a cognitive strategy he feels television can be substantially useful in recalling the rules and concepts that enter into the strategy, and helping the learner to transfer the strategy to new situations by showing concrete examples of its application. And finally, he feels that television can contribute to learning values and attitudes by presenting choice situations where one behavior must be chosen rather than another, and by presenting admired or identified-with models of the desired behavior.

FIGURE 3.15
William H. Allen's Chart of Instructional Media in Relationship to Learning Objectives (Allen, 1967)

Instructional Media Type	Learning Factual Information	Learning Visual Identifications	Learning Principles, Concepts and Rules	Learning Procedures	Performing Skilled Perceptual-Motor Acts	Developing Desirable Attitudes Opinions and Motivations
Still pictures	Medium	High	Medium	Medium	Low	Low
Motion Pictures	Medium	High	High	High	Medium	Medium
Television	Medium	Medium	High	Medium	Low	Medium
3-D Objects	Low	High	Low	Low	Low	Low
Audio Recordings	Medium	Low	Low	Medium	Low	Medium
Programmed Instruction	Medium	Medium	Medium	High	Low	Medium
Demonstration	Low	Medium	Low	High	Medium	Medium
Printed Textbooks	Medium	Low	Medium	Medium	Low	Medium
Oral Presentation	Medium	Low	Medium	Medium	Low	Medium

SUMMING UP

This is where we stand at the end of a review of pedagogic contributions to the theory of media choice.

We started with the hope of finding parallel taxonomies of learning, media, learners, and situations that might be interrelated in such a way as to illuminate the selection of media for instruction. Needless to say, we found very incomplete taxonomies, except in the instructional technology of men like Gagne and Briggs, and very little in media taxonomy to relate to it except on the practical managerial level represented by the kind of question a teacher might ask, "Do we need a picture here?" "Do we need a picture with motion?" "Is this the place for a lecture?" And so forth. It seems fairly clear that we shall have to go beyond that level into the symbolic systems of the media before we can work with media characteristics as subtly as pedagogical theory has dealt with the elements of learning and teaching. And until we do that we are not very well prepared to decide what media experiences best fit given learning needs.

Even the slight attention we were able to give to the symbolic coding systems of the media, however, suggested certain generalizations that may be useful. For one thing, the analogue code (music, movement in ballet, etc.) appears to be useful in instruction mostly as a complementary experience except where analogue experiences themselves are being taught—for example, music or ballet. In other cases, the analogue material in the media probably adds subtlety, strength, and enjoyment to the learning being offered by the other media codes.

It seems equally clear that the digital codes (print, spoken language, mathematics) are very widely useful through the events of instruction and the learning of the basic intellectual skills. Combined with some iconic material (as in an illustrated textbook, or a classroom with illustrative material available), they can do nearly anything that needs to be done during instruction.

The iconic codes (pictures, diagrams) are perhaps less widely useful than the digital, but in some tasks they are very strong. For example, they are effective in attracting attention; in recalling previously stored elements of a learning process; in presenting the main stimulus material, particularly when that requires something that an individual learner or a classroom teacher would find difficult to present; and in encouraging transfer of learned skills and knowledge to new problems. But they may also be useful in other ways—for example, in guiding a learner through an exercise in learning; and a glance back at the Open University's list will suggest the breadth of their usefulness.

Although not uniquely able to do so, the interactive media, notably computer-assisted instruction, are unequalled except perhaps by face-to-face communication, in providing feedback during learning.

What can we say, at the end of this chapter about Big versus Little Media? Two of the Big—television and sound films—are the only media that can provide all three coding systems and that can deliver the materials of learning simultaneously over a large area. As we have pointed out, the latter quality has both its advantages and its disadvantages for learning. The combination of coding systems, however, can be paralleled by a combination of smaller and less expensive media, or face-to-face teaching with the aid of one or more Little Media.

NOTES

1. Mowrer (1960) suggests that stimulus-response connections probably require signal learning (1) as a pre-requisite. Gagne is unwilling to draw this conclusion without further evidence (1965: 66).

CHAPTER 4

THE ECONOMIC EVIDENCE

With a given level of resources available, the task of an educational administrator is to select the policies, people, facilities, and equipment that will give the students the "best and biggest education per buck."

—James G. Miller
President, University of Louisville
(Quoted by Richard E. Speagle, in Tickton, 1970: 88)

A planner or an educator needs economic information in order to decides among instructional media systems.

The first need is for reliable information on the costs of alternative systems. It is necessary to know both capital and recurrent costs. By *capital* costs we mean the cost of equipment and facilities that will be in use longer than the current budget year: buildings, transmitters, receivers, projectors, books, and so forth. These are probably the "hardest" (most reliable) cost figures the educator will have to work with; and it is relatively easy to cost out the necessary components and the expense of delivering and installing them at a given place.

In accounting for the cost of a system, an economist usually "depreciates" or "annualizes" capital expenditures over several years. For example, if it is necessary to buy a transmitter which is supposed to last ten years, the cost is budgeted over the expected life of the equipment even though the actual purchase may have to be paid for in the first year. The economist usually does another thing, in handling capital costs, that may be surprising to the layman. He introduces a figure for "interest" or "social discount" that represents an estimated cost of investing in the necessary capital equipment rather than in something else, like bonds or industry, that might pay interest or profit each year. This amount, of course, nowhere appears on any voucher or other record of expenditure; it is purely a "notional" figure, the creation of the economist in trying to express the full cost of an educational investment. Because the concept may be puzzling, let us look at the reasoning behind it.

Jamison, with Klees (1973: 11) gives this example. Suppose that a country decides to buy $220,000 worth of radio equipment that has an expected life of ten years. And suppose that, by coincidence, this equipment could have been rented for about one-tenth of the total capital cost per year–$22,000. (The rental would probably be higher, but let us assume that level in order to make the computation simple.) If this were the case, the country would lose money by buying rather than renting, because if it paid only the rent it could take the remainder of its capital funds and invest in bonds or a savings account or a fertilizer plant, and draw income. If the interest or income were 7.5 percent annually, and the investment were reduced each year by the amount of the rent, there would still be a profit of $132,560 at the end of ten years. The economist usually includes in his accounts a percentage of capital cost corresponding to the probable return from investing those funds in the economy, because he is trying to bring to light the hidden costs, as well as the surface costs, of the investment. And, thus, his accounting of capital costs is, on the one hand, *less* than actual expenditures for the first year because it depreciates or annualizes the costs over the expected life of the equipment; on the other hand, *more* than actual cost because it includes an estimate of the return that is lost by investing in educational material rather than in something which actually earns additional money.

By *recurrent* costs we mean salaries, electricity, maintenance, rentals, disposable items like paper and pencils, and other such goods and services that depend upon the needs of the system in a given year. Thus, the cost of a transmitter is known for ten years, but the expense of hiring operators, paying the electric bill, and the like may vary from year to year. These recurrent expenses are predictable from existing experience and from operational plans, but are much more likely to be underestimated, at the beginning, than are the costs of basic equipment. It is obvious, too, that the recurrent costs will depend upon how much the system is used and the quality of product that is insisted upon (for instance, how "professional" the films or instructional television are expected to be).

The educator needs to ask two other cost questions also: how much it will cost to expand the system, and how much the total cost will be if, after a few years, it is decided to abandon the system and change to something else. The first of these ideas is simple enough. It is possible to divide system cost into *fixed* and *variable* costs. For example, in a radio or television system, the programming and transmission costs are about the same regardless of the number of students, until the coverage area reaches a size where a single station can no longer serve it. On the other hand, the reception cost depends upon the number of students, inasmuch as every classroom will need a receiver and every student will probably need workbooks or other supplementary materials. Consequently, as Jamison and Klees write (1973: 7), the simplest equation for the cost of an instructional media system is $TC(N) = F + VN$ where the total cost (TC) of a system serving a certain number (N) of students is the sum of the fixed costs (F) plus the variable costs per student (V) times the number of students. What the planner wants to know is the size of V: what does it cost, on the average, to add one more student to the system?

The other concept is equally important. Suppose that a country or a school system launches into an expensive system like instructional television, then discovers after a few years that it is not pleased with the decision. Obviously, the average cost would be greater if the project were abandoned early than if it were carried through to the point where the capital investment were amortized. Jamison and Klees illustrate (1973: 14ff.) how the cost of different time spans can be estimated, and these are figures that need to be considered in the process of decision.

These are the basic questions about costs that need to be answered in the process of deciding for media system A as against media system B. But estimating costs is only one step in planning. This first step will tell the educator whether a specified system will come within his resources, how much it will cost to operate the system at a given size or to expand it, and what are the cost considerations in possibly cutting the experiment short. So far as we have gone, the essential information can be expressed in financial terms and measured in such terms against other systems. But the really important measure is *product*. What will such an expenditure buy? The educator has specific goals in mind; he is thinking of investing in a media system to bring about certain changes he feels should be made. Consequently he must consider not only the cost of alternative systems but also whether one system will come closer than another to accomplishing the specified goal. In other words, he must weigh output against input, and compare that factor for different possible systems.

This is what the economist calls *cost-effectiveness analysis*. It is less specific and more difficult than simple cost-analysis because the outputs of education are less simple and specific than the costs. They are far from unidimensional. Thus, one goal of introducing instructional television into El Salvador was to offer middle-school opportunities to twice as many students at an acceptable cost; success or failure in achieving that goal can be readily measured. A further goal was to raise the level of education, which is not easy to measure. There are short-term and long-term results, effects on different kinds of learning and on attitudes toward learning, effects on different kinds of students and on the attitudes and performances of different kinds of teachers. On the whole, the present state of the art in measuring educational output, as illustrated in the preceding chapters, leads a planner to be more confident that a new system will extend learning opportunities to more students than that a certain system will contribute more to the quality of learning than will another certain system. This is the difficult area in which cost-effectiveness analysis must work.

There is still one more step between the simplicity of cost-analysis and an informed decision among media systems. Cost-effectiveness analysis is designed to determine the "best buy" in terms of immediate results (such as enrollments or results of learning tests), but education is designed also to serve long-range social and economic needs. Estimating the input of an educational system against its output into these long-range goals is called *cost-benefit* analysis. Economists have most often tried to express a cost-benefit ratio for education in terms of the cost of education versus its contribution to individual earnings. But a great many educational decisions today hang upon the cost of an investment in education against what it may be expected to contribute to the development goals of a country.

For example, El Salvador decided to use a system built around television to "reform" education in its seventh, eighth, and ninth grades. In so doing, it supposedly had to decide not only that the new system was within its resources but also that the system it chose was a "better buy" than other systems within its means—for example, one built around radio, or around the use of small classes—for opening those grades to a greatly expanded number of students. The system El Salvador chose also added a large number of upper-level technicians to the work force and thus helped meet one of the great needs of the country's developing economy.

An economist will find the above descriptions elementary and incomplete. We have included them to give other readers a brief introduction to the kind of thinking behind some of the cost estimates in this chapter. As a matter of fact, relatively few economists have worked on the analysis of instructional technology, and few media projects have been designed until recently with cost-effectiveness or cost-benefit analysis as any more than an afterthought. Nevertheless, the situation is changing, and decisions on the choice of instructional media systems are increasingly being made with the help of professional economists. For more technical treatment of educational cost-analysis in general see Coombs and Hallak (1972); for an introduction to cost-effectiveness analysis, Jamison (1972), and for an example of its application to instructional media, Jamison and Klees (1973); for reviews of economic cost-benefit techniques, Grilliches (1970) and Psacharoupoulos (1972). We will present below none of the theory represented by the titles just suggested, but rather some of the results of economic studies of media systems—first some summaries, then data from field projects.

THE GENERAL LEARNING STUDY

The most ambitious of the media cost summaries dates from 1968, and therefore is more useful for cross-media comparisons than for current cost figures. This is entitled *Cost Study of Educational Media Systems and Their Equipment Components* (General Learning Corporation, 1968.) The study examines the costs of instructional television with six different delivery systems—open-circuit broadcast, closed-circuit, ITFS, airborne broadcast, satellite broadcast, and distribution to school videotape recorders; also, film, radio broadcast, language laboratories, and classroom access (which means a variety of sound tapes available by teacher request to classroom loudspeakers). Except for radio and classroom-access audio, the study does not cover the smaller visual or audio media—filmstrips, slides, transparencies, graphics, nor classroom tape recorders as distinguished from language laboratories or dial access. The reason for excluding these is apparently that they would not ordinarily be asked to carry the bulk of teaching, as other devices might.

The General Learning Corporation study does not report the cost of any actual projects, but rather endeavors to calculate the *probable* cost of different media systems under different conditions. The data come from equipment costs at the time of the study, plus operating costs as projected from available experience. Thus the results of the GLC study will not apply precisely to *any* field situation, but make it possible to compare the costs of different media systems in specified situations.

For the purpose of analysis, it is assumed that an annual production of 1,000 hours of instructional material will be required of the system, and that this will have to be increased to as much as 1,600 hours when a very large region and over 1,000,000 students must be served. This is about half as much production as American Samoa provided at the height of its use of television for all twelve grades of a school system, and much more than Samoa presently provides. It is a great deal more than El Salvador provided for three grades, Colombia for six, or Niger for five. Thus we must keep in mind that the GLC estimates are for a very heavy use of instructional media, not for the cost of supplementing a course by a few films, filmstrips, or tapes.

The costs of providing necessary capital equipment, producing, and delivering this amount of instruction through each of the media systems are estimated for five different situations:

local: serving about 15,000 students

city: 150,000

metropolitan: 600,000

state: 1,000,000

region: 10,000,000

The smallest of these compares with Hagerstown and is about twice the size of American Samoa; the largest is the kind of area that would typically be served by airborne television (as was the American Middle West in the 1960s by transmitters in airplanes flying over northern Indiana), transmitters carried on tethered balloons (as in Korea), or a communication satellite. The city and metropolitan areas are of the general size to be served in the Ivory Coast, Colombia, or El Salvador. The state is about the same as the number being served by radio in Thailand.

The general conclusion of the study is that the costs of the different media tend to cluster in two broad bands, corresponding to what we have called Big and Little Media, and that Big Media (such as ITV and sound film) will cost between three and fifteen times as much as Little Media (like radio and audiotape), depending on the size of the coverage. Thus the scale of use becomes very important in calculating unit costs. Media like television and radio display what economists call *economies of scale* when used for large audiences, whereas media like film do not. Thus, as Table 4.1 shows, ITV is very expensive when used for only 15,000 students, but relatively cheap when used for ten times that many; whereas film is about the same cost per student regardless of numbers. (It must be remembered that we are dealing here with a very large amount of instruction per year.)

The GLC study made no comparable estimates for CAI or programmed tests. For these we shall rely on Hayman and Levin (1973) and Miller (1973), whose work will be discussed later in the chapter. As for the cost of the smaller visual media, such as filmstrips, which are also absent from the GLC study, we can assume that they would fall into the lower band, with or below radio. The fundamental assumption of the GLC study—that costs should be figured on a basis of 1,000 to 1,600 hours a year—makes it difficult to treat some of the smaller media—for example, an annual 1,000 hours of filmstrips?

Figure 4.1, from the GLC study, illustrates the significance of decisions concerning quality of instructional materials and size of area to be served. The cost of high-quality programming for a system of only 15,000 students would be $91.00 per student, which is beyond the capabilities of most schools. If the schools are willing to use lower-quality programs or programs from a central source, that cost can be decreased—dramatically so as the service area grows. High-quality programming is only a little over $10.00 a student at the level of the city, $6.00 for a metropolitan area, and $4.00 for a state. This is the tradeoff that an educational planner faces with a medium like television: The more programs are made to fit local needs and curricula, the less advantage can be had from economies of scale. The more central programming is used to bring about high-quality production, the less likely the programs are specifically to fit the local areas.

TABLE 4.1
Media Cost Estimates per Student per Year for Carrying a Considerable Part of the Instructional Load

	For 15,000 students	150,000	600,000
ITV	$40.00	$10.00	$ 9.00
Film	$52.00	$50.00	$52.00
Radio	$ 9.00	$ 3.00	$ 2.50
Dial access (one speaker per classroom)	$ 8.00	$ 4.00	$ 3.50

Source: General Learning Corporation 1968: 40 ff.

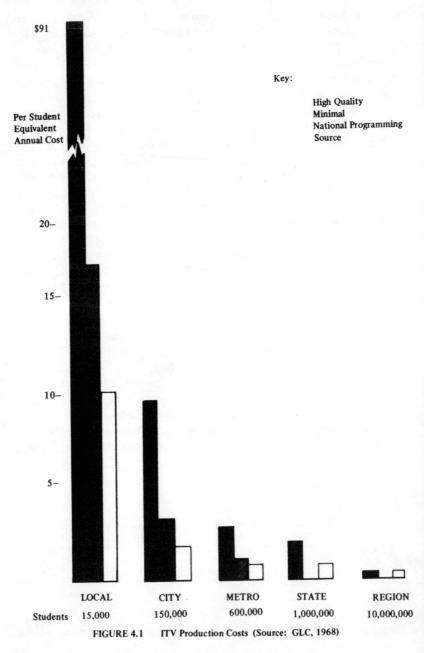

FIGURE 4.1   ITV Production Costs (Source: GLC, 1968)

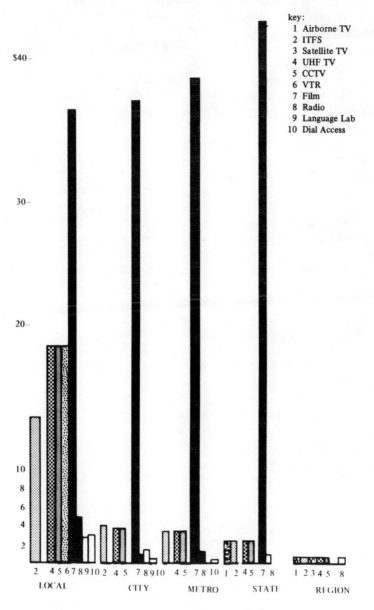

FIGURE 4.2   Production Cost Comparison

In Figure 4.2, we have reproduced the GLC summary of production costs per student for different media in different coverage areas. Note that the cost of producing television and film is assumed to be very high, and the cost of film remains high regardless of coverage area because of present practices in pricing film prints. The per capita cost of ITV production, however, declines rapidly as the audience increases. The production cost of radio is relatively high (about $4.00 at the local level) but, like television, benefits from the economies of scale. The production cost of material for language laboratories (or tape recorders used for language study) is really not comparable to the other media production costs because language laboratories do not need 1,000 hours of unique programming. The GLC study, therefore, assumed the need of 225 instead of 1,000 hours of unique programming for language laboratories; if this were 1,000 hours, the production costs for language tapes in Figure 3.10 would be roughly four times as high as they appear on that chart. The cost of producing material for a classroom dial access system may also not be strictly comparable with the others. It is assumed that a dial access system will be used by the teacher to call up short segments of illustrative material, rather than entire lessons. Therefore, GLC assumed that the 1,000 hours for a dial access system would include readings, music, recordings of events, and the like, which are now available at lost cost—perhaps $10.00 an hour.

Figure 4.2 includes a number of ways for delivering ITV—airborne broadcasts, ITFS, satellite TV, closed-circuit, UHF, and videotape. Of course, the production cost for all these will be the same; the differences will show up in the costs for distribution, in Figure 4.3.

As the figure demonstrates, satellite and airborne television are out of the question for anything less than very large coverage. VTR delivery of television is costly even for a local area, and out of question for larger areas, because of the high cost of videotape machines and raw tape; when video cassettes become available at low cost, the situation may be somewhat different. The least expensive way to deliver television to small areas is ITFS (2500 mH), and even that costs $6.00 per student in a local area. On the other hand, radio delivery is relatively inexpensive in a coverage area of any size. It is less than $2.00 at a local level, not more than $1.00 for other areas. Note that the projected delivery cost of satellite television at the regional level (the assumption is that a powerful satellite like the ATS-6 will be available) is competitive with other methods of delivery. Note also that closed-circuit television is closely competitive with UHF in cost of delivery at the city level (150,000 students), although in larger areas the open-circuit system has a cost advantage.

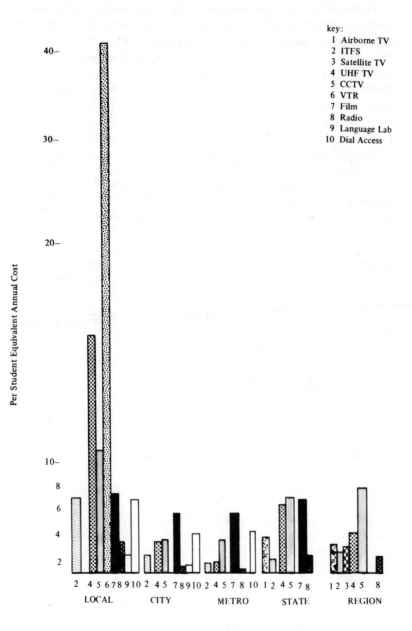

FIGURE 4.3   Distribution Cost Comparison

Estimates of reception cost are shown in Figure 4.4. They reflect the cost of such equipment as receivers and projectors and the training of teachers to use them. It is interesting, therefore, to note that the reception cost of ITV is calculated to fall between $5.00 and $7.00, according to the coverage area, and this includes $2.50 for teacher training. The GLC study may have underestimated the cost of receiving satellite TV, especially if this is to be done by direct broadcasting.

Let us now return to the total costs mentioned earlier. They are set forth in some detail in Figure 4.5, which distinguishes rather dramatically between the Big and the Little Media, insofar as they are represented in the GLC study. It is worth noting, however, that once the coverage area is expanded to 150,000 students there are several ways in which ITV can be delivered for $10.00 or less per year per student. Radio stands out as the bargain it is—one-third to one-fourth the cost of television (some practitioners estimate its cost as *one-tenth* that of television), and it is the only one of these "Little" Media usable for covering large areas.

Perhaps a word should be said about the film costs. These are figured on the basis of providing 1,000 hours of filmed instruction per year to the local area, increasing the hours with wider coverage. This is, of course, not the usual way that films are employed in schools. They are more often used for special tasks—for a demonstration or a change of pace—and it would be most uncommon for a school to use 1,000 hours of film a year. If the use is less, of course, the total cost would be less, but the hourly per student cost probably would be higher.

These are careful and considered estimates, and, as we have said, they check out well with available field estimates of the cost of large and extensive uses of the media. But let us not foreclose entirely the possibility of using Big Media for small audiences or small tasks, and let us not neglect the importance of level of quality.

Instructional television has been used, on occasion, for a very few students at what seems like a very low unit cost. For example, it has been reported that the break-even point for closed-circuit television in a college comes when the system enrolled 350 students. It was also reported that the Pennsylvania State University showed savings of $38,000 in one year through the use of closed-circuit television, with which they were able to reduce the cost per student credit-unit from $9.48 for conventional teaching to $5.44 for televised instruction. Their break-even point was said to come with an enrollment of 200. At Miami University it was estimated that televised instruction could break even with 220 enrolled.

Apparently these universities all had large lecture courses, the lectures being transferred to television rather than given in person. Whether the estimates included capital costs, amortization, full operational costs, and

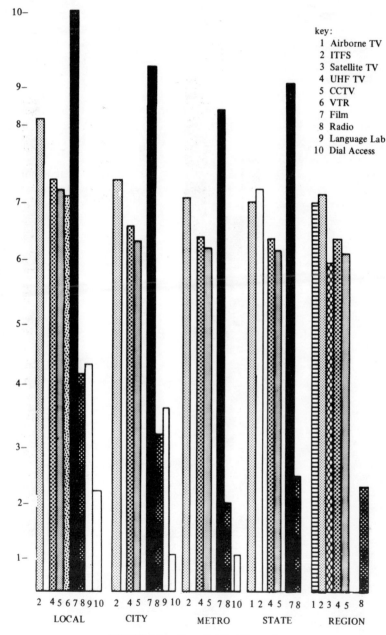

FIGURE 4.4   Reception Cost Comparison

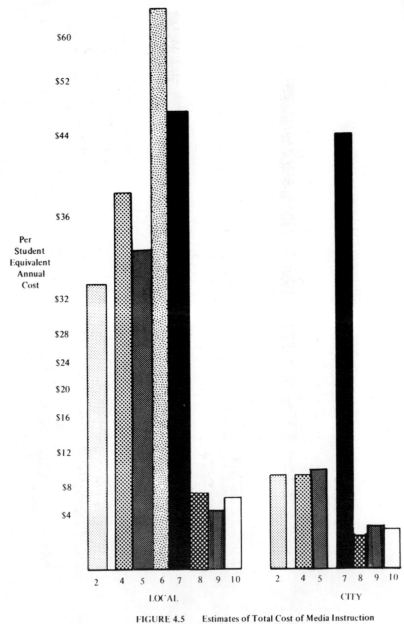

FIGURE 4.5   Estimates of Total Cost of Media Instruction
(Group Learning Corporation, 1968)

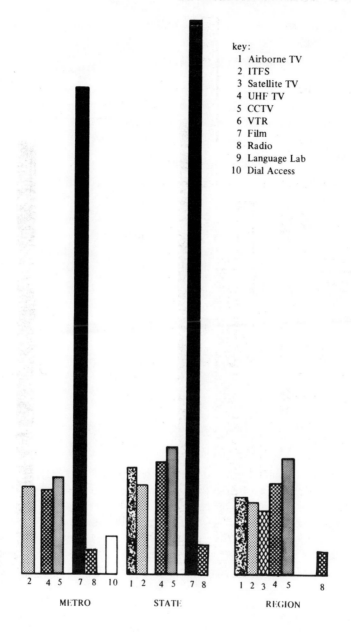

key:
 1 Airborne TV
 2 ITFS
 3 Satellite TV
 4 UHF TV
 5 CCTV
 6 VTR
 7 Film
 8 Radio
 9 Language Lab
10 Dial Access

FIGURE 4.5 Continued

general overhead, we do not know. We can assume, though, that ITV was used merely to pick up existing face-to-face lecturing with a minimum of the kind of program production usually expected of large television systems.

Hayman and Levin (1973) point out that, beyond the size of audience, the cost of instructional television depends principally on the cost of instructional preparation and the cost of the particular delivery system adopted. The following list is adapted from their four levels of production:

(1) Recording of a conventional live classroom.

(2) A teacher presents a lesson from a prepared script in front of a studio camera, with some technical editing.

(3) A teacher is trained and skillful in the use of television techniques. Props and graphics are used freely, and several rehearsals are held in preparation for recording each lesson. There may be modest use of techniques for technical editing of sound and visual tracks.

(4) Commercial production with all its professional implications, including the use of trained performers and sophisticated systems for sound and visual effect. Complete technical editing operations would be employed.

For these four levels they assign the following software costs per hour:

(1) 0

(2) $50

(3) $6,000 (amortizable over three years, at $2,000 per year)

(4) $500,000 (amortizable over five years, at $100,000 per year)

A person familiar with instructional television feels a bit uneasy with these estimates. The first seems too low, and the last, too high. For example, when a live class is televised there are still some costs—salaries in the control room, for example—and sooner or later the teacher will have to be compensated for wider use of his or her lectures. Furthermore, sooner or later this kind of teaching will prove unsatisfactory for the students who are not in the live classroom, and there will be extra expenses to satisfy their needs. The estimate of $500,000 an hour is much higher than any existing figures from field experience. *Sesame Street,* which certainly had commercial quality production, cost $42,000 an hour from idea to tape; *The Electric Company,* somewhere in the neighborhood of $75,000 an hour. The British Open University pays BBC $20,000 an hour for very professional television. The typical production cost of large ITV systems, such as the NHK educational program or those of American Samoa or El

Salvador, is in the range of $1,200 to $2,000 an hour. Therefore, it is a bit hard to use Hayman and Levin's four levels and the estimates that result from them. But they do serve to underline the undoubted fact that the cost of programming—whether television, radio, films, or the smaller media—varies greatly with the use intended and the audience to be served. If it is merely to feed a lecture to more lecture halls, the cost will be quite small, although this is employing television simply as a delivery system and is very far from using the full possibilities of the medium. If the program has to compete with commercial programs for a nonschool audience, then the costs will be of the order of those for *Sesame Street.* Somewhere between these two, most educational systems will find the level at which they choose to operate, balancing cost against optimum uses of the medium.

The General Learning Corporation study made some recommendations on the basis of their data as we have presented them. The study said some uses of instructional media were reasonable from a financial point of view, some were not, and some were questionable. The questionable uses raised questions either of production—was it desirable to enter into that level of production for a relatively restricted audience—or of technical matters—for example, is a school system prepared to equip and operate an airborne or a satellite system? In Table 4.2, we have adapted these recommendations (GLC, 1968: 17ff.) for easier reading. Uses they have called "reasonable" we have entered in the table as YES (meaning, it is reasonable to use medium X in situation Y). Those they consider unreasonable we have entered as NO. The questionable cases we have recorded as T? or P?,

TABLE 4.2
Is It Reasonable to use Medium X in Situation Y?
Answers from the General Learning Corporation Study

Medium	Local	City	Area Metro	State	Region
Airborne TV	NO	NO	NO	T?	T?
ITFS	P?	P?	YES	T?	T?
Satellite TV	NO	NO	NO	NO	T?
Open-circuit TV (UHF)	P?	P?	YES	T?	T?
Closed-circuit TV	P?	P?	YES	T?	T?
VTR	P?	P?	YES	YES	YES
Film	P?	P?	P?	P?	P?
Radio	P?	YES	YES	YES	YES
Language laboratories	YES	YES	NO	NO	NO
Classroom dial access	YES	YES	YES	NO	NO

Source: GLC, 1986, p. 17.

meaning that in this situation the user must consider very seriously the *technical* or the *production* problems involved.

This table says, in other words:

(1) The smaller media are reasonable in cost for smaller areas.

(2) Of all these media, radio is most widely usable over all the areas here examined.

(3) Television comes at a reasonable cost (according to GLC) under ordinary circumstances, beginning at about the middle level of the table—to serve a large metropolitan area. (Readers may wonder why technical questions were raised about the use of open-circuit television for areas larger than the metropolitan district. The authors of the GLC study are apparently questioning whether the system wants to build additional stations and connect them.)

(4) The very broad distribution systems, satellite and airborne, become competitive in cost only over an area larger than a state (unless the state is Alaska).

THE COST OF COMPUTER-ASSISTED INSTRUCTION AND PROGRAMMED INSTRUCTORS

It would be useful at this point to present a comparison of the cost of a "Big" medium, computer-assisted instruction (CAI), with those of a "Little" (or at least the smaller) medium, programmed instruction. The differences are considerable, although they may in the next years tend to converge somewhat in use for large audiences.

In a sense, CAI shows some of the cost characteristics of instructional films. Whereas it is quite possible for a system to make its own programs, or its own films, the distribution of programmed texts, as of teaching films, has been so largely absorbed by commercial organizations that the unit costs tend to resist the economies of scale. The only way to extend the use of instructional films is to buy additional copies, at a fairly large cost, or to rent a film at a unit cost which is related to the original purchase price. Similarly, the audience for a programmed text can only be extended by purchase of additional copies, which makes the unit cost for 50,000 users not much less than the cost for 5,000.

But the decrease in unit costs of CAI has been quite dramatic. Hayman and Levin (1973) list these estimates for different years from different studies:

$5.85 per student-hour, for a college course in physics during the period 1965-1969 (Hansen et al., 1968);

$3.73 per student-hour for elementary mathematics and English courses, in the period 1968-1971;

$1.06 to $2.18 per student-hour projected for a medium-size computer distributing to a few satellite centers in 1975;

$0.34 per student-hour, projected for a large computer system with wide distribution to satellite learning centers in the period 1972-1975 (Bitzer and Skaperdas, 1969).

This kind of comparison is not completely satisfactory because of the different assumptions used in making the estimates. Somewhat better are the estimates Hayman and Levin themselves have made, using comparable assumptions. They have drawn up five models of computer service and consequent cost—one for 1965-1969, another for 1968-1970, a third for a very large computer system like the one that is now being put into use to carry the "Plato" CAI services throughout much of Illinois, and two models representing the "present" (1971) state of the art, one for large systems, one for small. Their estimates are in Table 4.3.

To put these costs into perspective, it may be useful to recall that the costs of instructional television per student hour estimated large field projects have ranged from $0.14 for 25,000 students in El Salvador (Speagle, 1972) to $0.06 for 275,000 students in Columbia (Jamison and Klees, 1973). Therefore, even the most favorable of the projected CAI costs is still considerably above the unit cost of ITV for a large system. However, the CAI costs are converging on film costs and are at a point where they are justifiable for special needs and situations.

A rough estimate of the cost of programmed instruction can be made with the assumption that a programmed text sufficient for 10 hours instruction will cost $5.00 to $10.00. The variable is how many students will use that text. If it is used by five students, then the cost per hour per student will be $.10 to $.20; if by ten students, then the hourly cost is $.05 to $.10 cents, which is less expensive than most television, although more costly than radio.

THE SMALLER AUDIOVISUAL MEDIA

Up to this point we have said very little about comparisons of cost between "Little" audiovisual media—slides, filmstrips, audiotape, discs, and the like—and their "Big" counterparts such as television and film. The General Learning Corporation study included language labs and dial access, both using audiotape, and provided a comparison between their cost and that of radio, film, and television, but excluded slides and filmstrips, perhaps because it was felt that it would not be realistic to use them for 1,000 hours of instruction per year.

TABLE 4.3

Hayman and Levin's Estimates of CAI Costs, per Student Hour,
Taking into Account Advances in Technology over Time

Item	Model A 1965-1969	Model B 1968-1970	Model C 1972 Prototype	Model D Present Large Systems	Model E Present Small Systems
System Capacity Terminals	32	192	4000	32	8
Student hours per month	4224-7552	25,344-45,312	$5.28 \times 10^5 - 9.44 \times 10^5$	4224-7552	1056-1888
Costs, distributed to system capacity (dollars per student hour)					
1. Computer	$1.50-0.63	$1.22-0.51	$0.21-0.09	$0.22-0.15	$0.37-0.16
2. Terminal	1.80-0.75	0.59-0.25	0.73-0.31	0.73-0.31	0.73-0.31
3. Communications	incl. in 1	0.57-0.24	incl. in 2	incl. in 2	incl. in 1
Total, Hardware	3.30-1.38	2.38-1.00	0.94-0.40	0.95-0.45	1.10-0.47
4. Instructional Software	0.10-0.04	0.10-0.04	0.10-0.04	0.10-0.04	0.10-0.04
Subtotal, Items 1-4	3.40-1.42	2.48-1.04	1.04-0.44	1.05-0.50	1.20-0.51
5. Proctor	0.10	0.10	0.10	0.10	0.10
Subtotal, Items 1-5	3.50-1.52	2.58-1.14	1.14-0.54	1.15-0.60	1.30-0.61
6. Administrative Services, space	0.30	0.30	0.30	0.30	0.30
TOTAL	$3.80-1.82	$2.88-1.44	$1.44-0.84	$1.45-0.90	$1.60-0.91

Nevertheless, we can remind ourselves how much of educational media experience we ignore in not studying these smaller audiovisual media by looking at the results of a U.S. national survey made in July 1969 for the Commission on Instructional Technology (Tickton, 1970: 66). According to the estimates derived by Twyford for the commission, at the time of the survey, the average U.S. public school had ten record players, five projectors for filmstrips and slides, four tape recorders, and three film projectors. The average school also had 235 filmstrips, 78 recorded discs, 26 2x2 slides, 22 tape recordings, and 15 films. There were nearly twice as many filmstrips as still and flat pictures. Between 1955 and 1975, it was estimated that elementary and secondary schools would have spent nearly half a billion dollars for audiovisual equipment and materials.

One can read these figures either as enormous or as less than might be expected of a technological country where education is highly valued. On the negative side, it should be noted that the estimates add up to only one 16mm film projector for every 200 students, one tape recorder for every 156, one slide or filmstrip projector for every 117, and one record player for every 54. The commission also estimated that no more than 1 to 5 percent of public school time (15 to 75 minutes per week) is spent on *any* instructional medium other than the teacher, the book, the chalkboard, flat pictures, charts, and wall maps (Tickton, 1970: 65). But the numbers *are* enormous, at least in instructional potential, and it is a pity that no more economic attention has been given to cost comparisons involving the less expensive audiovisual tools.

From an article by Warren (in Butman, Rathjens, and Warren, 1973) and other sources, we can put together some rudimentary cost figures for these media. Their costs behave more like those of films than like those of radio and television, in that they show less effect than might be expected from economies of scale. They still must contend with the cost of duplicate prints, tapes, or discs, and those of distribution. Within the audiovisual media themselves, there can be a very wide variation in cost. For example, production cost ratios between filmstrips and films can be anything from 1:10 up according to how the time unit is figured and what level of quality is required. In fact, perhaps the greatest strength of the small audiovisual media is their ability to serve local needs at lost cost, rather than providing high-quality materials for general needs over a large area. Slides and filmstrips can be made at acceptable cost even by the teacher of a single course, and students can use audiotapes to hear their own voice in speaking a language or for practicing interviews or reading poetry.

Cost ratios between filmstrip projectors and 16mm film projectors are of the order of 1:8, although this difference disappears if sound is added to the filmstrip, and 8mm film is used instead. At the present time (1977), record players suitable for the hard use of a school classroom cost approximately half as much as audiocassette machines (which typically are made for the consumer market rather than for school use), and one-fourth as much as reel-to-reel tape recorders. Warren feels that there is a trend in developing countries as elsewhere from slides to filmstrips to film. Film is more expensive in every way, but has the advantage of movement, sound, and—at a cost—high-quality production. He notes no similar trend as among record players, cassette machines, and reel-to-reel tape recorders, although he feels that cassette recorders have greater potential than reel-to-reel machines for wide use, and that cassette machines and record players are not truly competitive, because against the cost advantages of the record players must be accounted the ability to record and play back on cassettes.

SOME FIGURES FOR COMPARISON

In 1969, Miller provided some "ballpark" estimates of the cost of different instructional media per user per hour. The wide variation between high and low boundaries of these estimates is probably due in part to the uncertainty of available figures, in part to the differences in quality and in scale of use. Miller's figures are given in Table 4.4.

TABLE 4.4
Estimates of Cost of Different Instructional Media
per Hour per User (Miller, 1969)

Medium	Estimated Cost per User-Hour
	(Dollars)
Class lecture	.15– 3.00
Small discussion group	.50–15.00
Books and journals	.05–10.00
Printed programmed instruction	.05–10.00
Computerized programmed instruction	2.00–25.00
Instructional radio	.01– 1.00
Dial access audiotape recordings	.01– 2.00
Broadcast ITV (live)	.02–10.00
Closed-circuit ITV (live)	.03– 3.00
Broadcast ITV (taped)	.01– 5.00
Closed-circuit ITV (taped)	.03– 3.00
Dial access ITV (taped)	.50– 5.00
Other standard audiovisual aids	.05– 8.00

Source: Adapted from Miller, 1973: 117-123

The wide spread in estimates for each medium makes these figures rather hard to use, and yet the very fact of this variation points to the possibility of using almost any medium in a relatively inexpensive way by fitting media to situations. Miller's item for "other standard audiovisual aids" apparently includes films, filmstrips, transparencies, and the like, with motion pictures at the upper end of the band and still pictures at the lower. The item on "books and journals" apparently covers at its lower end library materials rather than individually owned textbooks, which would on the average cost a student more than five cents per hour of use. Two of the most interesting items are "class lectures" and "small discussion groups." We sometimes lose sight of the fact that direct teaching costs money, and, because we have teachers in the school anyway, think of instructional media always as an add-on cost. But when it is possible to revise the use of classroom teachers—for example, when it is possible to replace local lectures and some practice, so as to make use of the classroom teacher for other duties or larger classes—it may be possible to deliver additional services at an appropriate cost.

ECONOMIC DATA FROM FIELD PROJECTS

Comparison of Radio and Television Costs

Let us turn now to economic data from actual projects. Most of the cost estimates so far presented have been projections from the cost of components and assumed averages, and consequently less realistic than field data although perhaps more carefully compiled and therefore suitable for comparative purposes. In the last decade, evaluators have made more and more efforts to collect economic information along with other data. The result has been an increasing awareness of this element in field projects, although the actual results are often hard to compare because they have been arrived at in different ways. We do have one comparison, however, made carefully by two economists (Jamison and Klees, 1973), using the best data they could obtain from eight projects, five using television and three radio. In addition they have included estimates of what costs will be when three projects reach their intended size. The authors are modest about the reliability of the data they have had to use, but their figures represent probably the most dependable picture we have of unit costs in large radio and television projects.

The projects they have analyzed are ITV in Colombia, American Samoa, Mexico, El Salvador, and the Ivory Coast; radio in Thailand, Mexico, and Indonesia. The projects in American Samoa, El Salvador, and the Ivory Coast are the large national educational reform activities described in Chapter 5. The Colombia figures come from a large program of supplementary television, as it was in 1965. The Mexico figures are from the Telesecundaria, which was intended to offer television-aided secondary school learning opportunities to villages where there was no secondary school. Among the radio projects was a large service offered by Thailand to provide to distant schools expert teaching in the English language, music, and social studies; and a Mexican project, called the radio primaria, which was designed to expand three-year elementary schools to six-year schools, mostly by radio, without the building of more schools or the addition of many teachers. The Indonesian figures are projected for an intended national radio service to the schools. Thus, the Indonesian, Ivory Coast, and more expensive El Salvador projections are not based on actual field experience; the Ivory Coast costs are already exceeding the Jamison and Klees estimates. However, these three simulations serve at least to show what instructional broadcasts might be if projects were developed to their full potential.

The principal findings of Jamison and Klees are shown in Tables 4.5 and 4.6. We have retained the authors' notes to explain the abbreviations and conventions.

These tables endorse everything already said about the importance of economies of scale in the cost structure of instructional radio and television. The costs per student hour in American Samoa are as high as they are because the very expensive installation is prevented from expanding its services beyond the approximately 8,000 students in the Territory. If it could serve numbers like those of El Salvador or Colombia, the unit costs would be quite different. A 1965 estimate of unit costs in Hagerstown was $.20 per student hour (Wade, 1967). Hagerstown, like Samoa and El Salvador, was a project in which the mainline teaching was done by television. Looking at these three projects together, we can see clearly the effect of scale:

Project	N of Students	Cost per Student Hour
American Samoa	8,100	$1.10
Hagerstown	20,900	.20
El Salvador	48,000	.14

If the television can be shared by still larger numbers of users (as in the 1980 projections for El Salvador), the cost may be reduced to as little as

$.02 per hour. It must be repeated that the latter estimate is based on projected planning, not on actual costs.

The radio projects, though not strictly comparable in every case to those on television, are definitely lower in unit cost. The Colombia use of television compares perhaps most closely with the Thai radio, but is approximately four and one-half times as expensive. (Figures for the Thai project for 1973 indicate that present costs are about $.02 per student hour, but no new data have been obtained on Colombia since 1965, and costs there also may have risen.) The planning study for Ivory Coast television is roughly comparable in size and educational purpose to the planning study for Indonesian radio, and the predicted television costs are about ten times as high.

The rule of thumb most commonly quoted by educational technologists is that teaching by television costs about five times as much as teaching by radio. This varies, of course, with economies of scale and the quality of production. Jamison and Klees took no account of quality in making their comparisons, but the wild variation in costs of production due to quality standards can be illustrated by these hourly costs of television production reported from different projects in 1971 or 1972:

Mexican Telesecundaria (Mayo, McAnany, and Klees, 1973) $ 470

Chicago TV College (McCombs, 1967) (This was an estimate for 1966. Rising costs alone would put it up to perhaps $800 today.) $ 583

Netherlands TELEAC (Wermer, in Internationales Zentralinstit Zentralinstitut, 1971) $ 1,055

NHK Gakuen (calculated from NHK Research Institute figures, by Goto, 1972) $ 1,973

German Telekolleg (from Dordick, 1972) $ 8,700

British Open University (Lumsden, 1973) $20,000

Perhaps the most justifiable comparison of radio and television production costs is within the same organization, where both radio and television are used for the same objective, and supposedly the same standard of quality is enforced. We have such a situation in NHK (Japan), where the costs per hour of producing instructional programs were estimated in 1972 as:

For an hour of television $1,937

For an hour of radio   356

In other words, an hour of instructional television NHK costs 5.4 times as much to produce as an hour of radio.

TABLE 4.5
Cost Summary of Five Instructional Television Projects [a,b]

Project	Year of Information Source	N	h	F	V	AC	AC/V	Student-Hour Cost
Colombia	1965	275,000	50.25	624,000	.859	3.13	3.95	.062
American Samoa	1972		145	1,268,000	3.06	159.60	52.2	.10
Mexico	1972		360	598,000	4.23	24.85	5.87	.069
El Salvador	1972							
(a) Total Costs, Sec. Only			170		1.10	24.35	22.14	.143
(b) GOES Costs,[d] Sec. Only			170		1.10	17.75	16.13	.104
(c) Total Costs, Elem. and Sec.			170		.94	2.88	3.06	.017
(d) GOES Costs,[d] Elem. and Sec.			170		.94	2.56	2.72	.015
Ivory Coast	1970		180		3.98	7.27	1.83	.040

[a] Values in this table were computed with a social discount rate of 7.5%; all values are in 1972 U.S. dollars.
[b] The symbols are defined as follows: N = number of students using project (in the given year, unless otherwise noted); h = number of hours per year a typical student views programs; F = annualized fixed costs; V = annualized variable costs; AC = average cost per student for the given value of N; and the student-hr. cost is the cost per student-hour of viewing for the given value of N.
[c] These values of N are planned student usage for 1980.
[d] Because of grants and loans. The costs to the government of El Salvador (GOES) were less than the full costs of the project.
Source: Jamison and Klees, 1973)

THE COST OF EXTENDED SCHOOLS

Cost estimates for the *Mexican Telesecundaria and Radioprimaria* have been given in the Jamison and Klees tables (Tables 4.5 and 4.6). Klees (in Mayo, McAnany, Klees, 1972) compared the estimated costs of these operations with the cost of doing the same thing by conventional means— school buildings and teachers. In the case of the Telesecundaria, the break-even point is about 10,000. At the present level of 28,000 students, and maintaining present class sizes of 50, the cost is about 1.5 times as much by conventional means as by television-extension. However, if the teacher-student ratio were reduced to 30, to make face-to-face teaching more effective, and if administration and building were to follow practices in the Secundaria elsewhere, then conventional means would cost about 2.8 times as much. Klees estimated also that adding three grades to elementary schools with the aid of radio would cost less than half as much as would the same job by the usual direct teaching method.

A full-length economic study of the British Open University has not been published, although the operation is being studied and reports should be available soon. Economists and administrators are understandably sensitive about costs to the university before it reaches a point of stability in registration and operation, and therefore most of the figures we have are not for publication. There is little doubt, however, that the Open University, which is probably the most elaborate such operation in the world, is costing less than residence universities. One preliminary study by an economist, given to us not for attribution, was based on cost figures when registration was in the neighborhood of 34,000, considerably fewer than the present number. The author of this study compared the cost per student of the Open University with the cost for certain other universities in Britain that, like the Open University, do not have large graduate or professional schools (for example, Exeter) and with certain other universities (like Cambridge, for example) that *do* have such expensive schools. He arrives at this comparison:

For the Open University	£ 489[1]	($1,173)
For campus universities without professional schools	£ 694	($1,666)
For campus universities with professional schools	£ 833	($1,992)

He believes that the unit costs of the campus universities would not decrease notably with increased enrollments, whereas the Open University would decrease its unit costs through being able to write off its television, radio, and field center costs over a larger number of students.

Two elements must be considered in evaluating costs of a university like this one. One is the proportion of dropouts. It has been estimated that the Open University when it reaches a "steady state" will be producing about 7,000 graduates a year. The cost per graduate will therefore be relatively higher than cost per year of instruction, and may approach that of a campus university. Against that negative consideration, however, must be measured the fact that many students at campus universities are given maintenance grants. Students at the Open University have no such assistance, inasmuch as most of them are working and living at home. Thus it is hard to believe that the total cost of instruction at the Open University will ever exceed that of residence universities.

The most recent cost estimates we have for the *Radio-Correspondence Schools of Australia* date from 1966 (Kinane, 1967, vol. 1: 169ff.). Kimmel (1971) made a case study of the Australian operation and reported merely that the 1966 estimates still applied.

At the time the cost figures were provided, costs per student of radio-correspondence were estimated at $310.00, plus the charge to the student for summer camp ($27.00) if he or she cared to go. Tuition, books, materials, and postage were all free to the student and covered by the estimate of central expense, except in secondary school where a government allowance did not cover the full cost of textbooks. This estimate is for New South Wales, where approximately 7,000 students were enrolled. In the state of Victoria, where enrollment was less than 1,000, the total cost per student was estimated at $611.00. The unit costs, as can be seen, are sensitive to economies of scale.

The $310.00 New South Wales cost corresponds to an average of $265.00 per student for classroom education. The break-even point is hard to calculate from available data but should be less than 10,000.

The figures we have given are for the radio-correspondence study alone. Australian Schools of the Air, where enrollments have to be considered in class units and necessarily kept small so that all the students can make use of the two-way radio (which costs additional money), are more expensive. The 1966 study estimated that a School of the Air, enrolling 100 pupils, would cost an additional $84.00 per student for capital and operating expenses, over and beyond the basic cost of radio-correspondence education. In other words, a school of 100 enrollment, with teachers and pupils talking directly to each other by radio, was estimated to cost just under $400.00 per student per year. If the class were only 60, the cost would be about $450.00 per student.

The real question, however, is what it would cost to do the same job in another way. It would be infeasible to build schools in the great open spaces of the Australian "outback." The only alternative is boarding schools. They cost $600.00 to $1,200.00 per student per year. This is the choice open to parents who settle their families in central Australia, and in that circumstance the radio-correspondence alternative seems very reasonable.

Dordick (1972) made an estimate of the annual cost per student of the German Telekolleg, using official figures from that institution and the Bavarian government. He calculated that the average cost per successful student is about DM 433, or roughly $122.00 per year. Note that this is the unit cost for a student who *graduates*. The annual cost of an *enrolled* student, who may or may not be intending to take examinations and seek credit (and who, if he does take the examination, may or may not pass) is less than one-third that much. Actual cost *to the student* is estimated at DM 24 ($6.90) per thirteen-week term, or about $21.00 a year. Therefore, the entire cost, so far as it can be estimated from available data, is about $143.00 per successful student for a year of education in the Telekolleg.

How does this compare with the cost of classroom schooling? The Ministry of Education in Bavaria (quoted in Dordick, 1972) gives these estimates for the unit costs of different levels of schooling:

Volkschule	DM 1,070	($301)
Realschule	DM 2,240	($631)
Gymnasium	DM 2,280	($642)

The precise parallel to the Telekolleg, the Berufsaufbauschule, is so new that reliable costs are not yet available. The Ministry estimates that its cost lies between that of the Volkschule and the Realschule, perhaps in the neighborhood of $400.00 to $500.00 a year. When we note that the Telekolleg students do at least as well in final examinations as do the students in residence, and that the Telekolleg graduates more students than all the Berufsaufbauschulen in Bavaria, then these costs make it seem quite a bargain.

Amagi, an economist of the Japanese government, made an estimate of unit costs of the NHK Gakuen (radio-television-correspondence *high school)* in 1966 (see Schramm, "Japan's broadcast-correspondence high school," 1967: 135FF.), although he was apparently unable to include all cost elements. His estimates have been updated and revised with the help of the Radio and Television Culture Research Institute of NHK.

The main cost inputs to the Gakuen in 1971 were these:

NHK contribution to the correspondence
    school (for preparation of texts, study

materials, grading of correspondence lessons, study days, etc.)	$1,350,000
Student fees to correspondence school	330,000
NHK expenses for producing and transmitting	
Television lessons	1,997,000
Radio lessons	434,000
TOTAL	**$4,111,000**

In 1971, the NHK Gakuen enrolled 17,789 students. This would make the cost per student about $231.00. For comparative purposes, however, it is necessary to multiply this by 4/3, because four years in the Gakuen (students of which are holding full-time jobs, in addition to studying) equals three years in an ordinary high school. Therefore, we can estimate that a year of high school in the NHK Gakuen costs about $308.00 per student. This is very reasonable in comparison to the cost of high school education in Japan, which in the last year for which such estimates are available was about $540.00.

However, the number of graduates from the radio-television-correspondence curriculum is rather small. During the last three years the cost per year per graduate has averaged about $2,143.00.

These are approximate figures only, but they make it clear that the NHK Gakuen is relatively inexpensive per student, relatively quite expensive per graduate.

Approximate costs for the Kenya radio-correspondence course of secondary education for teachers have also been estimated from official figures. The input to this project, over a start-up year and two years of operation, was:

Contribution from USAID, for preparing courses, training staff, and operations	$479,964
Contribution of a building from Denmark, amortized over 25 years	38,930
Contribution of Government of Kenya, for operations	410,556
Government of Kenya charges to students and payments to some employees	73,412
Notional interest	120,000
TOTAL	**$1,122,862**

During this time there were 27,467 separate course enrollments. Assuming that three courses would constitute a full-time year of study, we can estimate the full-time equivalent enrollment at 9,156. If this is correct, then the cost per full-time student per year was just under $123.00. This may be too high, because the start-up costs have not been allowed for. Certainly a correspondence course constructed in the first year would last for five years. On that basis, the total per student cost is probably somewhere near $100.00 per year.

A comparable figure on the cost of residence secondary school in Kenya is variously estimated from $200.00 to $400.00.

These later estimates should be read only as signposts, not as cost analyses by a trained economist.

THE COST OF RADIO GROUPS

We have no careful economic studies of radio groups. The finances of Acción Cultural Popular in Colombia are something of a marvel and much too complicated to be unraveled without direct study by an economist. The significant thing, however, is that a large operation like ACPO, serving hundreds of thousands of campesinos and budgeting over $4 million a year is still able to finance nearly three-fourths of its cost without help from public funds or contributions (see Brumberg, 1972). Its radio network, newspapers, and book publishing are expected to be completely self-supporting.

A number of cost estimates have been made on the Indian radio rural forums, but these have not had the benefit of work by a professional economist. Apparently the cost was about $87.00 to organize and maintain each of the 144 forums for ten weeks (twenty meetings) during the Poona pilot project. This would mean a little less than $4.50 per meeting, and the same per member for the whole period (twenty members). If it is indeed true, as the official report said, that each forum group averaged "six decisions for action," and if each of these decisions actually resulted in action, then the cost of bringing about each development project was about $14.50. If only *two* of the six decisions resulted in action, the cost per development project was about $43.50 (see Schramm, "Ten years of the radio rural forum in India," 1967: 105ff). Any development planner would be hard put to find a less expensive way to do that.

When India decided to expand the pilot project over the country and actually organized more than 10,000 forums, unit costs dropped considerably. In fact, it seems to have cost less to operate each of the larger number of forums for a year than to operate each of the pilot forums for ten weeks. Cost curves indicate that unit costs decreased sharply until about 700 forums were operating, and then leveled off. Although unit costs were lowered, performance appeared to have been less than expected. An effort was made to save perhaps too much money and to cut too much from the costs of training. Some of the challenge of starting a new project was missing. Therefore, the cost-effectiveness of expanding a pilot project is not merely a mathematical projection.

Little evidence exists on the cost of animation groups. Kahnert et al. (1967) estimated the cost of Togo radio clubs in 1965 at $.31 per meeting per member. Lefranc ("the radio clubs . . . ," 1967: 59ff.) estimated the budget of Niger radio clubs at $77,000 in 1965, McAnany (1972) as slightly more. In 1965 there were 42 clubs with 700 members. There was also a listening audience, outside the clubs, estimated as high as 100,000, and we do not know how to divide the cost between clubs and over-the-shoulder audience.

SOME CONCLUSIONS

As scarce as reliable unit cost figures are for instructional media systems, reliable cost-effectiveness estimates are scarcer, and cost-benefit ratios still scarcer. But this situation is changing. More and more economists are contributing to the study of educational media systems, more and more projects are being designed to bring in useful data on costs, and we now have made at least a beginning at understanding how media costs behave in different situations and for different purposes.

Everything we have been able to find out about the economics of instructional media systems reinforces the importance of two decisions which a media planner is required to make. One of these is the number of users he wants the system to serve. Radio and television, in particular, are extremely responsive to economies of scale. American Samoa, restricted from serving more than 8,000 students with its large television installation, found that it cost $1.00 per student hour to provide core teaching. El Salvador, on the other hand, could serve 48,000 students at $.14 per student hour. A competent economist estimated that if El Salvador could serve 1,000,000 students, as it hopes to do by 1980, the cost per student hour might be as low as $.02. Similarly with radio: It costs Mexico about $.06 per student hour to teach 2,800 students with the aid of radio, but Thailand can teach 800,000 for about $.02 per hour. On the other hand, film is not very responsive to economies of scale; it costs about as much per student to provide instructional films for a million students as for a few thousand. Printed materials are less affected by scale than are the broadcast media, and computer-assisted instruction is limited in its response to scale by the number of terminals that can interact on line with a central computer.

A second decision is the level of quality to be required of media teaching materials. A small sampling of ITV production costs for large systems shows a variation of more than 1:40 between the lowest and highest average figures. A thirty-minute teaching film can be made locally for a few hundred or a few thousand dollars; professionally, it may cost as much as $100,000. A filmstrip can be made locally for perhaps $100; professionally, for $5,000 to $10,000. By minimizing production cost it is possible to deliver even instructional television in one place by closed-circuit at an acceptable rate for a few hundred students. This is what certain universities have been able to do with closed-circuit television by simply photographing a teacher in the act of teaching a class, and distributing that to other classrooms. On the other hand, really high-class television production like that of *Sesame Street* ($42,000 per hour) or the British Open University ($20,000 an hour) requires large audiences before unit costs come down to an acceptable level.

Thus the interaction of scale and quality will determine in general the cost of using a given medium. But between Big and Little Media (television versus radio, film versus filmstrip, computer-assisted instruction versus programmed instruction), the cost ratio for comparable scale of use (except for very large or very small audiences) and comparable quality of production is usually 5:1 or more. The question that must necessarily be asked, therefore, is whether ITV will accomplish enough more than radio to justify paying five times as much, and so on with other such comparisons. There will certainly be times when anticipated cost-effectiveness will justify additional budget, but anyone selecting media must be prepared to justify the decision either on the basis of cost or of results or both. One of the strengths of the small audiovisual media is not an ability to respond to economies of scale, but rather to be usable at very low cost for local needs and purposes. For example, audiotape will permit a student in a language laboratory to record and listen to his own pronunciation; slides or filmstrips can be made, if necessary by the teacher himself, to illustrate lesson plans. This is the opposite of saving money through wide use, but in its way is just as important.

Evidence from field projects supports the relationships we have been discussing. One conclusion that emerges strongly is that systems, built around the broadcast media in particular, can be used with favorable economic results to extend and expand learning opportunities. In this case the media cost is not merely an add-on to the normal cost of instruction, as supplementary media instruction might be, but can be compared directly with the cost of doing the same thing by conventional means. Field evidence from the British Open University, the Mexican Telesecundaria and Radioprimaria, El Salvador, the Australian radio-correspondence school system, the German Telekollegg, the Kenya radio-correspondence schools for teachers, and others indicates not only that such projects furnish a high level of instruction, but also that they save money over doing the same task with the usual methods and facilities. Evidence on the effectiveness of radio groups is encouraging, but scant.

If we can assume, then, that favorable cost ratios can be expected from using media to do something that would otherwise have to be done by conventional means, what can we expect of the costs of simply adding media to ongoing class instruction? This is clearly an add-on cost, to be justified, if at all, by its contribution to quality of instruction, unless it makes possible a reduction of some kind in present costs. For example, if adding media instruction makes it possible for the same teacher to teach more students, without loss of effectiveness, then adding the media could be justified economically as well as educationally. Jamison and Klees (1973) present very interesting calculations on how much the student-teacher ratio would have to be increased in order to meet the additional cost of adding some media instruction without increasing the total budget. Their figures are reproduced in Table 4.6. The assumed salaries of teachers show that the table is for developing countries rather than for a country like the United States, although it is possible to extrapolate. The table is to be read this way: Suppose that the present ratio of students to teacher averages 25:1, that it costs $.10 per student per day ($18.00 per school

TABLE 4.6
Increase in Student to Teacher Ratio Required to Finance Technology[a]

Annual Cost per Student of New Technology	Teacher Annual Wage			
	$750	$1500	$2250	$3000
R[b] = 25 $ 1.80	1.60	0.77	0.51	0.38
$ 4.50	4.41	2.03	1.32	0.97
$ 9.00	10.71	4.41	2.78	2.03
$18.00	37.50	10.71	6.25	4.41
R[b] = 40 $ 1.80	4.25	2.02	1.32	0.98
$ 4.50	12.63	5.45	3.48	2.55
$ 9.00	36.92	12.63	7.62	5.45
$18.00	—	36.92	15.24	12.63

[a]This table shows the increase in avarage student to teacher ratio   that is required if per student instructional costs (teacher cost plus technology cost) is to remain unchanged after a technology costing A dollars per student per year is introduced into the system. The values of A chosen reflect costs per student per day of $.01, $.025, $.05, and $.10 if the school year is 180 days.

[b]R is the value of the student to teacher ration before the technology is introduced.
Source: Jamison and Klees, 1973.

year of 180 days) to introduce new media instruction, and the average salary of a teacher in the system is $3,000. Following through the appropriate rows and columns of the table, one sees that the student/ teacher ratio, in order to cover the additional cost, would have to be increased by 4.41—in other words, that an average class would have to number 29 or 30, rather than 25. For media that could make a real instructional contribution in the classroom, this would not seem an impossible price to pay.

It is clear from the evidence in this chapter that one can count realistically on being able to deliver ITV for, say, $.10 to $.20 per student hour, to an audience of 20,000 to 40,000, and instructional radio to an audience of the same size for perhaps $.03 to $.06 per student hour. Larger audiences or lower quality levels will reduce these costs; smaller audiences, higher quality, will raise them. The same amount of film to the same size audience would cost more. The cost of CAI is still very high but is moving down toward an acceptable unit cost as larger computers come into use. And the smaller audiovisual media, as we have indicated, have their own special advantage in being able to meet local needs at relatively low cost.

An economist would probably leave one additional warning with prospective users of instructional media. In a system of any size—ITV, for example—actual capital costs are very high at the start of the project. Therefore, in order to amortize these early investments and achieve an acceptable unit cost it is necessary to carry forward the project for at least five years, and preferably for ten or twenty. For example, if projects like the ones in Samoa or the Ivory Coast had been discontinued after two or three years, the cost per student, if accurately accounted, would have been astronomical.

NOTES

1. At the time this analysis was made, the conversion rate, pounds to dollars, was 1:2.4.

CHAPTER 5

EVIDENCE FROM THE FIELD:
National Educational Reform Projects

The universal surge of progress in the second half of the twentieth century offers to education an inspiring challenge. . . . Mere theoretical analysis will not show the way. Future action will have to be based on experience to date and a projection of this experience into the future.

Rene Maheu
Director General, UNESCO
1966-1974 [Foreword to *The New Media,*
1967, by Schramm et al.]

I n the last three decades, increasingly the newer "things" of education have moved into the organized learning process besides the slate and the textbook which so long supplemented the efforts of the teacher. This has been the case in developing as well as industrially developed countries: Witness distant teaching in Kenya and a national multimedia project in Korea. The obvious potency of media like television outside the school has helped encourage their use in the classroom. Margaret Mead noted that

> children learn, from television and from the ads, just what is happening in the world, about the pill and the IUD and organ transplantation and tissue propagation. They are learning about the possibility of test-tube babies while the schools are still cautiously producing a few carefully sterile remarks about reproduction [Tickton, 1970: 18].

A situation like the present, when the newer media are being introduced and experimented with, even though skill is often low and resistance high, is a good time to observe them, as we propose to do in the next chapters. We are going to examine four clusters of learning activity: movements for national educational reform, major uses of media for supporting the school, uses of media for extending the school, and media for nonformal education.

NATIONAL EDUCATIONAL REFORM

Perhaps the most spectacular use of the media of instruction in developing countries has been to try to accomplish a swift reform of a national or territorial system of education. Time is of the essence in this sort of project; changes that would ordinarily take fifty to one hundred years, at the usual measured pace of education, are projected to be achieved in ten or twenty years. Since 1960 five such projects have attracted world attention (see Table 5.1).

All the projects shown in Table 5.1 were carefully observed, and research has been an important component of some of them beginning in the late 1960s. Only the Niger, Samoa, and El Salvador projects have been in existence long enough to make it possible to speak of long-term results measured against objectives. Nevertheless, sufficient evidence exists to make it possible to draw some generalizations.

Why Were the Media Chosen?

The first four of these projects, as we have noted, were built around television; the fifth was, from the first, a multimedia concept, although television (delivered nationwide by transmitters in anchored balloons) was an important component. Why was television chosen to carry the weight of the first four projects, rather than, say, radio? Why was the media approach in the Korea project somewhat different from the others?

It is important to note that none of these projects came into being without substantial assistance from outside. Niger, for example, had capital assistance in the neighborhood of $1.5 million, and more than $500,000 annually in recurring costs, from France. France supplied 27 educators and 25 technicians, who, for most of the first seven years of the Niger program, were in sole charge of setting up both the new curriculum and the television programs.

Samoa, during the first eight years, had over $2.5 million in TV capital funds from the U.S. Department of the Interior, large capital appropriations for new schools, large numbers of expert advisers, educators, teleteachers, and producers from the mainland, and generous support from the annual budget of American Samoa, which also comes largely from Interior. Before 1964, the average annual expenditure per pupil in Samoa was

TABLE 5.1

Place	Starting Date	Serving what levels	Principal Medium Used
Niger	1964	First five grades.	ITV
American Samoa	1964	All primary and secondary grades, plus preschool and adult services.	ITV
El Salvador	1969	Seventh, eighth, ninth grades; now expanding to primary school, teacher training, and out-of-school education.	ITV
Ivory Coast	1971	First two grades; expanding a grade at a time to cover all six primary grades; also inservice teacher training.	ITV
Republic of Korea	1973	Elementary and middle school, with related teacher training.	Multi-media

Note: For basic information on these projects, see AUDECAM (1975) and Lefranc (1967) for Niger; Schramm, 1967b and 1973, for American Samoa; Hornik, Mayo, McAnany (1976) for El Salvador; Ministry of National Education, Ivory Coast, Report series of the Secretary of State in Charge of Primary Teaching and Educational Television, 1968- ; and for Korea, Research Reports of the Korean Educational Development Institute, 1973- .

between $50.00 and $60.00. By 1972, it had risen tenfold, to between $500.00 and $600.00. Only about $150.00 of this represented the added costs of television; the remainder was for schools and equipment, for educators, for considerably higher salaries to Samoans, and the like.

El Salvador had two grants from USAID, totalling $1.053 million for start-up costs, mainly technical assistance and equipment; a loan from AID of $1.9 million, largely for building; a loan of $4.9 million from the World Bank to be used mainly for new high schools; and an estimated additional $2 million in funds, equipment, and personnel, in smaller amounts than those previously mentioned, from UNESCO, UNICEF, Great Britain, Japan, and the United States. ILCE (Mexico) and UNESCO provided courses for television personnel, USAID provided curriculum and production advisers, and, indirectly, a research team.

The Ivory Coast, like Niger, has had extensive help from France. This will total somewhere in the neighborhood of $5 million over the first five years, and includes technical experts, equipment, and some operating expenses. UNDP, through UNESCO, is furnishing about $1 million in money and personnel. Canada's contribution has been for printers, editors, and printing, and may total as much as $1 million. The World Bank has made a loan of $11.2 million, largely for secondary schools. Lesser help has come from West Germany, Belgium, the United States, and elsewhere. The total is in the neighborhood of $18 million.

Korea, in addition to its own considerable budgetary input, has had generous and continuing support from USAID, but it is yet too early in the project to total the assistance.

The size of necessary support suggests that the willingness of the assisting agencies to support certain kinds of projects might have had something to do with the media that were chosen. An examination of the history of the projects lends some support to this conjecture.

The Niger project traces back to the Gaston Berger resolution presented by the former French Minister of Education to the UNESCO Conference of 1960. This influential resolution advocated the use of new technology to speed educational development in the less-developed countries. More specifically, the Niger project traces back to a UNESCO mission in that year, which made some suggestions about ways in which Niger might provide schooling for a larger proportion of its children. In 1962, President Diori instructed Radio Niger to make a study of the possible use of television for schools by day and for adults in the evenings. The French Ministry of Cooperation expressed interest in this idea, and planning began in France no later than 1963. In October 1964, a French production team of about fifty persons arrived in Niamey, and the first experimental program was presented to a test class on November 16 of the same year.

From the viewpoint of the Niger government, then, the main objective was to find a way to expand primary school enrollment rapidly. Only about 7 percent of children were in school. There was also an anticipated shortage of teachers, who would be needed if schools were expanded; some way had to be found to meet this need. On the part of the French Ministry of Cooperation, which furnished most of the financing, there were certain additional objectives, however. They wanted to test the assumptions that ITV could reduce dropout rates and failures in a developing system, that it would permit the use of briefly trained monitors in place of qualified teachers (who were in short supply), that it could be used to teach French to children who had never spoken the language until they came to school, and that it could be used effectively to build a desire to learn. The combination of these two sets of objectives helps to explain why the Niger project developed as it did.

The educational reform project in American Samoa was in part a response to a sense of guilt on the part of the U.S. government that it had "neglected" the territorial schools. Universal education had been extended through high school in 1961, but the teacher corps was composed mostly of persons who had gone no farther than the ninth grade and had little command of English (even though that was supposed to be the language of instruction). Primary education was offered mostly by one-room schools taught in open *fales* (a raised Samoan dwelling without walls). A congressional committee had recommended consolidation of schools in suitable buildings, a revision of the curriculum to make it more relevant to Samoan life, and, above all, an improvement in the standard of English in order to open doors to learning in school and permit Samoan graduates to move freely into American life if they so wished. The reform therefore was envisaged as a swift upgrading of Samoan education under the new conditions of universal participation, overleaping the time required to train teachers adequately, and concentration, especially in primary school, on mastery of English language.

The congressional visiting committee which we have mentioned came to Samoa in 1960, reported to Congress in 1961, at which time a vigorous governor, Rex M. Lee, was appointed and took office. He secured the approval of the Interior Department and Congress for some extraordinary efforts to change educational conditions quickly. In 1962, he brought to Samoa a committee, headed by Vernon Bronson, from the National Association of Educational Broadcasters. Bronson, who had once been in charge of instructional television in Miami, Florida, prepared a detailed report providing for a school reform built around multiple channels of ITV. The governor then asked an ad hoc committee of educators, headed by Dean Reller of the School of Education, University of California at

Berkeley, to look at the NAEB report. After hearing from them, he adopted the Bronson report, and work began in 1963 on the building of new consolidated schools and the installation of major television facilities. The first teleteachers and broadcasters from the mainland arrived in the summer of 1964. A six-week conference on curriculum and procedures was held that summer. By November of 1964 (a few weeks earlier than Niger), the station was on the air and the new system was in use.

El Salvador saw its "Plan Basico"—seventh through ninth grades—as the weakest link in its educational pipeline of manpower into economic and social development. Planners and educators felt that the quality of instruction needed to be improved generally, wastage of manpower needed to be reduced, and enrollment should be at least doubled. After the Reform was established in Plan Basico (renamed Third Cycle), El Salvador was to turn next to the Second Cycle (fourth through sixth grades, to the in-service training of elementary school teachers in the revised curriculum and new methods, and to the provision of second-chance opportunities to adults who had left school early.

El Salvador's introduction of instructional television represented a convergence of its own long interest in ITV with the wish of an American president to see a demonstration of ITV in Latin America. Possible uses of instructional television had been discussed in El Salvador as early as 1960. Walter Beneke, El Salvador's Ambassador to Japan, arranged for a technical study by engineers from NHK (the Japan Broadcasting Corporation) in 1962. They reported favorably on the potential of ITV for El Salvador. In 1963, President Rivera established an Educational Television Commission, unfortunately without staff or budget, and in 1964 created a Department of Educational Television in the Ministry of Education. Ambassador Beneke returned from Japan in 1964 and was named chairman of the ETV commission. Planning then began in earnest, surveys were made of needs for trained persons and of opinions among educators, and a few people were trained in the skills of television.

Inquiries were made of donor nations and international organizations concerning financial support for an educational reform project built around television, but nothing concrete happened on this front until President Sanchez heard U.S. President Johnson speak at the Punta del Este conference in 1967 of the possibility of supporting a demonstration project for ITV in Latin America. El Salvador carried its quest for funds to the United States. AID sent a team of experts to El Salvador to examine the feasibility of such a project. By this time, Ambassador Beneke had become Minister of Education, and was vigorously directing a reorganization of his Ministry and of the teacher training system. Advisers from the United States, UNESCO, and elsewhere were in El Salvador by 1968, assisting with the training of television personnel, revision of the curriculum and development of the teacher training school. The first programs went out to the schools early in 1969, nine years after people began to consider the use of ITV, seven years after the first feasibility study, five years after a Department of ETV had been formed within the Ministry.

The Ivory Coast, with only about 24.7 percent of its age cohort in school in the first grade in 1967-1968, 18.5 percent in the second grade, 16.3 in the third, and 13.8 in the fourth, wanted to achieve universal primary education (six grades) by 1980 or 1985. This was required, the national planners felt, by the country's ambitious plans for national growth. "Economic and social development must be backed up by a policy of promotion and training of manpower," they said in an official publication describing the new system. "[This] must be viewed both as a means and objective of development." They needed a system to "reach the greatest number of people [and] at the same time give training to teachers capable of discharging their mission."

The use of ITV in the Ivory Coast was stimulated apparently by UNESCO and French experts who visited the country in 1967. The idea was accepted by President Houphoet-Boigny. Planning for Ivory Coast ITV began in France in 1967 (and has resulted in nine volumes of planning documents). Ivory Coast officials signed an accord with France and UNESCO in 1968. A center for teacher training was established at the provincial town of Bouake in 1968, with the intention of training teachers to be principals and directors in the new schools. In 1970 and 1971, the television center was built at Bouake in order to put it near the training activities. Advisers and technicians were supplied by France, UNESCO, and Canada. Actual broadcast of programs began in the autumn of 1971.

Thus, the objectives in three countries were heavily quantitative. Niger and the Ivory Coast were teaching only a small fraction of their elementary school population. El Salvador needed to double or triple the enrollment of the three grades it considered key to its economic growth. American Samoa was already teaching most of its children but in what it considered a qualitatively unsatisfactory way.

The Republic of Korea, too, saw its objectives as chiefly qualitative. Although $300 million per year, 18 percent of the national budget, were allocated to education, and 85 percent of that amount went to primary and secondary schools, Korean educators were dissatisfied with the outcomes of education especially at the levels of elementary and middle school. Instructional materials were regarded as inadequate, and almost no such materials were available to the schools except textbooks. Educational technology was not well utilized. The Korean Educational Development Institute (1973) reported:

The use of instructional TV programs to improve the quality of instruction and to help the teachers to use their time more efficiently is seen as urgent. An effective use of ITV will reduce the differences of the educational quality among schools in the rural and the urban areas which are caused by the concentration of competent teachers in urban schools.

Finally, it was considered important to reform teaching methods.

Teachers commonly begin teaching a unit without trying to identify the efficiencies their students might have in learning the unit. They give hardly any consideration to the needs of accelerated or slow learners. . . . A new model of instructional system [is needed to] meet the needs of each individual student without overloading the teachers with teaching and management responsibilities [KEDI, 1973: 5].

Therefore, Korea was looking for a new educational system rather than merely for a delivery system. Although it is too early to expect a history of the Korea project, it is reasonable to assume that the interest of Korean educators and government officials coincided with the interests of a group of scholars and educators at Florida State University, including Gagne, Briggs, and Morgan, who were frequently mentioned in a preceding chapter, and that the parties to this cooperation were brought together by the benevolent interest of the U.S. Agency for International Development which has been a chief financial supporter of the Korean educational reform.

Thus, the nature of the problem, the country's own interest in using one instructional device or another, the particular interest of the funding agency or agencies, and the kind of advice received from experts in the field all have entered into the choice of media. It is not hard to see why television bulked so large in these plans. It is one of the two media able to deliver instruction over wide areas of a country simultaneously (radio is the other), and one of the two media able to use all the symbolic coding systems typically used in instruction (sound film is the other); and it is the only medium able to meet *both* those requirements. Furthermore, it has been the most glamorous of instructional media. In the earlier educational reform projects, television was counted upon without much help to do the tasks that needed doing, whereas the later projects devoted more attention to other components of the instructional system. In El Salvador, for example, a full year of teacher retraining was an essential part of the program. In the Ivory Coast, both teacher training and curriculum design bulked large. In Korea, it was the entire instructional system that was emphasized: the curriculum, the training of teachers, and the use of programmed instruction, texts, and other media in addition to television, and its use in an instructional system, was to a certain extent a reflection of changing knowledge and styles in education. Instructional technology was quite young, as a field of study, when the Samoa and Niger projects were being planned at the beginning of the 1960s, but much more sophisticated when Korea was planning its educational reform early in the 1970s. The use of television in these projects therefore reflected the kind of advice the national planners received. So far as we know, no one advised planners in the 1960s to build their national reform around a Little Medium like radio.

Some Differences in the Projects

It is neither easy nor fair to compare the Korean project, which is still in the stage of preparing to go into the field, with the others. Figure 5.1, therefore, sums up some details of only the four ITV television projects and demonstrates some of their differences and similarities.

One of the chief differences is the pace of introducing the new programs. Three of the four projects, Samoa excepted, moved at a careful and measured pace into their reforms.

The production team in Niger, for example, tried out its television programs, by closed circuit, on two experimental classes during the 1964-1965 school years. During this time, the team found it desirable to remake, in whole or in part, about 80 percent of the programs. Beginning in 1966, the revised programs (about 400 per school year) were presented to twenty first-grade classes (800 students), and second-grade programs were tried on the two experimental classes. In the third year, the second-grade programs, revised as necessary, were presented to the twenty classes, while new third-grade programs were tested on the two experimental ones. At this careful pace, the project moved through the elementary grades. In 1971, the four-year primary school was extended an additional year. In 1971, the project started over again with the first grade. Thus for the first ten years, Niger really had only a pilot project, never serving more than 800 students. In 1974, however, the government decided to expand the project to 122 classes, thanks to the installation of a new 10KW transmitter.

El Salvador began slowly, like Niger, but with vastly larger numbers. In the first year, the initial programs were tried out on 32 seventh-grade classes only. In the second year, these programs, some of them revised, were broadcast to all seventh-grade classes able to receive them, and eighth-grade programs were tried on 32 classes in the eighth grade. At this pace, the reform moved through the three years of the Third Cycle, accompanied by an extensive program of retraining teachers, which we shall mention a little later. By 1973, television, teacher training, and

FIGURE 5.1

	Niger	American Samoa	El Salvador	Ivory Coast
Major Objectives	Expand primary enrollment, make curriculum more relevant, test ITV	Swift improvement and expansion in schools, make curriculum fit Samoan life, concentrate on mastery of English	Greatly expand enrollment in Plan Basico without loss of quality, introduce new curriculum, then turn to other parts of system	Expand enrollment in in primary school, train teachers to carry load of new responsibility
Outside Support	France provided about $1.5 million capital, $600,000 annual operating	U.S. through territorial budget provided $2.5 million capital for TV, about $1 million annual operating, plus capital budget for new schools	From U.S. A.I.D. about $1 million in grant, $2 million loan; from IBRD, $4.9 million loan; from UNESCO, UNICEF, others, about $2 million	From France about $5 million over 5 years, $1 million from UNDP and UNESCO, $1 million from Canada, $11.2 million loan from IBRD
Preparation Time	About two years	About three years	About nine years general, two years specific planning	About four years (plus larger preliminary planning in France)
Use of TV	Core teaching	Core teaching	Core teaching	Core teaching
Support of TV	Classroom materials, feedback, inservice training, ITV team, curriculum revision — latter especially noteworthy in Niger	Same	Same	Same
Pace	One grade a year, never more than 800 pupils until 1974, when extended to 122 classes	12 grades in two years; reached every child in American Samoa in four years	One grade at a time; doubled enrollment in Plan Basico in 4 years	One grade at a time; 20,000 pupils first year, 60,000 second year

FIGURE 5.1 (Continued)

	Niger	American Samoa	El Salvador	Ivory Coast
Classroom Teachers	Monitors	Qualified teachers	Qualified teachers	Qualified teachers
Teacher Training	Six weeks before first term; repeated second year	Emphasized inservice training	Full year of retraining for each teacher	Extensive inservice training
Organization	Almost completely separate from Niger Ministry of Education; operated as experiment under French ITV team; recently incorporated into Niger system.	Integral part of Samoa Department of Education; under U.S. educators and broadcasters at first, administration now Samoan	Integral part of Ministry of Education; used advisers, but project always in Salvadoran hands	Integral part of Ministry of Education; large number of foreign experts
Television Facilities	One low-power TV transmitter, well-equipped production center with three studios	Six open-circuit VHF channels, two transmitter towers on mountain, four studios, 10 VTRs	Rented time on air for four years, and got along with one studio for three years; now has two transmitters of its own and building with three studios	Has building with two TV studios, one radio; national TV network provides time
Production	About 400 programs a year, representing about one hour a day: French, arithmetic, basic programs	6,000 programs a year (2,000 hours) until 1971 all subjects 12-year curriculum, plus preschool and adult services; now greatly reduced	13 programs per grade per week; about 500 per year in 5 subjects – between 4 and 5 hours a week	7 to 8.5 hours a week: French, math, basal education

extension of universal free education to the Third Cycle had made it possible nearly to triple enrollment in those three grades.

The Ivory Coast offered televised lessons in the first year of the reform, 1971-1972, to 447 first-grade classes (about 20,000 students). In the following year, another 979 first-grade classes (about 40,000 pupils) were taught with the aid of television, and television was also introduced into the second grade. In two years, therefore, approximately 60,000 pupils were being taught, in part, by television. Meanwhile, plans were under way to expand the national television network which is intended soon to cover the entire country. At the last report (Grant, 1974), 55 percent of the school-age population were being served by the new system. The target is 100 percent by 1986.

American Samoa, by contrast, offered television to all the elementary schools which could receive it during the first year of the project, and all the high schools in the second year of the project. There was thus little opportunity to try out programs; within two years, it was necessary to provide television teaching for twelve grades. By the third year of the project, about two-thirds of the students in American Samoa were in consolidated schools, with television; almost all the students, by the sixth year. Introducing the new system to so many grades at once made it necessary to have an upgraded primary school (unfortunately, without teachers well trained to conduct such a system). In the first year, television was presented on three levels only; during nine years, the three levels have differentiated into eight grades. However, this meant that a number of students sat in the same level for two or more years, and also that it was very difficult to record programs and use them in later years, both because the primary school was constantly differentiating into more grades and because the level of oral English competence was changing, thanks to new emphasis on language. Thus, until about four years ago, the teleteachers in Samoa were producing 6,000 live programs per year—a fantastic level of production unmatched by any educational station elsewhere in the world. In the first year, as we have noted, some teleteachers were responsible for twenty programs a week, and also for classroom materials to accompany the programs. The production load gradually sank to ten programs per teleteacher per week, then to five, and now live programming has, at least temporarily, been stopped. But the enormous load of live programming must have had an effect on the quality of the broadcasts to the Samoan schools.

Why was Samoa in such a hurry? There were political reasons to move swiftly, of course. But the chief reason may have been the reluctance of the Samoans themselves to introduce the new system one grade at a time. A Samoan cultural norm, or so it was reported at the time, provided that "all should go forward together." It was therefore repugnant to the chiefs and their families that one small group of children would be the sole beneficiaries of the new system during the first year, and children enrolled at that time in the other eleven grades would *never* be taught by television. Again it must be remembered that Samoa reflected the state of the art of instructional television about 1960, when the concept of the "master teacher" to be shared widely by television was the favorite doctrine. Thus, for the Samoa project, the important figure was the teacher in front of the camera doing mostly what he or she had learned to do in the classroom for students he or she knew much better than Samoan students.

Whatever the true reason for what Samoa did, the wisdom of hindsight says that a slow and careful approach, one grade at a time, making, trying out, and revising materials before committing them to wide use, is a safer approach.

In one very important detail, the Niger project was different from all the others. The architects of that project decided to use monitors with no pedagogical training, most of them with only a primary school education, rather than qualified teachers in the classroom. This decision was made for two reasons. For one thing, looking toward a possible very large expansion of the school system, the use of monitors was expected to save money. In the second place, the project directors felt that it would be easier to prepare relatively untrained monitors to fit their new curriculum and their new ideas on pedagogy than to try to retrain teachers who were already anchored in the classic pedagogy. All the other projects used qualified teachers in the classroom, although in-service or preservice training or both were provided for them. The Samoan teachers at first were, however, treated almost like monitors and given detailed instructions on how to "follow up" the television lessons.

As we have seen, all four projects tried to provide some in-service training for their classroom teachers. The preservice training that El Salvador gave its teachers, however, was unique among the four.

With a few exceptions, every teacher in the Third Cycle in El Salvador who was assigned to a classroom with television received a full year of retraining at the new teachers' training center, with full pay, before going to his new assignment. The retraining course included both subject matter and teaching method. Exceptions to this rule were the first group, who received intensive eight-week courses in the vacation period before and after their first year of teaching with television, and some teachers who had graduated from the advanced Escuela Normal Superior, who were thought to need only a short retraining course. This is the only case to our knowledge when a school system has made use of a new media project to upgrade its teacher corps by such an extensive program of retraining.

The monitors in Niger were given a six-week course before they were sent to do their first teaching and a refresher course before the second year. In American Samoa, the pace of the project was so swift that there was little time for retraining beforehand. The emphasis was therefore put on in-service training and summer workshops. In recent years, a number of formal courses have been provided for teachers in late afternoons and summers, and teachers have been helped to extend their education in the United States. A number of Samoan teachers have now returned with advanced degrees in education.

The Ivory Coast offered a three-year (now two-year) course at the new teachers' training center in Bouake to teachers who were expected to become administrators in the new system, and instruction for classroom use of television was added to existing one-year teacher training programs. Special one-month courses were offered to teachers who were to go into classrooms with television.

Television bulked much larger in the planning and preparation of the first four projects than of the Korean project.

This is not to say, however, that the ITV projects did not try to create instructional *systems,* but they tended to build the system *around television,* whereas the Korean planners did not.

Niger, American Samoa, El Salvador, and the Ivory Coast all had the concept of a "team" to make their teaching materials. In Samoa, it was principally the television teacher and producer, whose load was at least five programs a week plus classroom materials. In El Salvador, each team included five persons—two subject-matter specialists, a teleteacher, a producer, and a "coordinator," all of whom were assigned to one subject only and had to produce, typically, three twenty-minute programs a week plus accompanying teachers' guides and pupil study sheets. In both Niger and the Ivory Coast, the production staffs were large and less subject-specific.

Thus, in each case, a serious effort was made to coordinate class materials with the television teaching. Revision of the curriculum was also in the plans for all four of the projects. Except for Korea, the most completely new curriculum was developed in Niger. The same team that was making the new curriculum was also responsible for the programs and for the training of classroom monitors, thus being given a maximum opportunity to incorporate its plans into practice. El Salvador kept its curricular revision ahead of the introduction of television into each grade, but the revision was rather general and left much to the programmers. American Samoa was under pressure to introduce such a vast amount of television programming that there was little time for a thorough revision of the curriculum in advance. Furthermore, the curriculum had to change constantly as the initial three levels of primary expanded to eight grades, and as the pupils responded to the increased emphasis on oral English. Only in the last few years have detailed and formal curriculum guides been published. The Ivory Coast accomplished some curricular revision in advance of television, although the changes were greater in method than in the substance of the classic French plan of studies. However, innovations such as the "new math" were included, and efforts were made to use examples and problems from Ivory Coast life.

Each project also made efforts to obtain regular feedback from the classroom and to provide continuing in-service training for its classroom teachers by means of broadcasts or meetings or both.

But these steps toward creating instructional "systems" around television were far less detailed and formal than Korea's. The Korea planners are building their efforts around a KEDI (Korean Educational Development Institute) model of an instructional system in five steps, thus:

Planning ⟶ Diagnosis ⟶ Teaching ⟶ Extended ⟶ Evaluation
                                    Learning   Learning

Of the instructional time (which follows planning and precedes evaluation) 10 percent is to be devoted to diagnosis, 70 to 80 percent to teaching-learning and extended learning, and 10 to 20 percent to evaluation. Under planning, the model provides for identification of tasks and objectives, making a lesson plan, and making a management plan. Figure 5.2 spells this out in greater detail.

The activity required under diagnosis is identifying where the students fall short in the prerequisites required for the learning task, and providing some remedial work if necessary.

Then comes the major activity, which the model calls teaching-learning, and which takes up about three-quarters of the time. This is detailed in Figure 5.3. One of the more interesting things to notice is where ITV appears in the pattern in relation to classroom teacher instruction, programmed learning, simulation, field trips, and so forth. Clearly this is not a system built around television, but rather one that has television built into it to do what the planners think most needs doing.

Extended learning begins with a formative test to identify and help students who need special practice and students who have mastered the tasks and are ready to go on to special projects. Finally, the evaluation provides for a summative test in order to draw some conclusions about student achievement, the effectiveness of the teaching, and grades that should be assigned.

This is nothing particularly new to anyone who reads modern pedagogical theory, especially the work of Gagne and his colleagues, and yet it

FIGURE 5.2 Design of the KEDI project: Planning

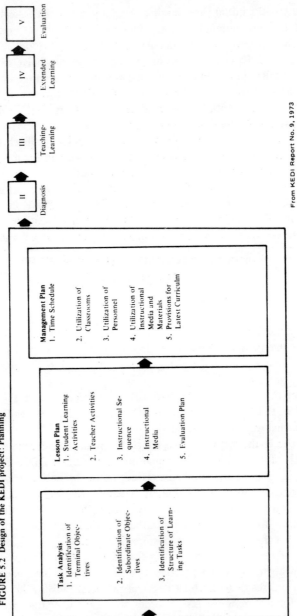

From KEDI Report No. 9, 1973

FIGURE 5.3   Teaching – Learning

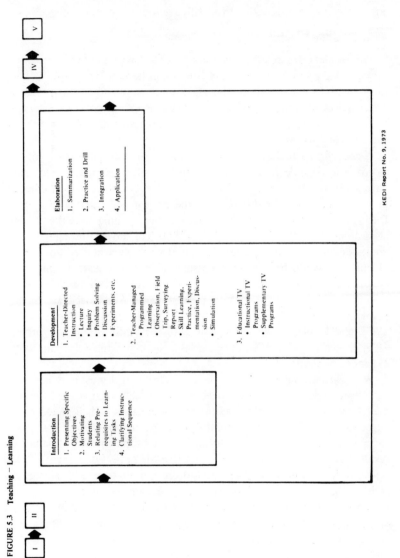

KEDI Report No. 9, 1973

is refreshing to see a project in the reform of national education begin with a theory of instruction rather than with a delivery system.

What Were the Results?

We have less research than we should like to have on the effects of these projects. Very few hard data have been published on Niger and the Ivory Coast, and Korea is still in the stage of making and testing materials. Nevertheless we can ask, of such evidence as exists, how the effects of these large and rather costly projects stack up against the objectives of the educational reforms.

Niger. Niger's basic reason for considering instructional television was to make it possible to increase primary school enrollment which, as we have said, was estimated at that time at about 7 percent of children of primary school age. In this respect, the project was less than a success. During the first ten years, it never succeeded in reaching more than twenty classrooms, 800 students. After these 800 had moved through the five grades of primary school, a second cohort of 800 was started through the pipeline. It would have seemed possible, at the very least, to put a new cohort into the first grade each year, so that in the fifth year the reform system would have been reaching 4,000 students. And indeed, the original plans had been much more grandiose—to expand from 800 to 18,000 by 1967, and to 40,000 by 1968. Not until the tenth year of the project, 1974, however, were 100 more classes added, and the total enrollment expanded to about 5,000.

Why did nothing like this happen earlier? In part it must have been that the Niger budget was unable to absorb large additional costs. In part, it may have been due to the traditional conservatism and suspicion of the Niger rural people. But it is hard not to believe that much of it was due to the passive resistance of the educational establishment. And this in turn resulted in no small part from the fact that the project was imported, was operated for the most part separately from the ministry, and rejected the trained Niger teachers in favor of untrained monitors and the traditional colonial curriculum in favor of a new and different curriculum. In other words, apparently little was done to integrate the project into Niger's plans and capabilities for carrying it on. It had few supporters in the ministry and was largely ignored by the officials responsible for the future of education in the country. It was treated much like a French experiment on Niger soil, and not until the end of its planned cycle did the establishment show much interest in whether the experiment continued to exist. Presently, things are looking up. Two thousand tested and revised programs for the first five grades are on tape, and there is new hope they will have the use they deserve. But from 1964 to 1974 the unit costs of the educational reform must have been discouraging indeed.

On the other hand, measured against some of the French objectives—to test the hypotheses that ITV could reduce dropouts and failures in an African culture, that it would make possible the use of (less-expensive) monitors instead of qualified teachers, that it could be used to teach French effectively to students who had never spoken it before coming to school, and that it could produce programs that stimulated the desire to learn—the project was far from a failure.

Dropouts in the television classroom were practically zero. Children came to school even when they were ill or the weather was bad, and they kept coming week after week, year after year. The monitors worked out very well; the project supervisors said that it was easier to train them to the new curriculum and the new methods than to try to retrain traditional teachers. Observers noted that the monitors established a remarkably fine rapport with the children.

No very useful studies of learning from the Niger project have yet come to light. A series of criterion-references tests were given in the first year, and the children scored very well as measured against passing grade scores set by the testmakers (see *Television Scolaire du Niger,* 1965: 67ff.; for later information, see AUDECAM, 1975). French visitors were surprised at how well the children were speaking the language after only two or three years. But the chief success of the project, by the general verdict of people who saw the twenty schools in Niger, was in the instructional programs it was able to produce.

The quality of ITV programs in many projects has been a source of dissatisfaction to project heads, to educational administrators, and to observers alike. It is perhaps ironic that higher standards are applied to television teaching than to classroom teaching, but they certainly are; and among the reasons are that television costs more and is far more public. In Niger, however, the programs have been almost universally praised by visitors. Relatively few programs were made in Niger each year (one-fifteenth as many as were made in Samoa). The pedagogical and production staffs were talented and large. The programs were tried in advance on two classes, and remade if necessary. The result was a series of programs in which typically "les enfants sont *plus acteurs* que spectateurs" as *Television Scolaire du Niger* explained (1965: 31). There was very little overt teaching on television; rather, the programs tended to be like "shows for children." They kept the pupils interested and active and provided many opportunities for them to act out skits they had seen on the tube, or to finish a playlet that had been begun on television—meanwhile, of course, practicing their French and their arithmetic, and enjoying the experience hugely. Officials in the Niger educational system protested that the project was not teaching the skills and knowledge expected of the classic curriculum, and in many cases the programs were modified so as to bring them closer to the traditional pattern. To the best of our knowledge, there are no reliable comparisons of what was learned in the twenty experimental schools and a comparable twenty traditional schools, but there seemed to visitors little doubt that the experimental classes were *enjoying* the experience of education very much more.

American Samoa. The objectives of reform in American Samoa were to accomplish a swift upgrading of the system after a long period of apparent neglect, and especially to improve the use of English in the schools, both as a door to learning and a door to later entrance into the U.S. economy for the 40 percent or so if Samoan school graduates who choose to go to the United States.

There is very little doubt that the second of these objectives has been achieved, so far as *oral* English is concerned. Two linguists visited American Samoa in 1963 and 1964, just before the project began, and described the kind of language, alleged to be English, spoken by pupils and teachers. Four quantitative studies were made between 1966 and 1969, comparing the English language usage of students who had been in the new system for different numbers of years. We ourselves have tested all the school children on the one Samoan island that had never received television, and compared their performance with that of the children in an isolated school on the main island that had little contact with spoken English except in school and on television, and a third school that was not isolated. The results of this study are impressive. Only three out of ten children on the non-television island (who had received no part of their education in the new system) could make any English response at all to simple questions, although the Samoan schools now, as in 1964, are supposed to be conducted in English. The fourth, fifth, and sixth grades on the nontelevision island scored considerably below the *third* grade of schools on the main island of Tutuila, which has television. This is true of their performance in understanding English, speaking English, and reading English. The scores we have been speaking of are for students who received *all* their education on the island where television did not reach. However, there were five students in school on that island who had spent one or more years in school on a Samoan island where they were taught in part by television. The scores of these five students, given in Table 5.2, are in some ways more revealing than the total scores. The n's in Table 5.2 are small, but represent the total population of each school in the grades tested.

We are thus able to compare students who have had *all* their education in the new system, with students who have had *none* of their education in the new system, with students who have had *part* of their education in it. Those who have spent all their time in the new system with television do very much better in English than those who have spent no time in it; and

TABLE 5.2
Comparison of Scores in Schools on Main Island of Tutuila Where ITV Was Used with Those of Students in School in an Isolated Island without Television

	Grade	Understanding Spoken English (Maximum = 50)	Speaking English (Maximum = 114)	Reading (Maximum = 32)
Non-TV students on isolated island (N=10)	4,5,6	18.5	*	4.9
3rd grade TV students on main island (N=14)	3	32.6	69.6	12.0
6th grade TV students on main island (N=15)	6	42.1	102.7	21.9
Student 1 on isolated island (Spent one grade on main island)	3	29	9	4
Student 2 (one grade on main island)	3	25	19	5
Student 3 (two grades on main island)	4	31	14	9
Student 4 (three grades on main island)	5	25	44	17
Student 5 (four grades on main island)	6	39	97	17

*Too little to record

those who have spent part of their time in the new system are between the two other groups, and, in general, the more time they have spent in the new schools, the better they do.

However, there are puzzling aspects in the main research results from American Samoa. For one, the improvement in oral English seems not to have spilled over into corresponding improvement in reading skill. Standardized tests given in Samoa in 1963 and 1964 have been lost, but annual tests from 1970 through 1976 indicate that the lowest average scores are in reading, although the reading average has improved about one academic year in the last five years. Of course, enrollments have increased, and therefore later scores may represent a less select group. But we might expect that this would also be reflected more than it is in the oral English scores.

Standardized tests given in Samoa show that the children do much better on questions based on rote learning than on questions requiring abstract thinking or reasoning. This is a phenomenon seen also in "disadvantaged" groups on the American mainland, particularly in those who come from homes where English is not spoken or where there is no reading matter—which also describes most Samoan homes. There is a plausible theory that one can never learn a foreign language better than his own language. If he does not have practice in reading outside school, he is unlikely to learn to read well in school. And consider the peculiarly cruel situation of the Samoan child: He has been taught in a primitive form of a foreign language by a teacher who is also handicapped in that language, throughout the primary school years when the child should be filling his mind and learning the skills of conceptualizing, reasoning, and problem-solving. Is a child taught in that way likely to be handicapped in those skills forever? The Samoan schools have begun to investigate this by experimenting with a bilingual curriculum.

What kind of test performance can we reasonably expect of students like those in American Samoa? Their school, for the most part, is in English. But they are actively discouraged from using English at home, and, unlike American children, they have no English reading material there. In studying and taking tests in English, they are therefore "disadvantaged"—quite as disadvantaged as many minority groups on the mainland. And if their performance on standardized tests is compared with that of mainland minority groups, they compare satisfactorily. They begin school below the test norm of mainland white middle-class students, and as they move through school, most of them fall farther behind. This is precisely what the Coleman Report found to be true of many Black, Puerto Rican, Spanish-American, and Native American groups on the mainland. The Samoan children typically do a little better than these disadvantaged mainland groups in arithmetic, a little worse in reading, as Figure 5.4 shows.

The evidence does not exist to make possible a clear comparison on Samoan test performance today with performance when the system started. The only thing we can say with some confidence about trends in performance (because the Samoan project, wisely or unwisely, resisted such research in its first five years) is that skill in oral English clearly has improved.

In a sense, the institutional changes that have come about as a part of the educational reform are more revealing than the test scores. To an observer (if not to a tester), the system looks a great deal better than it did in 1964. The new schools are attractive and efficient. The teaching seems better. Discussion in the classrooms is replacing much of the chanting of rote responses. Perhaps most important, in these last eight years the system has been turned over almost entirely to Samoan leadership. In 1964, Samoans held little except subordinate positions. The top jobs were all filled by educators from stateside. For four years now almost all school principals have been Samoan, as have most of the assistant and deputy directors in the Department of Education. In 1973, the first Samoan Director of Education in the territory's history took office. The second Samoan Director has now succeeded him. This is an accomplishment of educational reform which should not be undervalued.

Television was cut back in 1971 from 6,000 live programs to 2,200 per year. That was a sign of maturity and rising standards, rather than lack of confidence in the medium. Teachers, especially in the secondary schools, felt better able to teach their own classes without a crutch. Neither

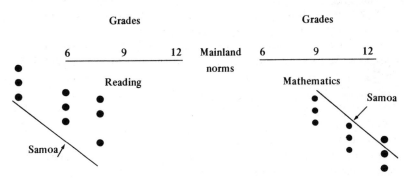

FIGURE 5.4

Comparison of American Samoa scores on U.S. standardized tests, in terms of grade levels below mainland norms, with that of three "disadvantaged" groups on the mainland. The dots represent the special groups; the line represents Samoa average public school scores in 6th, 9th, and 12th grades.

teachers nor administrators are satisfied any longer with the "talking face" kind of television that almost necessarily had to be the staple diet of Samoan schools when so many programs were being produced; they are asking what jobs television can do best, and how many programs of really high quality their system can produce.

In 1975, television was further cut—indeed, so severely that live programming had practically to be eliminated and only previously recorded programs broadcast. This latter cut is not a sign of educational maturation, but rather of hard times and shrinking financial support from the U.S. government. Achievement tests in 1974 showed signs of lower scores in some classes where television had been eliminated, and it will be interesting to see, in the 1975-1976 year, whether elimination of all live programming will have a substantial effect on student scores.

The appearance of detailed curriculum outlines, however, the establishment of a tests and measurements service, the new disposition to try different kinds of educational practices like team teaching, programmed instruction, and learning games—developments like these represent a long jump from 1964 when the schools were mostly one room in which the children chanted back whatever responses the teacher had made them memorize.

Therefore, despite some of the puzzling and mixed evidence, it seems possible to say that reform and ITV in Samoa have made considerable changes in the system and in what goes on in the schools.

El Salvador. The central objective of the El Salvador educational reform—to extend universal education through the Third Cycle without loss of quality, and by so doing to relate the educational system more closely to the needs of the country for trained manpower—has been achieved at least with regard to enrollment and quality.

Free universal education has been extended through the ninth grade, and the enrollment in the Third Cycle has nearly tripled. There is no reason (from test evidence) to believe there has been a loss in quality. Whether the kinds of manpower that are being produced by the revised Third Cycle are contributing in greater degree to the needs of economic and social development is not yet clear, but there are some signs that might lead us to question it.

Although the El Salvador project has been studied for five years, the evidence still does not provide a ready answer to the question of whether or not quality has risen. Do we define quality of education as what can be learned from a criterion-referenced test? If so, there has been only one true comparison between the new system and the old. That was in the seventh grade in 1969. At that time the relevant comparisons between learning gains in the Old and New (ITV) System Classes showed substantial advantage for the TV classes. After that year, however, it was impossible to test one system against the other because the New System was extended throughout. For the next three years, during which two complete cohorts moved through the middle school and a third cohort passed through two of the three school years, the comparisons had to be between classes that had all the New System *including* television and other classes that had all the New System *except* television. These latter comparisons, like the laboratory experiments that have held all variables constant except the delivery of a teacher by television rather than in person, tended to show no very substantial differences. Overall, there was a slight and cumulative advantage for the classes with television, as Table 5.3 shows. However, inspection of that table will indicate that the chief differences were in the seventh grade (where they might have been due either to the Hawthorne [novelty] effect or to the fact that more time was given to prepare the broadcasts for that year) and that after the seventh grade relatively few annual learning gains whatever the type of class, were even as much as 20 percent. Of course, the criterion tests may have been less than completely satisfactory. But if there is no simple explanation like that, then the El Salvador educators have little cause for elation over how much their students were learning.

There *was* cause for satisfaction, however, in the growth of general abilities in the El Salvador schools. The test instrument was a standardized one made for Latin American populations and containing items on verbal ability (tested by sentence completion and word relationships), nonverbal ability (tested by analogies and classification), and numerical ability (tested by computation and number series). All students gained in general ability, of course, as they passed through the three-year middle school. However, in all three cohorts the students who had ITV gained 15 to 25 percent more in general ability than the students who had all features of the New System *except* television. Thus the TV students were ahead after the first year and lengthened their lead as they moved through the two

TABLE 5.3
Number of Cases in which Average Annual Gains in Test Scores,
By Classes with TV and Classes without TV, Were of a Given Size.

	7th grade		8th grade		9th grade	
	ITV	No ITV	ITV	No ITV	ITV	No ITV
Over 20% gain	9	2	1	2	2	2
10 - 20% gain	0	6	6	4	1	2
Less than 10% gain	0	1	2	3	3	2

After Hornik et al., 1973: 60

following school years. This is an impressive result. The fact that the nonverbal part of the test contributed most to the total mean of the TV students provides additional reason to believe that the television experience may indeed have been chiefly responsible for the difference. If so, what does the result say about television? The question can be answered more confidently, of course, when it has been tested elsewhere. But the most widely favored explanation is that the general ability test minimizes the result of verbal rote learning as emphasized in the classroom, and maximizes the result of ability to generalize and apply classroom learning to situations and problems such as were illustrated by television.

The El Salvador study collected more than test data, and some of these results are even more interesting than the comparisons of means. For example, striking and important institutional changes were accomplished in a very short time. The Ministry of Education was completely reorganized and integrated, something that had been needed for a long time but was accomplished at last under the stimulus of general change. The system of teacher training was completely reorganized; most of the normal schools of the country were closed, and a new high-quality central teacher training facility was created. The curriculum was revised. The Third Cycle was combined with the first two cycles, and put under a single director. New and much improved study materials were made for the Third Cycle. A new concept of supervisors—as advisers rather than inspectors—was adopted and, to a certain extent, implemented. The concept of evaluation was widely spread throughout the Third Cycle. Most of the 900 teachers in the seventh, eighth, and ninth grades were given a year of retraining with pay, free from teaching duties. The "taxi-teacher," who taught an hour at one school then hurried to another, and then another, teaching the same subject but never seeing his students outside class, was replaced with full-time teachers. These are dramatic changes, and the fact that they and others all occurred within three years indicates that the reform movement had the power to bring about changes that otherwise might have taken many years or might never have happened at all. Furthermore, when administrators and planners were queried as to how such changes came about, most of them mentioned the ability of television to act as a stimulus and set a timetable for needed institutional change.

What was the effect on quality of teaching? The presence of certain manifestations of "modern" teaching in the classroom were measured—for example, less lecturing, more discussion, thought questions rather than rote questions, more questions asked and opinions given by students, more individual and group projects, and so forth. It was found that the New System classes had significantly more of this "modern" teaching than did Old System classes. The part of the teacher's experience that seemed to correlate with such teaching was the year of retraining. If a teacher had that, he was likely to teach in the way we have described; if he had not been through the retraining course, he was less likely to do so.

What was the effect on attitudes? These were considerably different by courses. Both TV and non-TV students were positive toward social science and science classes, negative toward mathematics and Spanish language. (Math was particularly disliked by TV classes, and it was generally concluded that the nature of the television teaching was responsible.) English language was well liked by TV students, little liked by students who did not have TV classes. Perhaps the most significant attitudinal finding, however, was that the high initial enthusiasm for ITV declined steadily as students moved through the three years of the school. Several reasons have been advanced for this. One is that the reality of ITV could not match anticipation. Another possible reason is continuing dissatisfaction on the part of teachers with employment conditions, which caused many of them to relate the cost of ITV to their own small salaries. In one year there was an exceedingly unpleasant teachers' strike that had the effect, among other things, of completely disrupting the television schedule for the rest of the school year.

The implication of these hypotheses is that the declining enthusiasm for ITV may have been related largely to the situation in El Salvador. However, much the same curve of attitudes was found in American Samoa. In Samoa, where attitude studies were begun only in the fifth year of the project, the decline was by grade, more than by time. That is, over several years, attitudes in primary school remained quite favorable. In the higher grades and in high school, however, the decline was steady by grade and evident, although less so, over time. It may be, therefore, that not only does the first magic of instructional television wear off, but also as students move into upper school years they become increasingly impatient with one-way educational communication, particularly when it is less than truly expert. Still another interpretation, and one that has much evidence behind it both in Samoa and in El Salvador, is that teachers in higher grades become increasingly impatient with the invasion of their classroom by an outside teacher and with having to make *their* schedule and *their* judgment of the needs and readiness of their own pupils fit the inflexible schedule of a television broadcast.

It will be recalled that one of El Salvador's chief reasons for experimenting with television in the seventh through ninth grades was that it was felt necessary to produce more middle-level technicians for the economy—accountants, repairmen, etc. Two studies of student aspirations resulting from the experience were made and reported in Hornik et al, (1973): 103ff.). The results were mildly startling, for the students were aiming not at the middle-level jobs where the need was felt to be greatest, but rather toward the professions. Actually, they were aiming far above their fathers, both in education and occupation. Whereas less than two percent of the fathers had gone to universities, 40 percent of the students were aspiring to a university education. Although 70 percent of the fathers were working as unskilled laborers, 40 percent of the children were aiming toward professional occupations requiring highly specialized training. These results raised questions of whether the occupational system and the higher education system of the country could possibly handle the tidal wave of students now moving through Third Cycle, and whether such aspirations might not lead to widespread frustration rather than filling the ranks of middle-level technical employees where El Salvador most needed trained people. A study of what actually happened to the Third Cycle graduating class of 1971, which was the first class to go through entirely under the New System, found that 86 percent of the graduates had been able to go on with their education—hoping ultimately to reach the university—and another 4 percent were studying and working part time. The crunch will apparently come in another few years when they seek university entrace.

Ivory Coast. It is too early yet, and too few data are available to say how close the Ivory Coast project is to achieving its objectives. It is evident, though, that the project is moving toward the goal of universal primary education. In the first year, 20,000 were taught with the aid of television in first grade; in the second year, 20,000 in grade two and 40,000 in grade one. In the third year about 100,000 were in the new system classes. Thus this project is moving forward very strongly. Unfortunately, no reports on learning gains and attitudes have come to us.

Korea. No systemwide figures are as yet available for Korea, where time so far has been spent on preparing and testing both hardware and software for the national project. However, test results from unit tryouts are being reported, and these indicate that the new materials are working effectively. Table 5.4, for example, carries the results of a comparison between a large experimental group using the new materials in two subjects, and a control group using the previous materials. The groups were equated by a diagnostic test which showed the control group scoring slightly (but not significantly) higher at the beginning of the unit. At the end of the unit, as will be seen from the table, the experimental groups were significantly higher than the controls (.01 level). Furthermore, when the students were divided according to the percentage who attained "mastery" (80 percent or over), and "near mastery" (60 to 79 percent), again the experimental students did noticeably better.

TABLE 5.4
Achievement of Experimental and Control Groups on Unit Tests for Two Subjects.

Subject	Experimental Group			Control Group		
	No. of Students	Mean	S.D.	No. of Students	Mean	S.D.
Korean	860	86.38	15.59	475	82.31	13.79
Arithmetic	865	84.86	21.60	558	75.71	18.54

Difference between means of experimental and control groups significant at .01 level

Subject	Experimental Group			Control Group		
	No. of Students	Mastery (80-100)	Near Mastery (60-79)	Non Mastery (0-59)		
Korean	860	82%	13%	5%		
Arithmetic	865	75%	18%	7%		

Subject	No. of Students	Mastery (80-100)	Near Mastery (60-79)	Non Mastery (0-59)
Korean	475	70%	23%	4%
Arithmetic	558	56%	25%	19%

KEDI, Research Report, No. 8, March 1974

SOME CONCLUSIONS

We can conclude that these national reform projects have been able to bring about important changes, expand opportunities to learn, and contribute to the quality of education. They have not in every case done all that was intended, and sometimes not in the way intended, but nevertheless each has been able to make considerable change, in a short time, in one of the most change-resistant of social institutions, the formal school system.

The Korean multimedia project is not yet far enough along to tell us how much a project works in national educational reform. In the case of the four projects which are built around television, we have not yet answered the question of whether such a project has to be done with television.

There is no really hard evidence on the question; apparently no one (except the Korean group) has ever tried to bring about national educational reform with radio, films, or any other medium, large or small, in the position of prime mover *except television.* We put the question about television to representatives of the reform projects built around ITV. They replied, with variations but no essential disagreement, that such a task would be harder to do without television and harder to do with a medium other than television.

Their arguments run like this:

—The size of television and its logistic demands require a major commitment to change, and consequently make other changes easier.

—Television imposes a schedule on change. The decision to go on the air at a certain time requires curriculum revision in advance of that, requires financing to be arranged still farther in advance, requires professional training before the equipment is in hand, requires that teachers be prepared and that classroom guides and other materials be ready, and so forth.

—The dramatic quality of the technology attracts wide interest and symbolizes for a wide audience that change and "modernization" are occurring.

—The excitement of television sometimes leads participants in a project to undertake tasks they might otherwise hesitate to attempt. This is what Hirschman was talking about when he wrote:

Since we necessarily underestimate our creativity, it is desirable we underestimate to a roughly similar extent the difficulties of the tasks we face so as to be tricked by these two offsetting underestimates into undertaking tasks that we can, but otherwise would not dare, tackle. The principle is important enough to deserve a name; since we are apparently on the trail here of some sort of invisible or hidden hand that beneficially hides difficulties from us, I propose "the Hiding Hand" [Hirschman, 1967: 13].

—Television catches the interest of the pupils, who think of its introduction as something new in an old routine.

—Television makes it easier to obtain financial help from outside.

—In other words, they say, television is a mover, a catalyst of other changes in the system, and its effect as such may be more significant than its direct effect on learning.

They also feel that television can do more things than radio and is vastly easier to prepare and deliver than films.

We present these ideas for what they are worth. They come, of course, from people who have been involved in a project with television and, consequently, would perhaps be inclined to defend their use of it. We still would like to see an attempt to bring about national educational reform with radio, rather than television, as the chief media component. The evidence now says merely that television can be used as an important component of national educational reform. It remains to be proved that another instructional medium can do as well. And the Korean project will tell us how it works to put television elsewhere than front and center.

From the four ITV experiences reported in this chapter, however, we can draw some conclusions about the effective use of instructional television for widespread reform:

(1) None of these projects could have gone forward successfully without substantial support—financial, logistic, and technical—from outside. This raises the question of whether such "forced feeding" is the best way to encourage national educational reform, or whether a simpler, less expensive method, supportable largely by local resources, might be more lasting even if somewhat slower. For example, one reason the Niger project stalled after reaching twenty classrooms was the feeling of the host government that its budget would not support a broad expansion. Similarly, the ITV station that UNESCO helped build in Senegal went dark when the UNESCO project ended. This seems wasteful of resources. On the other hand, both El Salvador and the Ivory Coast will probably be able to absorb the cost and technical demands of their national projects, although outside help was required to get them started; and American Samoa is having financial troubles but has accomplished the rather remarkable feat of "Samoanizing" its educational system in only eight years.

(2) None of these television projects could have come into existence, and none of them could have continued for very long, without strong

support from the top. In Samoa it was the vigorous backing of Governor Lee; in El Salvador, the strong support of Minister Beneke; in the Ivory Coast, the support of President Houphoet-Boigny. In Niger, President Diori's interest made possible the existence of the project, and the fact that almost no other strong support existed in the government made it difficult for the project to expand beyond the experimental stage.

(3) Each of these projects encountered strong resistance at some time in its development. The principle seems to be that change of such magnitude always rouses defenses. In Niger, the opposition came from the educational establishment—the ministry whose curriculum and methods were rejected and who did not have control over the new classes, the Teachers Union whose members were rejected in favor of untrained monitors. In Samoa, the first opposition came from members of the Department of Education who did not believe in teaching by television; this was overcome by Governor Lee's determination to change the system quickly. Later there was political opposition, apparently using the schools as a device to strike at territorial officials. Still later, the secondary school teachers, feeling more confident, became dissatisfied with having to share so much of the teaching with the television teacher. In El Salvador, the chief opposition came from the Teachers Union, which was dissatisfied with salaries, and struck at television mainly because they felt the money it cost should have gone into higher pay for classroom teachers. In the Ivory Coast, like Samoa and Niger, not all members of the ministry were convinced that television should be brought in to change the established patterns. A minister had to be replaced, apparently because of his opposition, and the reform put in the charge of a new Secretary of State for Television and Primary Education.

(4) It is at least a reasonable hypothesis that after a certain time the newness of television wears off, and after that occurs the use of television or the gadgets of television must be somewhat changed. For example, in Samoa, after eight years, television was asked to take on a different function—no longer being used to carry the core of all teaching, but rather to do the things it can do best, and to be used more sparingly and more discriminatingly. The analogy is to a "spot" pitcher in baseball, who is brought in to pitch in a situation where his particular kind of skills is most useful. In El Salvador, television is being turned toward other targets—the primary schools, the adult audience, the primary teachers who need in-service instruction—and it is predictable that in time the amount of television used in the Third Cycle will be reduced and its uses will become moe specialized, as in Samoa. In Niger, the situation is a bit different because television is supporting the monitors, and, in any case, is not conceived to the same degree as presenting a "master teacher." More often

it presents, as one of the leaders of the Niger project said, an instructional "show." Programs of this kind are less likely to be seen as competitive with the classroom teacher, even when the monitors grow in skill and confidence, or when qualified teachers are used in the classroom.

(5) It is clear that none of these projects is really a "television" project, except in the sense that television is a principal component. Television is hardly a self-sufficient instructional tool. It needs teachers' guides, study materials for students, visuals for classroom use, and all the other tools of instruction that a live classroom needs. Looking at the experience of El Salvador, for example, one can say that the retraining of teachers was at least as important an influence on educational opportunities offered students as was television, and the provision of new and excellent teachers' guides and classroom study materials was not far behind in importance. Furthermore, institutional changes in the system of the kind we have mentioned may in the long run be responsible for more "reform" than anything television may contribute to learning. In other words, television must be built into a *system,* and its ability to help bring other elements of the system into existence may be more important than its direct effect on students.

(6) If one introduces such a televised system faster than one grade at a time, one risks serious administrative difficulties. This is well illustrated by the experience of American Samoa, which would have found its task vastly easier technically and administratively—although perhaps not politically—if it had not decided to serve all twelve grades at once.

(7) If a national educational reform project is expected to continue, to reach national dimensions, and to be absorbed into national budgets and plans, it needs to be integrated from the first, not only into the local culture, but also into the local power structure. This was done in El Salvador, and apparently is being done in the Ivory Coast. It was assisted in Samoa by turning the system over to Samoan leadership and operation in eight years. It was not accomplished for a long time in Niger, where the excellent television teaching was regarded as a foreign experiment, to be staffed and supported from outside.

CHAPTER 6

EVIDENCE FROM THE FIELD:

Media to Supplement the School

A human being should not be wasted in doing what forty sheets of paper or two phonographs can do. Just because personal teaching is precious and can do what books and apparatus cannot, it should be saved for its peculiar work [Edward L. Thorndike, 1912: 162].

Thorndike's sentences sound oddly at one and the same time modern and old-fashioned. To read over a date line of 1912 that instructional media should be used wherever possible to lighten the chores of teaching causes us to reconsider how new the field of instructional technology really is. To see print and phonographs used in 1912 as the only examples of media of instruction reminds us how new the electronic media really are. Films were the new medium in 1912. There was no radio in common use, no television, no computers.

Yet Thorndike was directly on target when he chose to talk about the use of media in support of the classroom teacher. That has been from the very first the most common use of the media of instruction. The teacher in the classroom has been in charge. His or her teaching has been "supplemented" by a chapter from the textbook, a page of problems from the workbook—later, a film, a television program, a simulation game, or something else. Rudy Bretz has urged us to distinguish between use of the media to "supplement" or "enrich." Supplementary use of media is directly related to the curriculum, but carrying a minor part of the responsibility, in comparison to the teacher. Media used for enrichment are less directly related to the syllabus, but rather are intended to contribute new insights, new experiences, variety, or enjoyment. Obviously there is no hard and fast line where supplement becomes enrichment, or vice versa. But these two uses of the media have been the ones most readily accepted by the teacher and most often experienced by the pupil. Not until the last few decades have media been used (as, for example, in Niger and Samoa) to carry the *primary* task of teaching, so that the teacher becomes supplementary; or to extend learning opportunities beyond the classroom or the campus so that the school itself becomes supplementary. These are the most dramatic uses, the ones on which we shall spend the most time in describing field projects. But they are understandably not the ones about which classroom teachers have been most enthusiastic.

The research reported in Chapter 2—the studies done under quasi-laboratory conditions, mostly in controlled classrooms—dealt largely with supplementary use of instructional media. This is particularly true of Tables 2.3 (films), 2.6 (radio), and 2.7 (tapes, transparencies, and the like). The findings of these studies were overwhelmingly that a great deal is learned from such use, and when they can validly be compared with direct teaching the result does not discredit the media.

There is no particular reason, therefore, to expect a radically different result when supplementary use of the media is studied in the field. It may be useful, however, to see what additional understandings can be derived from the field studies.

SOME EXAMPLES OF ITV AS SUPPLEMENT

Hagerstown

Hagerstown (the schools of Washington County, Maryland) is the oldest of the large ITV projects. It began in 1956, eight years before Samoa and Niger, nearly twenty years before the Korea multimedia project. The line of inheritance from Hagerstown to Samoa is clear, but between the two there is a fundamental difference. Television in Hagerstown was controlled by the teachers, and television teachers were drawn from among the classroom teachers. In Samoa, the television looked to be, at first, in charge of the *television* teachers, most of whom came from the United States, and who were to a considerable extent responsible for both what was broadcast and what happened before and after it in the Samoan classrooms.

How did Hagerstown happen to choose television as a medium of instruction? (For a basic introduction, see Wade, 1967.) In February 1956, Washington County schools were considering whether to provide for closed-circuit television in the construction of new schools. At that time the schools were invited to submit a proposal to the Ford Foundation and the Electronics Industries Association for a major project to study possible uses of television in the classroom. Thus, as in most of the projects described in the preceding chapter, felt needs of a school system coincided with interests of an outside donor. Washington County wanted to improve classroom instruction notably by sharing its best teachers and by offering specialized subjects like music for which there were not enough specialized teachers; to expand in-service teacher training; and to meet some of the growing problems of school overcrowding (for example, by teaching classes in large groups where appropriate and by sharing teachers over larger numbers of pupils). The interest of the Ford Foundation and the industry association was in ascertaining how television could be used practically to contribute to the effectiveness of education. The Foundation made a grant of $1 million, and the industry association donated about $300,000 worth of equipment for closed-circuit television (closed-circuit was necessary because open-circuit channels were not then available in sufficient numbers around Hagerstown). The Chesapeake and Potomac Company installed coaxial cables from the studios to the schools and operated them without charge for the first two years of the project, scaling later charges to amortize those of the first years.

Thanks to this help and to consultation from outside, Hagerstown began to broadcast in September 1956. In the first year, about 6,000 students were served, and within two years almost the entire school population was receiving television. As the schools grew, the number of students served reached 20,853 in 1965.

The system has been broadcasting about seventy hours a week, fifteen of them elective. The largest number of TV courses are in seventh, eighth, and ninth grades. Which courses are to be offered on television is decided at the administrative level. Classroom teachers are assigned to television teaching (Wade, in Unesco, 1967: 64) on the basis of "rapport with teachers in the classroom ... attendance record ... dramatic flair ... ability to handle criticism, and ... special preparation in the field." The television assignment is usually for one or two years; then the teacher returns to classroom teaching. Consequently, most programs are live, rather than recorded. Asked to list qualities that were "very important" in effective television teaching, a sample of Washington County teachers with at least two years' experience named the following characteristics, which are listed in Table 6.1 in order of agreement. Number 1 was named by 89 percent of the teachers; number 10, by 75.

Hagerstown believes that "enough skillful and imaginative individuals from the classroom can be found to form a satisfactory television staff, although the task of selection is a difficult one" (Wade, 1967: 66). Furthermore, it believes that, given enough preparation time (typically fifteen hours per program) a teleteacher can act as his own producer, gather the necessary visual aids, and decide upon the organization of the

TABLE 6.1
Characteristics Listed by Hagerstown Teachers as Most Important for Effective Teaching on Television.

1. A sympathetic understanding and concern for the problems of the class-room teacher.
2. Receptivity to ideas and suggestions.
3. A thorough knowledge of the subject to be taught.
4. Enthusiasm.
5. The ability to promote activity on the part of the student.
6. Professional training required for class-room teaching.
7. Command of an expressive vocabulary suitable to the instructional level of the student.
8. Correctness of enunciation.
9. Poise.
10. Emotional stability in dealing with criticism.

Quoted, Wade, 1967: 66 .

program. The Hagerstown teleteacher receives feedback cards from the classroom and takes part in periodic meetings with classroom teachers to discuss the televised lessons.

Programming by teachers for teachers has apparently succeeded in establishing rapport between studio and classroom teachers in Hagerstown. This is demonstrated in a survey of attitudes made for the Ford Foundation in 1965 (International Research Associates, 1965), which varied little from a survey of teachers and administrators made by the school board itself in 1961. Even in the highly favorable Hagerstown situation, the degree of favorableness declined noticeably from elementary through high school. That is to say, the higher the grade, the less favorable the teacher toward televised classes, as Table 6.2 shows. The similarity of the curves to results of opinion surveys in Samoa and El Salvador is striking.

Studies of learning in the Washington County system in the late 1950s and early 1960s have shown impressive results. For example, in Table 6.3 are scores made by rural Washington County students whose classes were supplemented by televised arithmetic. Before television, these students averaged half a grade below national norms (on the Iowa test of basic skills). After one or two years of television, each grade exceeded the national norms.

TABLE 6.2

Percentage of Opinion at Different Levels of the Hagerstown School System as to What Television Contributes

Comments	Admin-istrators	Primary	Inter-mediate	Junior High School	Senior High School
Much or some help in teaching	83.3	76.9	80.9	62.5	40.9
Provides richer experience	98.7	98.4	96.4	90.0	76.3
Enriches and expands curriculum	91.1	94.2	90.7	77.8	76.0
Limits or reduces curriculum	3.8	3.3	6.4	15.3	18.6
Has no effect on curriculum	5.0	2.5	2.8	6.9	5.4
Improves curriculum planning	91.0	94.0	88.0	81.0	68.0
Improves quality of over-all programme	97.0	94.0	88.0	81.0	66.0

Quoted, Wade, 1967: 73

TABLE 6.3

Elementary School Means on Nationally Standardized Test,
Compared to National Norms, Hagerstown, 1958 to 1961.

	Grade 3	Grade 4	Grade 5	Grade 6
National norm in May	3.90	4.90	5.90	6.90
1958 (before television)	3.59	4.43	5.26	6.49
1959 (first year of television)	4.06	4.97	5.77	6.83
1960	4.18	5.01	6.13	7.17
1961	4.30	5.08	6.19	7.28

Wade, 1967: 70

Because television was introduced later in some schools than in others, it was possible to make a few comparisons of television versus conventional teaching. Table 6.4 shows how this comparison worked out for sixth-grade general science.

In eighth-grade general science, achievement averaged two years higher after three years of television than it had been before television was introduced. In junior high school mathematics, the average achievement level of urban pupils on a standardized test of concepts rose after four years of television teaching from thirty-first to eighty-fourth percentile on national norms, and in the rural schools from fourteenth to thirty-eighth percentile. Rural schools that had scored on the twenty-eighth percentile of national norms in U.S. history rose after one year of television to the forty-fifth percentile, and after two more years to the fifteenth percentile.

Some results were less than expected. The same rural pupils who had gained so substantially on a national test of math concepts made very small gains in actual problem-solving. Teachers hypothesized that, for these students, problem-solving required mainly classroom practice, to which television made little contribution. Again, the pupils who had made

TABLE 6.4

Comparison of Scores on Sixth-Grade Science Pupils
in Hagerstown Taught with or without Television.

Ability level (grade 6 science)	Average I.Q.[a]	Achievement growth	Average I.Q.[a]	Achievement growth
111–140	117	12 months	118	15 months
90–110	100	11 months	100	14 months
57– 89	83	6 months	83	13 months

[a]Intelligence Quotient.
Wade, 1967: 71

such striking gains in elementary school arithmetic made very small gains in reading. Was this because the reading classes were offered on a voluntary basis, or because reading, like arithmetic problem-solving, is mostly a matter of practice? Also, gains in some of the core courses like social studies and language were less than in arithmetic and science. Was this because there was less difference between the expertise of the classroom teacher and the selected television teacher in the core courses than in the more specialized ones?

Hagerstown school administrators, interviewed in 1965, pointed out that television had been advantageous in certain other ways. It made it possible for the schools to offer for the first time a sequence of science courses from grades one through twelve, modern language from grade three, and expert instruction in art and music, as well as high-school calculus—none of which would have been possible in many schools without sharing teachers on the tube. Television also made it possible to assist elementary school teachers in the fields where they were least well prepared, for inexperienced teachers to watch expert teaching in their own fields, and for steps to be taken toward equalizing opportunities between large and small, urban and rural schools.

Asked what they thought of television versus nontelevision classes, Hagerstown students identified the chief advantage of nontelevision classrooms as freedom for students to ask questions, get personal help from the teacher, and participate actively in discussions. The chief advantages of television teaching, they thought, were that without it they would not have the visuals and other materials presented by the television teacher; furthermore, the television classes were better prepared and the teleteachers, in general, more expert in their subjects.

But the real test of the Hagerstown experiment came in 1961 when the Ford grant ran out and the school system had to decide whether to continue the television on its own money. The opinion of teachers and administrators was overwhelmingly that they should do so, and that was the decision taken by the school board, which said: "Washington County personnel feel . . . that the instructional program of a school system is handicapped without the use of television as a resource."

Supplementary TV in an Isolated Village

It must not be assumed, even in view of the enormous size and extent of Japan's instructional services, that every Japanese school makes major use of media. Japan is a mountainous country with many small, isolated villages, and radio and television have come slowly to many such schools. The Japanese Ministry of Education had been disturbed by the test scores of children in these isolated villages. These can be illustrated by a selection from the ministry's 1959-1960 survey (Tsuji, 1964) which classified primary schools by their location and by their average scores on achievement tests (see Table 6.5).

Translate some of the location names into urban, suburban, rural, northeastern, southern, and so forth, and such a distribution of scores would not be uncommon for the United States. But the Japanese ministry decided to find out what instructional television could do about raising some of the lower scores, and for that purpose chose four mountainous villages only seventy-five miles from Tokyo but difficult to reach by surface transportation.

Fifth grades in two of these four schools were given television receivers and agreed to make use of ITV in science and social studies. The other two schools were used as a control group. No teacher in the TV group had previous experience in teaching in a classroom with television. Pretests were given all the fifth grades in science, social studies, and intelligence. The Tanaka-B test was used for the latter measure and standardized tests for course achievement. No significant differences were found between TV and control groups on any of the pretests, although the control schools scored slightly higher in intelligence and the TV schools slightly higher in both subject areas. Pupils whose scores were subnormal were removed from the sample, and the result was a close match of mean scores for 130 TV children and 72 controls.

The TV classes received one science and one social studies program per week, each twenty minutes in length. At the end of the school year, both

TABLE 6.5
Average Scores of Japanese Schools, 1960, by Location.

Location	Scores in Japanese Language	Arithmetic	Soc. Studies	Science
National average	49.2	43.6	44.5	51.7
Residential district	58.4	52.1	52.2	55.8
Business district	57.2	50.0	53.6	56.5
Mining, industrial district	53.5	47.2	44.7	50.5
Agricultural district	43.3	38.6	39.7	50.2
Mountain villages	41.0	36.0	32.9	46.6
Out-of-the-way district	40.0	35.8	34.0	46.3

experimental and control classes were tested again, with the results shown in Table 6.6.

Thus, at the end of the year, the TV classes in all three measures had moved significantly ahead of the non-TV groups. The gains were impressive in science and intelligence, but disappointing in social studies, as we see from Table 6.7.

The superiority of the TV group's gains in both intelligence and science were also significant at beyond the .01 level. There were no significant differences in social studies.

In some ways, the most interesting results of the study, however, came from analysis of the scores against ability. When the groups were dichotomized on the basis of scoring above or below 45.5 on the intelligence

TABLE 6.6
Scores after One Year, NHK Study of ITV in Isolated Villages.

Subject	TV Group (n=130)	Control Group (n-72)
Intelligence	52.6	48.9 *
Standard deviation	9.64	13.0
Social Studies	45.9	43.1 *
Standard deviation	7.71	9.67
Science	47.9	42.3 **
Standard deviation	7.16	8.64

* = .05   confidence level
** = .001 confidence level
Tsuji, 1964: 9

TABLE 6.7
Gain Scores in One Year, NHK Study of ITV in Isolated Villages.

Group and Subject	Scores Before	After	Difference
Intelligence			
Television	45.4	52.6	7.2**
Control	46.2	48.9	2.7**
Social Studies			
Television	44.9	45.9	1.0
Control	43.2	43.1	−0.1
Science			
Television	42.9	47.9	5.0**
Control	41.0	42.3	1.3

** = .01 level
others not significant
Tsuji, 1964: 10-11

pretest (50 being the national mean), then it was seen that the lower intelligence group in the TV-receiving classes in every case gained significantly more than the lower intelligence group among the controls. This difference was in all three tests significant at beyond the .01 level. When higher-intelligence groups were compared, however, the only real difference was in science, where the TV group came out significantly higher. Thus, the ITV experience seemed to have greater effect on lower-ability than higher-ability students. The trend was strongly for students who scored low on the pretest to move closer to the class mean on the after-test. If this conclusion holds up in other non-American, non-European countries, it will be of great interest to developing countries that are trying to serve isolated communities and educationally disadvantaged children.

School Television in India

India's first television station was in Delhi, and much of its transmission time in the first years was for schools. In 1964 and 1965, when 22,000 students in 227 schools near Delhi were studying science with the aid of television, Paul Neurath (who had previously evaluated the Poona radio rural forums) was called in to study the effectiveness of school broadcasts in physics and chemistry.

Dr. Neurath went about his task carefully and thoughtfully, trying to allow for obvious irregularities in the situation that kept the design from approaching the precision of an experiment in natural science. He gave four rounds of tests (one of which had to be thrown out because of incomplete collection). Each round was given to a different sample of 250-350 television students and 100-250 control students.

His main hypotheses had to do with the kinds of knowledge that would be better learned with television than without it. He divided the test questions into three types: factual—things learned by heart from books or lectures; visual—where the student draws primarily on experiments, diagrams, or pictures; and understanding—where the student has to draw on his ability to generalize, to make deductions, to recognize a problem or a connection even when it comes in an unfamiliar form. He hypothesized that television students would do better with visual questions, and about the same as the controls on factual questions; he left open the question of which group would do beter with the "understanding" questions.

What did he find? Without citing figures, which become rather cumbersome because of his methods of tabulation, we can report that the television students did somewhat better overall and on all types of questions. They did best comparatively on visual questions, and the difference was least on factual questions, thus being in general agreement with the hypotheses. The result that most surprised the experimenter was that television students did distinctly better on the understanding (problem-solving) questions.

He also gave one of the tests over again, after a month's interval. Again the television students did better on all three kinds of questions, but the difference between television and nontelevision students was less on the delayed test.

Dr. Neurath, therefore, gave a good report card to instructional television as teacher of physics and chemistry. Some of his conclusions about the impact of television on the Delhi schools (especially on teachers and teaching) are as interesting as his quantitative results:

> Whether he cheers or jeers at the television teacher, whether he finds him a better, an equal, or a worse teacher than himself, a friend, an aider, an intruder into his classroom—the classroom teacher is forced so and so many times a week to become aware of another teacher's performance in front of his own students and thus to become aware of his performance as well.

> The whole teaching process, though not necessarily the teaching performance of every single teacher, is slowly improving.

> Science teachers are becoming aware (from seeing the television teacher) not only of the necessity but also of the possibility to mobilize their own, even though in most cases rather meager, laboratory resources . . . more vociferous in their clamor for more laboratory space and equipment.

His conclusions about the impact on the student and the school system also merit examination:

> Television lessons provide a break in the routine, thus making school itself more interesting.

> The impact of the television lessons themselves is less than the impact of television as an innovation within the whole teaching process.

> Principals . . . come almost invariably to the same point: teachers have to adhere more closely to the syllabus. Before television they saw relatively little possibility to check up on whether their teachers were folowing the syllabus or not.

> Syllabi are being revised [quotations from Neurath, 1968: 71-81].

School Television in Colombia

In 1965, Lyle and others made a case study of Colombian school television during its second year. This study may be read in UNESCO (1967, vol. 2: 49-75). From our point of view, even more interesting features of the Colombia findings may be in some learning studies made in the same year as the case study, by Comstock and Maccoby (1966).

At the time it was studied, the Colombian system was broadcasting forty fifteen-minute programs per week (ten of which were repeats) to the first five grades of primary school. It was also broadcasting some teacher in-service training. The audience was very large: 275,000 in 1965, and over 400,000 two years later.

In 1965, Comstock and Maccoby, who were in Colombia to study the problems and performance of the U.S. Peace Corps in the field, tested about 5,000 primary school pupils from the District of Bogota, who had been taught with the aid of television against a similar group who had been taught from the same syllabus but not by television. Tests were based on the course syllabi.

Eight comparisons, in the second, third, fourth, and fifth grades, were possible. In three of the eight—grade 2 language, grade 5 mathematics, and grade 4 science—the means were significantly different in favor of the television classes. In the other five—grades 3 and 5 science, grades 3, 4, and 5 social science—there were no significant differences.

This was not a surprising result, but Comstock and Maccoby noticed something else they wanted to test. They found a great variety in the learning contexts being provided for television in the classroom. A few teachers actively rehearsed their students in the points made on television; a few others invited questions; more simply lectured on the same subject as the television program; still others did very little of anything related to the broadcasts. So another experiment was designed. One group of teachers was assigned to direct a purposeful question-and-answer session based on the television program during the remaining minutes of the period. Another group was assigned to lecture on the main points made in the broadcast. Still another group did what they had always been doing, different methods for different teachers.

The question-and-answer pattern proved to be superior in all cases, apparently because it provided more chances to practice. We can conclude, therefore, that what happens in the classroom makes a great difference in the effectiveness of supplementary ITV.

OTHER SUPPLEMENTARY EDUCATIONAL MEDIA

Teaching by Radio in Thailand

Instructional school radio in Thailand dates to 1958, although the Ministry of Education had broadcast an educational home service for four years prior to that. The first school broadcasts went out to 286 selected schools on May 20, 1958. In 1959, the number of schools using the service was about 500; in 1963, about 2,000; in 1965, 5,000; and in 1972, an estimated 6,245. The number of students has grown correspondingly, from about 30,000 in the first year to betwen 800,000 and 1 million today.

All programs originate in the ministry studios in Bangkok. They are broadcast by a 10Kw short-wave transmitter. Because of interference from the large number of radio stations in Thailand, tapes are also sent to and rebroadcast from nine other medium-wave stations in various parts of the country.

The annual program service includes two social studies programs of fifteen minutes each per week for each of four grade levels, one music program of twenty minutes per fortnight for each of five levels, and one English program of twenty minutes per week for each of eight levels. In general, the music programs go to all the seven grades of primary school; social studies, to the first five primary grades; and English, to the upper three primary grades (5, 6, 7) and the five forms of secondary school. On the average, each lesson is repeated four times. Thus, between 400 and 500 different programs are on the air each year, in about 3,000 repetitions. The total time of different programs on the air is about 165 hours per year, and the estimated total number of student listening hours to these programs is over 8 million.

This is a very typical program for supplementary radio. No *course* gets more than forty minutes a week. Pupils in the first four grades get a total of forty minutes of radio per week. Pupils in the fifth grade get sixty minutes; those in grades six and seven, forty minutes; and all the secondary school students, twenty minutes per week. Obviously radio is not dominating the classroom; it may lead, it may stimulate, but it is far from taking over.

In 1958 and 1959, representatives of the ministry conducted a large field study to evaluate the learning from instructional radio (Xoomsai and Ratanamangala, 1962). Schools were selected at random from among those receiving the radio programs, and controls chosen from those nearest and most similar to the experimental schools. In grades two and three, 622 students were tested on music and social studies; 572 from grades six and seven, on their ability to understand and write English.

The chief purpose of social studies in the primary grades in Thailand is to help pupils develop attitudes and values desirable in the Thai culture. In twenty-six of the twenty-eight items of the grade three test, and eighteen of twenty-eight in grade two, the radio students scored higher (i.e., more in favor of the desired attitudes) than the controls. Sixteen of the differences in grade three, and twelve in grade two were significant at the .05 level or beyond.

Music students were tested on their ability to identify songs and musical instruments and rated by classrooms on their singing and dancing. In the written tests of identification, experimental groups were reported to be superior to controls at the .001 level or beyond. Classroom ratings on singing and dancing were also significantly higher in the experimental schools, and observers noted that the variability in performance was reduced in the experimental over the control groups, hypothesizing that the radio instruction had brought the performance of the less skillful pupils nearer the level of the others.

No significant differences were found between experimental and control groups on ability to understand English. On tests of writing English, the radio group was superior in grade seven, the control group in grade six.

The experimenters concluded that the radio teaching appeared to be effective in social studies and music in lower primary, and that the results with radio English in the upper primary were inconclusive.

In 1972, an experiment similar to this was conducted with sixteen matched pairs of seventh-grade schools in three districts of Thailand. Sixteen schools received supplementary instruction by radio in English and music, and sixteen did not. Students of English were tested on listening (comprehension) and writing. Students of music were tested on writing, listening, and singing. Ns were, for each group, approximately 450. (Data came to us by personal communication.)

Overall average gains, pretest to post-test, were slightly larger in the broadcast groups in both English listening and English writing. In tests of music listening, there was a slight advantage for radio students in the test of listening, but higher scores for the schools *without* radio in both writing and singing.

Unfortunately, we did not have the data from which confidently to compute the statistical significance of these results. We were able to compute significances per school, however. Here the schools with radio had a slight advantage over those without radio in tests of listening to English.

In other words, these field tests were no more effective than most of the laboratory experiments in discriminating between media teaching and face-to-face instruction.

Rather more interesting than the quantitative results were the answers to an opinion survey administered to over 1,800 classroom teachers in 1972.

To the question of what proportion of the schools were using the different broadcasts, the answers are: music, 64 percent; social studies, 53 percent; English, 25 percent. Other questions are:

(1) How often is the reception poor? Sometimes, 76 percent; occasionally, 13 percent.

(2) Why do you use the school broadcasts? As supplementary teaching material, 71 percent.

(3) Do you agree that school broadcast programs can help the teachers? Strongly agree, 54 percent; agree, 39 percent.

(4) Do you agree that teachers have a good opportunity to learn teaching techniques from school radio programs? Strongly agree, 51 percent; agree, 42 percent.

(5) Should there be more broadcast programs? Strongly agree, 40 percent; agree, 32 percent; uncertain, 11 percent.

(6) Do you agree that the quality of education will not decrease if we give up school broadcast programs? Disagree, 41 percent; strongly disagree, 12 percent; uncertain, 22 percent; agree, 19 percent.

(7) Do you agree that school broadcast programs can make pupils more interested in their learning? Strongly agree, 47 percent; agree, 42 percent.

Asked to rate the quality of the different subject programs, 74 percent rated music first; 6 percent rated social studies first (52 percent, second); 13 percent rated English first (20 percent, second).[1] So the supplementary broadcasts, regardless of whether students learn more from them than from other methods, seem to have convinced the teachers that they are a good thing.

Radiovision in Developing Areas

We have been disappointed in not being able to turn up new evidence on the effectiveness of radiovision in developing regions. This combination of filmstrips with voice (radio broadcast, tape recorder, or teacher) is inexpensive and relatively simple. It allows a school system to make its own materials and teachers (especially if they depend upon tape or script rather than upon radio for the sound) to control the timing and repetition. It would seem to be precisely the kind of audiovisual tool that is readily adaptable to education in the newer countries.

Radiovision has been used most impressively by Britain and France, where teachers are accustomed to audiovisual methods and schools are equipped to provide them. It is being used in the Central African Republic, and has been used experimentally in Niger, Malawi, and some countries of Southern Asia. Lefranc in 1965-1966 observed its use for literacy programs in Niger and came up with no hard evidence and a mixed report as to how it was working. For one thing, it played a very small part in literacy teaching. There were often problems with the projectors, and with coordinating radio and projection. When radiovision was used, the voice of the teacher rather than audio from the radio usually provided the commentary.

Until we have more evidence, then, all we can say is that filmstrips, accompanied by teacher commentary and discussion, by a tape cassette or a radio broadcast, would seem to be worth the attention of a developing country that seeks to enrich and extend the learning opportunities it offers.

Programmed Instruction in Central Africa

When Rhodesia made its Unilateral Declaration of Independence in late 1965, that signalled the end of one of the most remarkable developments of programmed learning anywhere in the developing regions. Within a year, most of the individuals who had played key parts in this project had left the faculty of the University College of Rhodesia and were carrying on their work in other countries. David G. Hawkridge, who had been head of the operation in the Faculty of Education of the university, came to the United States and later became Director of the Institute of Educational Technology of the British Open University.

But in the years before 1966, the Rhodesia center had proved most convincingly that programmed instruction is not solely for the "developed" countries. Thousands of miles from any other center for the study of programmed learning, the members of that Rhodesia group had produced seventy-five programs, which were in various stages of testing at the time of the general exodus. They had used these programs successfully with both African and European students, with professionals, skilled workmen, and many others. They had assembled an excellent collection of programs, studies of programming, and teaching machines from different countries, and had an active research program going. It was unfortunate for Rhodesia, and for Africa in general, that the program was terminated when it was. What it might have become can be imagined from a modest monograph (eighty-eight pages) by Hawkridge (1966).

This monograph is full of evidence on the teaching effectiveness of programmed instruction in the Rhodesian situation. Here, for example, are the results of an experimental comparison between two groups of agricultural extension recruits with only primary schooling. They were to learn the necessary arithmetic to measure and peg soil contours. One group was taught by means of a program; the other, by traditional classroom methods. These were the results (Hawkridge, 1966: 28):

	Pretest	*Post-test*
Program group (n = 22)	32.9	67.3
Class group (n = 20)	36.4	48.6

Most such comparisons were part of the process of validating and improving programs. Such programs ordinarily went through several revisions before they were ready for wide use. As an example, take a program entitled "How People Learn," intended for the use of adults with eight years of schooling who were preparing to be teachers or trainers (see Hawkridge, 1966: 29-31). The program was first tested on twenty-eight participants in a course for prospective extension agents. Their pretest score was 45.6, their post-test, 91.2. The test was thought to be too easy and was accordingly modified, and a number of items in the program were changed. Next, the program was tested on three classes of different kinds. Their gains were larger than those of the first group, but the program proved to need still further improvement in individual frames. This was done, and it was tested for a third time, on twenty-five assistants. Their mean scores were:

Pretest	*Post-test*
21.8	75.7
(range 0-50)	(range 44-100)

The program was then judged to be satisfactory and released for use in the extension service training program. The test results from Rhodesia leave little doubt that programmed instruction works as well in developing as in economically more advanced regions.

One of the interesting accounts in Hawkridge (1966) is by a teacher who was attracted to Rhodesia by the opportunity to participate in the work on programming. His story links experiences in Singapore and Rhodesia.

> I remember well some four years ago talking with several R.A.F. Education Officers at F.E.A.F. Headquarters, Changi, Singapore. The subject of teaching machines came up. This was the first time I had heard of such contraptions, and being a teacher of some 30 years' standing I was very skeptical and rather rude. Unfortunately, these officers knew very little about the machines or the ideas behind them, and I was left in complacent ignorance for several months until I read an article in the *Times Educational Supplement* and another in the *Reader's Digest* about programmed learning.

I had been teaching mathematics for much of my teaching life, and had felt frustration for a long time, especially with the average and not so bright pupils. The bright boys were all right; the response was there and the end product most satisfying, but these were only a small proportion of the pupils passing through my hands. How could I make the subject more interesting? How could I give more individual attention to the slower members of the class without holding back the brighter ones? How could I restore confidence to the "can't-doers" and the "blind-spotters" of mathematics? How could I increase the pupils' input comparative to my output of knowledge? What was the point in carrying home piles of exercise books and ploughing through them in the absence of the pupils, and not being able to do something constructive about it? These were questions which had forced themselves on me over the years, and I hadn't found a satisfactory answer by the time I read the articles on programmed learning.

I was always ready to give any method a try, and this method seemed reasonable. I started to programme a course in mathematics for a fourth year form, quite prepared at any moment to find that this was just another gimmick. I put into the programme as much experience as I had gleaned over the years in presenting the concepts I wished to teach, and away we went. I fed the knowledge to them in small doses, following each dose with appropriate questions and emphasizing points where, from experience, I knew snags would arise.

From the beginning the interest was there; the amount of work turned out was amazing; the atmosphere in the class was one of concentrated effort; the "can't-doers" were getting the answers right and were very happy about it. I was busy flitting up and down the class-room sorting out snags, keeping each pupil supplied with programme sheets, and still able to give individual attention where it was needed.

Then I had a piece of luck. After I had been doing this for about three months the R.A.F. Education people heard of my experiment, and sent one of their experts on programmed learning to Singapore. They had been experimenting for a long time in the training of apprentices and saw the possibility of using programmed learning in Service schools. They sent out S/L Thomas, now co-author of *Programmed Learning in Perspective;* he stayed some ten days, lecturing on the subject in the evenings and spending most of the days with me, since I was the only one doing this work in Singapore.

Fortunately for me, he found that I was on the right lines, and I learnt a lot from him, especially on the preparation of material before writing the programme.

I hadn't any teaching machines; the answers were on the back of the programme sheets, and the pupils checked by turning over these sheets to find the correct answer. This wasn't entirely satisfactory, since it did not eliminate cheating, but the pupils were very good about it on the whole. To get the *maximum* benefit, however, one must use a presentation device which is cheatproof, I have concluded.

The work continued for a year, and at the end of the year this form and a parallel form, which had had formal teaching on the same syllabus, sat the same examination—a London GCE Algebra '0'-level paper they had never seen before.

The results in the two classes, expressed as percentages, were as follows:

Programmed Instruction: 86 76 70 68 67 65 64 64 53 49 47 47 45 42 35 14 13.

Conventional Instruction: 56 48 42 37 33 32 30 29 26 26 22 21 14 13 13 12 11.

Averages: Programmed Instruction 53.1 Conventional Instruction 26.7

These results, and the fact that there was no diminution of effort during the year, convinced me that there was something in the method, and on coming to Salisbury I was permitted to continue with the experiment, but this time with a IVc class, whose record of work was very poor. It meant working from the beginning in Algebra. Again, the interest was there from the start—it always is with a new method, but the test comes in maintaining this interest. There was no trouble at all on this point, and the class went ahead steadily, working all the time and enjoying the work. They made such progress that I was asked to enter them for the '0' level GCE at the end of the year—a year before they were due to take the examination. I wasn't too keen, knowing the amount of work to be covered: the basics had to be covered in addition to the examination syllabus. I decided to go ahead, and although the Algebra was covered adequately we could not finish the Arithmetic, Geometry and Trigonometry. There was, however, rather an interesting side issue. The programmes had stimulated the boys to work and this was reflected in their other subjects. So much so that three other masters decided to enter some of the boys for the examination.

Ten boys were entered for mathematics; the resulting grades were: 1 4 5 7 7 8 8 9 9 9. These were considered satisfactory in the circumstances. They were C-stream pupils taking the examination a year before their time. They did satisfactorily in other subjects, and some of the boys were given tests at frequent intervals to assess their gains in knowledge, and the results were most encouraging.

The experiment is being continued this year, with a Third Form included, to try to cover the syllabus thoroughly and give ample time for revision.

Both the third and fourth form classes have taken to the programmes as enthusiastically as their predecessors [Hawkridge, 1966: 44-45).

SOME CONCLUSIONS

These findings are encouragingly consistent with the experiments reported earlier.

Used as supplements to classroom teaching, the media of instruction are effective. They work as well as other classroom teaching. Used in the right place, in the right way, for an appropriate purpose, they will improve on classroom experience. They can introduce demonstrations otherwise impossible in the classroom, take the student to a part of the world he or she could not otherwise experience, bring into the classroom a distinguished visitor or a teacher with special expertise. Beyond that, they can offer a change of pace from the routine of everyday teaching.

Used this way, any medium can be effective. Television works in a mountain village of Japan or a county in Maryland. Films work anywhere. Radio works in a technical school in Germany or the uplands of Thailand. Programmed instruction has proved effective not only in the laboratory schools of the United States but also on the plains and in the forests of central Africa. Of course, different media will do different things. If it is drill that is needed, programmed or computer-assisted instruction will fit the need better than television. If it is necessary to share experiences over a wide area so that the unit costs of a large operation are acceptable, then television commends itself over programmed instruction or films. Other things being equal, the ideal medium for supplementary use is one over which the classroom teacher has a maximum amount of control. That is, supplementary instruction should be introduced into a given classroom when the class is ready for it. The teacher should be able to repeat it, or stop it in the middle, or delay it for a question, or combine it with such other classroom experiences as the situation seems to require. Obviously, some media meet these requirements better than others, but the interesting thing is that there seem to be important supplementary uses for almost any medium used well.

Of all the uses of the media of instruction, supplementary use is most likely to win the approval of the classroom teacher. The teacher is somewhat suspicious of the large educational reform projects when they are built around media and particularly when the media are used for core teaching; this arrangement threatens the classroom teacher with replacement. Teachers tend also to be suspicious of the uses of media to extend the school; these, too, threaten to turn over the job of the classroom teacher to someone or something else. But the supplementary use of media to assist the teacher is under the teacher's own control and threatens nothing except an attack on ignorance and boredom.

NOTES

1. The percentages do not sum to 100 for a single question because, in the interests of brevity, some of the responses have not been reported. Thus, for example, five answers were possible to most of the attitude questions: strongly agree, agree, uncertain, disagree, strongly disagree. The percentages for only two or three of these possible answers are reported when they are sufficient to show the trend of responses.

CHAPTER 7

EVIDENCE FROM THE FIELD:
Extending the School

The young of many countries continue daily to manifest revulsion against the traditional effort to contain the educational process in the bureaucratic and homogenized spaces of existing schools and colleges and curricula. . . . To go on building 19th century spaces for the storing and dissemination of information is perfectly natural. It is also fatal [Marshall McLuhan, 1968: 1].

The 1960s were the decade in which colleges and schools stretched beyond the campus and the classroom to bring learning opportunities to students wherever they were. But the movement did not begin in that decade, nor did it come about primarily because of the revulsion McLuhan talks about. It happened chiefly because of the practical needs and capabilities of education.

In the 1960s, the war babies were ready for college; the immediate postwar babies, for secondary school. Education came to seem like a magic charm for both individual mobility and economic and social development. Enrollment began to rise swiftly, and the pressure was on the system's higher parts, which in many countries had typically been reserved for the elite. In the decade of the 1960s, many countries were feeling affluent enough or under sufficient pressure to respond positively to that pressure. There was also an upsweep of popularity for adult education, and strong currents in education were emphasizing the usefulness of self-study and individualized instruction.

Extended education—"distant teaching," some educators called it—was not new. Planners could look back over a long history of evening classes, correspondence study, agriculture and home economics extension, and other services designed to share educational resources widely. Correspondence study, in particular, has been used almost as long as there have been reliable postal services. Most correspondence schools have been privately owned and operated for profit, but in many countries, including the United States, correspondence courses have been offered by universities for academic credit. In Japan alone, about 200,000 persons are now believed to be studying by correspondence, and the total number of correspondence students in the world is in the neighborhood of millions.

The problem with studying by correspondence has always been the isolation of the student, the lack of a schedule to encourage him to keep his work up to date, and the very high dropout rate. Australia was perhaps the first country to add radio to correspondence study in an attempt to solve some of these problems. Australia felt an obligation to offer educational opportunities to children who lived in the remote central part of the continent, far from schools, usually far from neighbors. Beginning in 1933, the Australian state school system combined radio with correspondence programs in the hope of adding liveness, immediacy, and motivation to the lessons. A few years later, New Zealand adopted the same combination. Even today in Australia and New Zealand thousands of school children, studying at home, don their school uniforms and sing the school song along with the radio at the weekly broadcast school assembly.

Beginning in 1956, the Chicago City College offered by television a complete two-year college curriculum, leading to the degree of Associate in Arts. In some European countries experiments were under way also, in the 1950s, to use one or another of the broadcast media in support of adult education. But the real flowering of this movement took place in the 1960s, in a great variety of forms and places, as the Figure 7.1 will illustrate.

THE VARIETY OF PATTERNS

In Figure 7.1 we have set down thumbnail descriptions of twenty-one media extension projects, most of which began in the 1960s and on all of which we have a respectable amount of information. The figure begins with one project in which formal education was offered almost wholly by correspondence, and another in which it is being offered almost wholly by radio. Then it moves on to a group of projects built around radio, another group built around television, and finally a group attempting truly to be multimedia.

FIGURE 7.1
Examples of the Use of Instructional Media to Extend the School.

Country	Starting Date	Nature of Program	Under Auspices of
(Almost wholly correspondence study)			
India	1962	A number of required and elective courses offered to school-leavers who could not attend university classes on campus. 41% of all B.A. students at Delhi have in recent years been in correspondence study. Radio programs and some television have now been added to the correspondence work.	School of Correspndence Study and Continuing Education, University of Delhi
(Almost wholly radio)			
U.S.A.	1969	Regular college courses offered by radio in approximately same form as in classroom. Reading lists and sample exams sold for $2.00. Students al-	Purdue University

FIGURE 7.1 (cont.)

Country	Starting Date	Nature of Program	Under Auspices of
		ready registered in University may take examinations for credit in this program free of charge; others pay $25 per examination. 15 courses offered in 1971-72, more in 1972-73. Students of radio courses will now be able to go to campus to hear tapes of classes and use other materials.	

(Built around radio)

Country	Starting Date	Nature of Program	Under Auspices of
Australia	1933	Radio correspondence school offers 12 grades of instruction to children in remote parts of continent. Children earn diplomas and can transfer to residence schools or apply on equal terms to universities. Some of these schools now supplemented by use of "Flying Doctor's" radio, which permits radio contact with teacher and other students. Summer residence school available.	Australian state educational systems
France	1963	Paris University III offers courses by radio and correspondence, with practical work supervised by the University, for students who cannot attend regular classes and want to pass state examinations *(agregation,* or CAPES) entitling them to teach in a school or university.	Education division of University plans and administers courses. Broadcasts produced by French broadcasting system.
France	1963	University courses by radio, correspondence, and periodic group meetings at a number of cooperating universities, for students who wish to earn the *license* (corresponding to the American B.A.) or the *maitrise* (M.A.) in the regular university examination. Teaching is becoming more and more multimedia.	Cooperating ministries, five television-teaching centers, and cooperating universities.

FIGURE 7.1 (cont.)

Country	Starting Date	Nature of Program	Under Auspices of
West Germany	1966	"Funkkolleg" — radio schools for post-secondary adults, who can earn state certificates in a number of courses. Reading and study groups integral with the rest of the program. Now becoming truly multimedia.	Collaboration of state radio organization, adult education associations, universities, and Ministry of Education.
Kenya	1968	Two years of secondary school courses for teachers in service, leading to Kenya Junior Secondary Exam and promotion. Radio plus correspondence and home study exercises.	Institute of Adult Education, University of Nairobi, with support of Ministry of Education.
Austria	1969	Broad course in "Living Economics" offered by radio, with textbooks, printed scripts, available for purchase, and a few group meetings arranged. State diploma for completed course.	Austria association of schools of adult education, with collaboration of federal Ministry of Education.
Mexico	1971	"Radioprimaria" — radio programs used to expand three-year primary schools to six years without new buildings and with minimum addition of teachers. Full school credit given.	Ministry of Education.

(Built around television)

Country	Starting Date	Nature of Program	Under Auspices of
U.S.A.	1956	Chicago TV College offers complete two-year junior college leading to degree of A.A. and possibility of transferring to four-year university. Television plus texts plus assigned papers plus, in some cases, class meetings on campus.	City educational system through Chicago City College.
East Germany	1961	"Television Academy" offers variety of adult cultural and vocational subjects. Television plus some printed materials. No credit except in a few courses where the TV teaching supplements already existing credit courses.	Government boradcasting organization

FIGURE 7.1 (cont.)

Country	Starting Date	Nature of Program	Under Auspices of
Netherlands	1964	TELEAC offers 13 to 15 courses a year in general adult education and occupational refreshers. Television plus study groups. No credit or degree, but certificates awarded for passing courses.	Ministry of Culture, Leisure Time, and Welfare.
Poland	1966	Television Technical College offers TV courses to supplement study in correspondence and evening technical schools. Courses mostly science, math, and applied technology.	Ministry of Education.
Mexico	1966	"Telesecundaria" offers complete secondary school curriculum to groups assembled in towns that have no secondary schools. Television plus textual materials plus one teacher for entire school. Students can earn diplomas.	Ministry of Education
West Germany	1967	"Telekolleg", intermediate school preparatory to trade and technical study, offers basic language, mathematics, science, history, and technical electives to students who are working and unable to attend school. Television, correspondence study, five-hour meeting every three weeks. Leads to diploma and entrance into higher school.	Bavarian broadcasting system and Ministry of Education
France	1968	"RTS-Promotion" offers variety of courses for broadening general knowledge, learning foreign languages, and contributing to vocational and professional skills. Television, printed study materials for	Institut Pedagogigue National

FIGURE 7.1 (cont.)

Country	Starting Date	Nature of Program	Under Auspices of
		students willing to pay for them, in some courses correspondence study or CAI. No credit.	
Thailand	1969	Ramkhamhaeng University, established by parliament to take care of overflow of university applicants, offers a complete college curriculum by closed-circuit television in vary large lecture halls. Textbooks are used in each course, and in some cases large discussion groups. Degrees are offered to students who complete the courses satisfactorily.	University established by national parliament

(Built around radio and television)

Country	Starting Date	Nature of Program	Under Auspices of
Japan	1973	"NHK Gakuen", a radio-television-correspondence high school, offers complete high school curriculum — three years in four — for students who did not find places in residence high school and (most of them) went to work. Students can use either radio or television, or both. Correspondence lessons, texts, one day a month and five summer days in supplementary classes. Diplomas given.	Japan Broadcasting Corporation (NHK) with cooperation of correspondence instruction association.
Sweden	1967	"TRU" (radio or television committee) offers very wide variety of courses, extending from preschool to adult education. Some lead to exams and formal credit; others do not. Some are vocational and refresher courses, some are for general adult education. Truly	TRU is relatively independent, but financed by out-of-state funds and closely cooperative with Swedish Broadcasting Corporation and various

FIGURE 7.1 (cont.)

Country	Starting Date	Nature of Program	Under Auspices of
		multi-media, using TV, radio, textbooks, correspondence, recordings, home study kits, as needed.	adult educational organizations.
U.K.	1971	"Open University" offers complete university curriculum, with one TV, one radio program per course, per week, home study materials, some exercises to be self-corrected and some by computers, some correspondence papers marked by tutors, and study centers that provide opportunities to consult tutors, use study materials, and meet with other students. There are also opportunities for short-term residential study in the summers. Degrees are awarded.	University chartered by parliament and supported chiefly by parliamentary appropriation
West Germany	1974	Four-year pilot tests, offering university courses leading to degrees, for students unable to attend classes, or for interested adults. Planned as fully multimedia teaching, with support of radio and television stations, printed materials, correspondence study, and opportunities for study meetings.	Association for Distant Studies (Verbund für Fernstudien - VFF) comprising the 11 states of West Germany, institutions of higher education, and the Institute for Distant Studies (Deutsches Institut fur Fernstudien - DIFF) of the University of Tubingen.

This is far from a complete list. "Extended" university study is now available in Australia, along with the time-tested elementary and secondary courses. An open university is under way in West Germany, and an "Everyman's University" is about to offer courses by correspondence and broadcast in Israel. In the United States, the University of Nebraska is setting up a regional university system making use of television and textual materials, and the system seems to be growing beyond Nebraska. Stanford University, as we have noted, is offering many of its engineering courses by 2,500 mH television to employees of nearby industries and research laboratories. In other parts of the country, consortia of colleges and universities are joining together to produce credit courses and offer them by television and correspondence. In other words, the movement is still live and widespread.

What Level, What Medium?

One of the most interesting aspects of Figure 7.1 is that it demonstrates the use of extended schooling for every level of the educational system, and for both academic and vocational studies. Of course, there is every reason to believe that the need for this kind of instruction will be most demanding at the advanced level, to serve working adults and the increasing number of workers who find it necessary to pick up some of the courses they missed or to retrain themselves for technical changes in their occupations. Distant teaching will probably become the great vehicle for "lifelong education." But it is clearly not restricted to that use.

The listing also makes it clear that extended teaching is not simply teaching by television or radio. It has often been remarked that the "open" universities, many of which were described first as "universities of the air," are more properly called "universities of the post office." The chief learning activity of the student is with textual materials, and the chief two-way communication between school and student is over correspondence assignments. Correspondence study is the basis of these learning experiences just as it had been for a hundred years with correspondence schools. Yet radio, television, and other media have made a fundamental difference in the old correspondence systems, and that difference is reflected in the proportion of students who complete courses. The broadcast media contribute a liveliness to extended study that correspondence alone can hardly be expected to provide. Furthermore, they require a student to keep a schedule to keep up with the broadcasts; and it is this quality, more than others, that is responsible for the increased proportion of course completions.

Print, therefore, must be regarded as the basic medium of extended teaching, in the form of self-study texts and homework assignments that can be graded and criticized by correspondence tutors. Radio and television are the chief supporting media, because they can deliver live teaching widely and relatively cheaply, considering unit costs, to homes, meeting places, or schools. But programmed instruction is already appearing in many of the media-extension programs, and one can anticipate that CAI will become an important element as its costs decrease. The more affluent countries are more likely to use television than radio, and adult noncredit programs that have to compete with entertainment attractions are most likely to be on television. However, one of the large land grant universities in the United States offers many of its courses by radio, and Austria teaches a noncredit course in economics very widely by radio. A developing country, looking toward this kind of teaching, can therefore be relatively confident that either radio or television will be effective, and that numerous combinations of media and learning practice can be used to fit the needs and capabilities of a given country or school system. This is one of the trends of which a potential user—country or system—should take note.

THE TREND TOWARD MULTIMEDIA

No single medium ever has proved entirely satisfactory for extending the experiences of schooling. The University of Delhi, which had been able to teach so many of its students by correspondence study, has now found it desirable to introduce a radio program, a television program, and optional class meetings in five cities in addition to the correspondence study (see Figure 7.1). Purdue University, which offered its classroom courses for credit by radio (as the Stanford School of Engineering does for many of its courses by 2,500 mH television) now records the broadcasts so that students may come to the campus or other centers and listen to them again. It also provides other study materials for use by students who want to supplement their radio classes. The Chicago Television College, which started with television and textbooks, found that it was desirable to provide consultation hours in which students could talk with teachers by telephone and also to bring students to campus, where possible, for a few meetings each semester.

In other words, there has been a strong trend in this as in other branches of instruction, toward multimedia learning. The *simplest* combination that has seemed satisfactory is correspondence study plus either radio or television. The broadcast media, as we have noted, provide a sense of live teaching and a reason for the student to stay on schedule; the correspondence assignments require learning activity and provide a two-way link with a live teacher who can go over a student's work and provide guidance. No country seems yet to have found a feasible way to substitute films or tapes for the broadcast media, although films and tapes have often been made available at study centers, and meetings and study groups have been used in part to substitute for individual written work. But the other media and learning devices are mostly used to improve upon the functions performed by the basic media. Programmed instruction, CAI, and home study science kits, for example, contribute to active learning. The opportunity to consult a tutor fills even more fully than correspondence assignments the need for two-way communication and guidance. The opportunity to meet with a group adds reinforcement and gives the chance for group practice.

Not many school systems or countries have gone as far as Sweden or the British Open University toward multimedia teaching, but the trend is to enlarge the combinations and enrich the variety of opportunities for learning.

THE TREND TOWARD ACTIVE LEARNING

More and more attention, in distant teaching, has been devoted to the problem of how to keep the student learning *actively*. This means essentially going beyond the correspondence assignments which have to be turned in every two to four weeks. Programmed instruction is a very promising tool for this purpose, inasmuch as exercises do not have to be corrected centrally. Computer-corrected exercises which can be quickly returned to the student have also been used. Home study kits provided for science students by the British Open University are designed to let a student learn science by practicing it in his own environment. The use of radio transceivers in Australia has made it possible for a certain number of radio-correspondence students to exchange ideas and questions with their teachers and fellow students and practice some skills, such as reading aloud, that would be difficult to demonstrate by correspondence. And related to this are a number of plans (like the "School without Walls") which are designed to help the nonresident student make active use of his whole environment for instruction.

THE TREND TOWARD "OPEN" ENTRANCE

Still another trend, which promises to become even more important, is a challenge to the entrance requirements of resident school systems and universities. In general, the schools-out-of-school have been more permissive than ordinary schools in accepting students without entrance examinations and sometimes without the required previous education.

Surprisingly enough, many of these students have done very well. The British Open University, where 17,000 out of 19,000 students in the first year did not have A-level qualifications, proved that. Most of the students in the NHK Gakuen did not have good enough records to earn places in resident secondary schools, yet many of them did very well in the examinations, and 30 percent graduated from high school. In general, courses for adults out-of-school have been open to anyone who wants to try them. This opportunity is increasingly being extended to academic courses and is leading many schools and universities to review their requirements, and some of them to establish external degree programs by which credit can be earned through examination regardless of prerequisite study.

How Effective Is This Teaching?

Data on learning and cost, even on audience, from these projects are scarce. Only a few of the projects have had the benefit either of adequately designed field research or attention by a trained economist. The presence or absence of some of the kinds of data we should like to see is indicated in Table 7.1.

TABLE 7.1
Availability of Output Measures on Projects Designed to Extend the School

	Size	Audience Composition	Completion Rate	Learning	Costs
Austria	X	X	X	X	X
Australia	X	X			X
Germany, East					
Germany, West					
Funkkolleg	X	X	X	X	X
Telekolleg	X	X	X	X	X
France	X	X			
India (Delhi)	X	X		X	
Japan	X	X	X	X	X
Kenya	X			X	X
Mexico					
Radioprimaria				X	X
Telesecundaria	X	X		X	X
Netherlands	X				
Poland		X		X	
Sweden	X	X			
Thailand	X				
U.S.A.					
Chicago	X	X	X	X	X
Purdue	X	X			
U.K.					
Open University	X	X	X	X	X

Even this table, despite its many unfilled boxes, more than does justice to the data. For example, only three of the projects have measured learning with an experimental design; the others, if they collected evidence at all, have only the record of passes and failures in the course examinations.

But let us review what there is.

How Large Are The Audiences These Programs Serve?

The general adult education programs attract very large audiences. The four examples on which we have data are all in economically advanced countries; it is too bad we have no comparable evidence from a developing area.

When the East German Television Academy broadcast a series on mathematics for popular viewing, it received 200,000 letters from viewers. A series on "English for You" brought in 35,000; broadcasts on chemistry and physics, about 100,000 each. A series of televised lessons in Russian drew 500,000 letters (Paulu, 1969: 66-67)!

Audiences of the five most popular noncredit courses offered by France's RTS-Promotion were estimated by the Institut Francais d'Opinion Publique as follows:

Series	Number of Viewers
Mathematics for all	1,000,000
Electronics	720,000
Labour legislation	670,000
Business management	560,000
Methods of mental work	530,000

(Garnier, 1971: 115)

A report on the Netherlands' TELEAC listed both the active participants (meaning that they obtained the materials and supposedly worked along with the course) and the estimated number of viewers who were not active participants. For these figures, and those on Sweden's very broad program of televised education, see Table 7.2.

The figures in the table are obviously projections from sample surveys, which are not described in the reports, and must be regarded as very rough estimates. However, they leave little doubt that a European country can attract a sizable proportion of its adult population to serious instructional television. It would be interesting to know what Brazil, Uganda, or Korea, for example, could do with similar adult programs.

The school-extension projects that offer examinations and credit, and therefore are bound into formal schooling and curricula, attract smaller

TABLE 7.2

Course	Active Participants	Other Viewers
Netherlands[a]		
Television for teaching and instruction		70,000
Mathematics: surfaces, contents, and tangents	5,014	80,000
Building and living	2,435	90,000
Astronomy	4,677	100,000
Studying		68,000
First aid in accidents	3,582	400,000
Further training for general medical practitioners	978	85,000

	Mean number of viewers	
	1970 Autum	1971 Spring
Sweden[b]		
Psychology	235,000	136,000
The community of many	185,000	136,000
Let's do some more mathematics	225,000	361,000
It's for you	280,000	198,000
The labour market	70,000	68,000
Know your world	70,000	48,000
Information for adult students	265,000	136,000
Do you know? – a televised dictionary	105,000	89,000

a. Wermer, 1971: 151
b. Anderssohn and Bohlin, 1971: 182

audiences than the general adult programs which place no requirements upon their viewers. Yet they are able to take care of large numbers of students, as the following list shows:

Project	*Registered Students*
Australia, radio-correspondence school (primary-secondary)	6,000 in New South Wales alone (Kimmel, 1971: 27)
West Germany, Funkkolleg (radio course in pedagogy)	12,000 first term, 9,350 second (Hoffbauer, 1971: 93)
West German, Telekolleg (televised intermediate technical school)	Varies between 8,000 and 10,000 (Dordick, 1972: 18)
India, University of Delhi curriculum by correspondence with radio supplement	8,400 (Pant, 1971: 22)

Japan, NHK Gakuen (radio-television correspondence high school)	17,000 (Goto, 1972: 3)
Kenya (radio-correspondence in-service course for teachers)	1,900 in Form I, 2,000 in Form II in second year of project (Krival et al., 1970-1971: 26)
Mexico, Telesecondaria (televised secondary school)	29,000 (Mayo, McAnany, Klees, 1973: ch. 4, p. 1)
Thailand Ramkhamhaeng University (closed-circuit)	43,000 (official report of the university)
Chicago TV College	6,900 (McCombs, 1967, updated by Schramm, 1970: 6)
Purdue (radio courses for university credit)	Average of 2,000 a year (Forsythe, 1972: vi)
British Open University	42,000 in third year (official report)

These figures must be interpreted in light of related considerations. For one thing, very few of the projects represented in the list are operating near their maximum capacity; if they were, considerable savings in unit costs would probably result. In the second place, some of those that are near capacity are hemmed in by facilities or other restrictions in a way that makes expansion difficult. For example, the India correspondence-plus-radio curriculum mentioned above now includes 45 percent of all the B.A. candidates in the University of Delhi. The German Telekolleg now graduates more students than all the residence schools at its level in the entire state of Bavaria. Ramkhamhaeng University now fills its physical plant nearly to capacity, although some of the halls it uses for students to receive the televised lectures hold 2,000 persons. (Some of the Ramkhamhaeng classes enroll over 7,000 students!) In the third place, most of the school-extension projects that include open-circuit broadcasts have a large unregistered and unenrolled audience listening or viewing in addition to the students. We have already illustrated, in the case of the Netherlands' TELEAC, the disparity between the total viewing audience and the portion of the audience that is serious enough to order the materials. In Chicago, the noncredit viewers vary from 10,000 to 40,000 per program, according to ARB measurements, as compared to perhaps 1,000 to 2,000 registered students. In West Germany, although the total enrollment of the Telekolleg is only 10,000, more than 10 percent of all the television receivers in Bavaria are tuned in to the broadcasts of physics and history courses (Dordick, 1972: 23).

The over-the-shoulder audience is therefore a bonus for school-extension courses that have ostensibly been made for registered students. These audience figures say something about the appetite, at least in economically advanced countries, for continuing education. However, they also say something about choice of media. Nonregistered users do not pay the cost of teaching. If it is important enough to reach such an audience, the country can probably afford to pay the cost centrally. But if it is not, and if it is necessary to cover the cost of distant teaching by means of student fees, then the use of a medium like television must be weighed against the number of students who are likely to be served. Thus, Britain, with 53 million people, will find it easier to finance television teaching from student fees than will Israel, with less than 3 million. Israel, with 119 television receivers per 1,000 people, is more likely to find television teaching productive than Senegal which has a million more people, but less than one television receiver for every 1,000. Senegal, on the other hand, has 67 radio receivers per 1,000 people, and might find radio a more feasible medium with which to supplement correspondence teaching. In moving toward multimedia opportunities for distant students, therefore, smaller countries and those at an earlier stage of development are likely to depend upon the small media, like radio and programmed texts.

Who is in the Audience?

Whereas two-thirds of the registered students of the Chicago TV College are in their twenties and thirties, almost half the noncredit viewers are in their forties and fifties. Wherever such information is available for the school-extension projects, it backs up the Chicago finding. The younger people who need degrees or diplomas for their careers are likely to be registered students, but the listening audience not registered is likely to be older, to have missed some work when they were in school, to want to refresh their knowledge of it, or to be intellectually curious.

However, the school-extension programs also attract active registrants older than would be expected at a school in residence. The programs offer a second chance to persons who are a bit beyond the school age. Consider, for example, the registration in the NHK Gakuen which offers a high school curriculum out of school, chiefly to working students. The Japanese youth would ordinarily enter high school at about the age of seventeen. But in the radio-television-correspondence Gakuen, only 38 percent of the students are in their teens; 36 percent are in their twenties, and 20 percent are in their thirties (Goto, 1972).

The enrollment of the German Telekolleg is much the same. Only 44 percent are twenty-five or under, 38 percent are between twenty-five and thirty-five, and 18 percent are still older (Dordick, 1972: 14). Fifty-six percent of the students in the Polish Television Academy, which is supposed to prepare students for a technical school, are over twenty-two (Tymowsky, 1971: 162). A course in Austria, "Living Economics," drew half its audience from the thirty to fifty bracket.

Courses addressed to working people usually attract a disproportionate percentage of men. For example, the Austrian radio course (economics) drew an 86 percent male enrollment; Germany's Telekolleg (technical preparation), 79 percent male; Poland Television Academy (chiefly technical), 89 percent male. On the other hand, for Chicago TV College, which is intended mostly for home viewing, 75 percent of the credit students were women. They were home-bound with illness, children, or other responsibilities, and welcomed this chance to get in more college work, perhaps looking ahead to a job when they were able to dispense with the home responsibilities. Germany's Funkkolleg, when it offered a course in pedagogy, had 62 percent female enrollment, most of them teachers or future teachers. The British Open University also had more female students than expected, perhaps because 34 percent of its first class were teachers.

With the exception of the Australia and New Zealand radio-correspondence programs, which are for school-age children, the Delhi project, which is for college students, and the Ramkhamhaeng University in Bangkok, which is for all practical purposes a campus university doing most of its teaching by closed-circuit television, these extension projects have proved extremely attractive to working and home-bound adults. Over 80 percent of the credit audiences of the Austrian, the German, the Japanese, and the British programs, among others, come from people working at full-time jobs. The Japanese radio-television correspondence high school has detailed figures on employment. Thirty-three percent of its students work in factories, 12 percent are nurses, 18 percent in business, 8 percent in some kind of office work. The Japanese surveys show, however that the school is increasingly being used by adult women who married or were otherwise distracted from high school, and are now trying to pick up the courses they need for graduation. For them it truly represents a "second chance."

One other pattern of audience composition is worth noting. In the first class of the British Open University, as we have said, almost 90 percent of the students did not have the A-level qualifications that would have been required of them for entrance into a campus university in Britain. Still, 16,000 out of 19,000 passed the rigorous examinations at the end of the year. What Britain has thus impressively proved is what other projects also have been discovering: Given a chance to compete, many people who do not have the required academic prerequisites, and who in many cases are beyond the usual ages for education, can still do very well in difficult studies.

How Many Out-Of-School Students Finish?

One of the problems with asking students to study by themselves outside a school is that there is invariably a considerable shrinkage in numbers between registration and completion. Many commercial correspondence schools, for example, are believed to have completion rates no higher than 10 percent.

From the data at hand, it is possible to estimate the degree of shrinkage in the kinds of out-of-school education we are examining in this chapter, which typically combine broadcasts with correspondence study and/or other activities. The rate varies by the type of course, and particularly by the amount of control and support given the student. For example, about 75 percent of the students formally registered in the Chicago TV College complete the particular course for which they have registered (McCombs, 1967, vol. 2: 114). These home students are highly motivated to earn a college credit. About 84 percent of the students who finally registered in the first year class of the British Open University (1973) completed their courses and passed the examination. These students had the benefit not only of correspondence and self-study exercises, but also of radio and television, and tutorial centers nearby when needed (about half made some use of the tutorial centers).

The Austrian radio course on "Living Economics" was less tightly structured than the two courses just mentioned. There was no formal registration requirement, but certain steps along the road to the examination measured the seriousness of the students. Thus:

- —6,400 students enrolled "on their own" (meaning not in factory classes). Of these,

    - —5,069 (80 percent) ordered the scripts at 25 schillings (about $1.00)

    - —1,729 (28 percent) ordered the textbooks at 169 schillings (about $6.50)

- —579 students (8 percent of the original enrollees) actually did take the test (Wagner, 1971: 33-36).

Another course which was loosely structured and gave no credit toward a degree was the German Funkkolleg course in pedagogy. Here is the record of shrinkage in the active class members through two terms:

	First term	*Second term*
Originally enrolled	13,495	
Ordered the printed material —8 study letters at DM 24 (about $6.00)	12,100	9,350
Did the required homework and thus were eligible to take the final examination	5,997	4,048
Actually took examinations	3,825	3,563
	(67 percent eligible; 28 percent of original enrollees)	(88 percent of eligible; 26 percent of original enrollees)

(Hoffbauer, 1971: 103)

It seems, from this last record, that after an out-of-school program has reduced its audience to those who seriously intend to complete the work, subsequent shrinkage is relatively small.

So far we have dealt only with single courses. What is the rate of shrinkage in a whole curriculum offered outside school—for example, a high school? We have evidence on this question from two sources: the German Telekolleg, which offers a two and one-half year technical school curriculum, and the Japanese NHK Gakuen, which is a four-year high school curriculum. The final completion rate in both of these seems to be in the neighborhood of 30 percent. Here are the available figures on the first two classes enrolled in the Telekolleg:

	First class	*Second class*
Took exam at end of first 10-month term	41	36
Took exam at end of second 10-month term	31	30
Took exam at end of final 6-month term	27	(not yet available)

(Dordick, 1972: 20)

And here are comparable figures from the first six classes of the NHK Gakuen:

Of	who entered in	after	proportion graduated
11,721	1963	9 yrs.	25.3
6,673	1964	8 yrs.	30.5
5,779	1965	7 yrs.	30.2
5,327	1966	6 yrs.	27.5
6,188	1967	5 yrs.	26.1
6,162	1968	4 yrs.	20.5

(Goto, 1972: 1)

It is reasonable to suppose that the first class of the school was somewhat atypical: Students entered without really knowing what to expect or what was expected of them. Therefore, a slightly lower completion score is understandable. The 1964 class should have graduated at the end of 1967. By 1972, when the laggards had another four years to finish their work, 30.5 percent had graduated. The 1968 class, which should have completed its work by the end of 1971, had by that time graduated 20.5 percent. We can assume, then, that in a situation like that of the NHK Gakuen, which serves students who are working full-time while they complete three years of high school in four, a little over 20 percent will finish their course work and graduate on time, and over the next four years another 10 percent will graduate. Both from the Japanese and the German cases, then, it can be assumed that a little less than one-third of out-of-school students in a demanding curriculum parallel in every way to a school in residence will ultimately complete their work and graduate.

How Much Do They Learn?

At this writing, from only three of the school-extension projects do we have evidence derived from an experimental design on how the students learned. These are the Mexican Telesecundaria and Radioprimaria and the Chicago TV College.

However, this is not the extent of the evidence. From a number of different projects, we have data on the proportion of students who passed the final examination. And in addition to those, we have the record of a project like Australian radio-correspondence schools which, for forty years, have been graduating hundreds or thousands of students each year from primary and secondary school curricula, from which a considerable proportion have transferred to boarding schools or entered universities.

Even though learning scores are lacking, one can hardly call a project like that unsuccessful.

All three experimental comparisons were carefully done, but suffered from the common inability of field researchers to assign subjects randomly among treatments. For example, it was impossible for the Chicago researchers, if they sought a realistic situation, to assign certain students to study at home and others to study in the classroom. Those who actually registered for the course at home could *not* have taken it in the classroom; those who took the course in the classroom would have been unwilling to take it at home. Those who did take it at home had a special reason for doing so, and their gratitude for being able to do so was a significant element in the experiment. Similarly, the researchers in Mexico could not have assigned students randomly from the population to either experimental or control groups. No high schools were available for the Telesecundaria students to attend unless they moved to another town. Attempts were made, in these experiments, to equate the experimental and control groups or to allow for measured differences by means of covariance, but still the conditions of a completely rigorous experiment were not attained.

In Chicago, students who registered for a TV College course at home were compared with groups of day students and groups of evening students taking the same course on campus. Altogether, twenty-seven experimental comparisons were made, over three years, between face-to-face and home television students. Twelve of these were significantly different, ten in favor of the home television group. The results in more detail are in Table 7.3.

TABLE 7.3
Chicago TV College Learning Comparisons

Subject	Method	N	First Year Criterion	Score	Statistics	Significance
English 101	home TV	354	final	75.41	covariance	n.s.d.
	class	101	exam	71.13		
Social Science 101	home TV	90	final and	158.45	matched	n.s.d.
	class	90	midterm	153.33	pairs	
Biology 101	home TV	259	final	110.31	analysis of	favors home
	class	98	exam	101.01	variance	TV, .05
Political Science	home TV	244	final	108.69	analysis of	n.s.d.
	class	58	exam		variance	
English 101	home TV	33	final	23.85	matched	n.s.d.
	class	33	exam	23.79	pairs	
English 102	home TV	69	final	21.75	analysis of	n.s.d.
	class	24	exam	21.95	variance	

TABLE 7.3 (continued)

Subject	Method	N	Criterion	Score	Statistics	Significance
Social Science 102	home TV class	45 45	final exam	74.64 73.89	matched pairs	n.s.d.
Biology 102	home TV class	153 153	final exam	110.16 106.30	analysis of variance	favors home TV, .05
Mathematics	home TV class	28 28	course grade	2.97 3.17	covariance	n.s.d.
Second year						
Accounting 101	home TV class	53 44	final and midterm	79.38 76.05	covariance	n.s.d.
English 101-102	home TV class	53 40	not available	Not available	covariance	n.s.d.
Humanities 201-202	home TV class	69 73	final and other tests	379.16 345.73	covariance	favors home TV, .05
Social Science 101	home TV class	56 23	critical thinking post-test	29.0 26.47	covariance	n.s.d.
Biology 101	home TV class	26 26	final and other tests	n.a.	covariance	n.s.d.
Biology 102	home TV class	153 153	final and other tests	n.a.	covariance	favors home TV, .05
Child Psychology	home TV class	46 46	final	74.46 69.89	t. test	n.s.d.
Shorthand	home TV class	26 64	final	109.22 104.64	n.a.	n.s.d.
Third Year						
Social Science 102	home TV class	29 29	course exams	129.13 121.0	covariance	favors home TV, .01
Physical Science 101	home TV class	n.a.	exams	212.41 230.85	covariance	favors class, .01
Physical Science 101	home TV class		exams	212.41 185.29	covariance	favors home TV, .01
Humanities 201	home TV class	31 44	course exams	176.16 181.11	covariance	n.s.d.

TABLE 7.3 (continued)

Subject	Method	N	Criterion	Score	Statistics	Significance
Humanities 202	home TV class	20 31	exams	152.01 176.10	covariance	favors class, .01
Psycho- logy	home TV class	60 30	exams	187.27 178.83	covariance	n.s.d.
Psycho- logy	home TV class	60 21	exams	187.27 164.48	covariance	favors home TV, .01
Mathema- tics	home TV class	35 30	exams	140.23 122.76	t. test	favors home TV, .01
Speech	home TV class	17 48	exams	118.34 106.19	covariance	favors home TV, .01
Speech	home TV class	17 37	exams	118.34 106.19		favors home TV, .01

Source: Erickson and Chausow, 1960

The researchers who studied the Mexican Telesecundaria compared samples of schools (*not* students) in each of four districts of Mexico from among the schools teaching face to face and from the Telesecundaria groups taught with the aid of television. They used before and after tests, and obtained the results in Table 7.4.

Because of the difficulties with design, the researchers declined to claim statistical significance for these results, and pointed out merely that the Telesecundaria students were obviously doing at least as well as comparable classes in the schools.

Table 7.5 presents similar comparisons for the Mexican Radioprimaria. This is an ingenious use of radio to expand three-year primary schools to six grades without adding three additional teachers. Sometimes the fourth, fifth, and sixth grades are taught by one teacher in the same room, and in a few instances the third, fourth, fifth, and sixth grades are all taught together by one teacher. The most common pattern, however, is to put the fifth and sixth grades together under one teacher, sometimes combining the third and fourth grades, sometimes not. In any case, the radio broadcasts are used to help teach the three upper grades, with fewer teachers.

All the sixth grades in the Radioprimaria were compared with the sixth grades not taught by radio in the province of San Luis Potosi. Since the Radioprimaria schools were all in villages or small towns, suburban and city schools were eliminated from the nonradio sample. This resulted in the figures shown in Table 7.5.

These gains were significant, but the author of the study preferred not to make any claim of statistical significance, in view of the conditions of

TABLE 7.4
Mexican Telesecundaria Learning Comparisons, 1972

	Telesecundaria			Direct Teaching		
Subject	Means	Gain	N	Means	Gain	N
Mathematics						
February	20.24			20.15		
June	25.92	5.68	1,151		2.61	836
Spanish						
February	26.39			24.54		
June	31.50	5.11	1,110	27.19	2.65	781
Chemistry						
February	18.06			18.49		
June	24.31	6.25	1,132	22.70	4.21	713

Source: Mayo, McAnany, and Klees, 1973

TABLE 7.5
Mexican Radioprimaria Learning Comparisons, Sixth Grade, 1972

	Radioprimaria			Direct Teaching		
	Mean	S.D.	Gain	Mean	S.D.	Gain
Mathematics						
September	15.7	6.3		17.5	6.8	
December	19.0	6.6	3.3	20.3	6.9	2.8
Spanish						
September	26.4	9.5		28.3	9.0	
December	30.1	8.9	3.7	30.1	9.1	1.8

Source: Spain, 1973: 17

field experimentation, but only to point out that the Radioprimaria students appeared to be gaining at least as much as the students taught in the usual fashion, without radio, one teacher to a classroom.

What if the suburban schools were not removed from the sample? This comparison was made, and showed that the nonradio group gained no more than without the suburban schools (and less than the Radioprimaria group), but their beginning scores were higher. What if only the Radioprimaria schools that added sixth grades in the year of the test were included? That comparison also was made. The scores of the new radio schools were insignificantly different from those of the older schools. Thus, it is reasonable to assume that the sixth-grade students in the Radioprimaria were not learning any less than their peers in the ordinary classrooms.

The remaining quantitative data on learning are mostly records of the proportion of students who passed course examinations. This says nothing about how much was learned in comparison to how much might have been learned from another method of teaching. Rather, it measures what proportion of the registered students were learning what they were expected to learn from the course. Thus, for example, among the Austrian students who took the exam in the course on "Living Economics," only 1 percent failed, which must have been encouraging to the teachers, although they would have recalled that only about 20 percent of those who originally said they intended to take the examination did so (Wagner, 1971: 36).

In general, all the examination figures on school-extension courses are encouraging. In the case of the German Telekolleg, only 60 of the 7,214 students who took final examinations in the first enrolled class failed (less than 1 percent). When this first class came to the end of its three-year curriculum, 97 percent of the students who took the final examination passed. The average grades were slightly better than those made by students in the Berufsaufbauschulen, which teach the same curriculum in classrooms (Dordick, 1972: 16 gg.).

In the University of Delhi correspondence curriculum (now supplemented by radio and other learning aids), the passing rate for the final B.A. varied between 42 and 50 percent, which is just under the passing rate of all students in the university (Pant, 1971: 22).

In the radio-correspondence course (secondary education) for teachers in service in Kenya, the passing rates compare favorably with those of residence students, both in public and in private schools. The average passing rate in public secondary schools is just under 25 percent. For all private secondary schools, the rate is just under 12 percent. But the radio-correspondence students who took exams in six or seven subjects had a passing rate of 34 percent; those who took only four or five exams had a rate of 44 percent; and those who took only two or three subjects had 60 percent passes. Furthermore, it is possible to compare the records of the students in different courses—subjects they had studied in the radio-correspondence course versus subjects they had studied otherwise. In all subjects, the average passing rate for study by radio and correspondence was 49 percent. In all subjects *not* studied by radio and correspondence, for the same students, the passing rate was 20 percent (Krival et al., 1970-1971: 59 ff.).

A similar comparison can be made in the case of the Polish Television Academy. This institution is intended to supplement studies already offered in correspondence and face-to-face evening schools. A field survey identified students who viewed all or almost all the programs, and others who viewed only occasionally. This is what the records showed:

	Regular viewers (in %)	Occasional viewers (in %)
Did not take examination	30.6	49.2
Failed examination	10.2	11.5
Passed examination	45.1	19.6

(Tymowsky et al., 1969: 45)

The remaining students in the sample said they had never intended to take the examination or intended to take it later, or the like.

So far as this evidence is conclusive, therefore, it seems to show that students in one of the systems designed to extend the school learn on the average at least as well as students in comparable classroom systems. This seems to be the case whether the course is in an economically advanced country (e.g., West Germany) or a developing country (e.g., Kenya). It seems to be the case whether the broadcast medium is radio (Australia, Kenya) or television (Mexico, Germany) or both (Japan, Britain). And it seems to apply whether the course is at the level of primary or secondary (Mexico, Australia, Kenya, Japan), technical school (Germany, Poland), or higher education (Britain, Chicago).

SOME CONCLUSIONS

The import of this rather impressive evidence is that distant teaching, well-conceived, well-supported with the proper media, really works.

It works in developing countries or in highly industrialized ones, and at many different levels of education. Where data are available, they appear to show that students in one of these media-extended programs learn at least as well as students in the same curriculum in traditional classrooms. We shall see in a later chapter that unit costs of extended education can be less than in conventional settings, and that in places where educational opportunities are not now available, those opportunities can usually be offered by media-extension for considerably less than it would cost to provide the same opportunities in the same places by building, staffing, and operating conventional schools.

The basic medium of distant teaching is *print,* as it has been since correspondence schools began. The fundamental difference, however, between the new and the old forms of distant teaching is the addition of broadcast media to provide live teaching and scheduling discipline.

Other things being equal, a planner would probably choose television rather than radio for a program of distant teaching, because it would allow the presentation of visual materials as well as sound. But the field evidence on this kind of teaching, as on other kinds, leads one not to disparage the potential of radio. For example, it cannot be said that television is necessarily the medium for economically advanced countries, and radio for developing countries. Radio is used and seems to work well in both Australia and Germany, which are far from primitive, and television has demonstrated that it can work well in Mexico and was the choice of Thailand when that country wanted to extend university opportunities almost overnight to a vast number of students. A point to remember is that things are *not* always equal, in choice of media. Japan spends five times as much to produce an hour of television as to produce an hour of radio. Japan can afford to use both radio and television with its distant teaching programs, as also does the Open University in Britain. But some other countries might prefer to deliver the visual experiences in another way than by television, and make maximum use of the capabilities of radio at one-fifth the cost.

Any school system or any country entering upon distant teaching must be aware of the tendency of such systems to grow into truly multimedia systems. The British Open University and certain other systems in affluent countries might be expected to do this, but the trend is far broader. Even the University of Delhi, which started to use correspondence study to relieve the demands it could not meet for entrance to its undergraduate program, soon decided to add radio programs to its instruction, and has now made some use of television also. None of these programs has found it sufficient to use *only* radio or television, or even radio or television plus print. Invariably, the planners of the system have found they would be well-advised to provide additional study and practice materials where possible—programmed instruction, kits, reading assignments, problems or experiments to be done in the student's own environment—and also some additional two-way communication—occasional classes, summer terms, study groups, telephone consultation, tutorial centers, or even, as Australia does, a few classes by two-way radio. In other words, although this pattern of instruction is designed to work at a distance and to place more responsibility on a student to work alone where there are no schools or teachers, it tends to develop in such a way as to provide, by media or by different organization, as many as possible of the learning experiences of a classroom.

The problem of designing distance teaching, therefore, is not troubled by whether a well-designed system will work effectively, but rather by the practical question of how sparse or how rich to make the system. An effective system can be designed with radio and correspondence; or it can be designed with television, tutorial centers, kits, programmed or computer-assisted instruction, and any number of other devices. The availability of resources—human, technical, and economic—therefore is an element in the decision.

CHAPTER 8

EVIDENCE FROM THE FIELD:
Nonformal Education

Any major political program of the Seventies should be evaluated by this measure: How clearly does it state the need for de-schooling—and how clearly does it provide guidelines for the educational quality of the society for which it aims? . . . Hope for education begins when it moves outside the school [Ivan Illich, *New York Review of Books,* January 7, 1971].

Nonformal education is not a sharply bounded concept. The most common alternative name for it—out-of-school education, which is used by UNESCO—is no sharper. It may or may not take place in a school building; it may or may not be under the auspices and control of a school system; it may or may not be conducted formally; it may or may not lead ultimately to a diploma or a degree. However, it is *not* the kind of education we think of as going on in the government primary schools of Niger or the Plan Basico schools of El Salvador or Samoana High School in Pago Pago or Harvard University; on that, educators agree. Beyond that, nonformal education is whatever a writer chooses to call by the name.

Between "formal" education, such as we have discussed in three preceding chapters, and "nonformal" education, which is the subject of this chapter, there is a shifting and shadowy border. The only excuse for having such a concept as nonformal education at all is its central purpose, rather than its boundaries. And for this reason it is well not to waste time defining the boundaries, but to concentrate at once on the central purpose, which is to provide the population, young and old, some of the learning opportunities they have not had or cannot easily obtain in formal schooling.

We find the approach taken by Ahmed and Coombs, in the volume of case studies they prepared for the World Bank and UNICEF, a practical and useful one. Nonformal education, they say,

> refers to the motley assortment of organized and semi-organized educational activities operating outside the regular structure and routines of the formal system, aimed at serving a great variety of learning needs of different subgroups in the population, both young and old. Some nonformal programs cater to the same learning needs as the schools and in effect are substitutes for formal schooling. Examples are the "second chance" program in Thailand, the radio-correspondence "school equivalency" program in Kenya, the Rural Education Centers in Upper Volta, portions of ACPO's program in Colombia, and functional literacy programs in such countries as Mali and Thailand.

> But most nonformal education programs covered by the case studies are directed at serving important learning needs and benefiting clienteles not generally catered to by the formal schools. These learning needs relate, for example, to health, nutrition, family planning, and other requisites for improving family life; to developing good personal character traits and positive attitudes; to increasing

economic productivity, family incomes, and employment opportunities; and to strengthening local institutions of self-help and self-government and broadening participation in them. Most of the programs are aimed at benefiting particular subgroups in the local population—such as small farmers, craftsmen, and entrepreneurs; older girls and women; infants and young children (through the education of their elders); unemployed out-of-school youth; members and leaders of community organizations such as cooperatives, farmer societies, and local councils. But several multipurpose programs—such as the Sarvodaya Movement in Sri Lanka—seek to serve all members of the family and community and a broad spectrum of learning needs.

The extreme diversity of nonformal education programs—not only in their target audiences and learning objectives but in their forms and structures and educational technologies and methods, precludes fitting them neatly into a refined classification system [Ahmed and Coombs, 1975: xxix].

They proceed then to report on seventeen programs in fifteen countries, which do indeed represent a diversity of structures and functions.

The reason why nonformal education has taken on such importance in our time and especially in the less-developed countries is precisely the failure of the formal school system to meet all the educational needs of the society. The formal system, worldwide, fails to reach half the school-age population. The rate of dropouts is very high. The curriculum is largely irrelevant to the needs of many of the potential students. The system is very expensive, measured against the resources available. Educational expenditures now average 16 percent of national budgets in the less-developed countries; in at least ten countries they are more than 25 percent of the total budget. A sharp rise in educational investment since 1950 has more than doubled enrollments in the LDCs, but this, in turn, has resulted in loss of quality and in widespread unemployment and dissatisfaction among school leavers. The great push to expand formal education has not been geared into the capacity of developing countries to absorb educated youth, nor the needs of these countries for particular kinds of workers in particular places. It has tended to slight the adult segment of the adult population which also needs opportunities to learn in order to be maximally useful to national development. Nonformal education has risen in response to the conclusions of planners, educators, and users alike that there must be a better way to expand educational opportunities than by means of the present formal systems.

Nonformal education is therefore distinguished by the part it plays, rather than by its boundaries.

It is not limited to developing countries. Indeed, Kato (1974: 10) notes that there is one "miscellaneous school," meaning a private non-degree, noncredit school, for every 670 inhabitants of Tokyo. These offer instruction in a great variety of skills such as typing, penmanship, flower arranging, cooking, foreign languages, automobile driving. In countries as well-developed as Japan, and in countries much less well-developed, non-formal education exists to do what the formal education system does not. Its curriculum derives, not from the classic model, but rather from an estimate of today's needs and tomorrow's challenges, in a particular locality and country, and with reference to a particular group of people.

THE MEDIA OF NONFORMAL EDUCATION

If there is *a* medium for nonformal education, it is radio. The reason for this is illustrated by Paul Theroux's study of rural radio in Uganda, which reports that whereas 87.7 percent of all the rural families sampled in that study have no electricity, 86.3 percent nevertheless have radios (Theroux, n.d.: 21). In other words, radio is the only broad channel to the rural regions, the one long-range, relatively inexpensive, easily deliverable medium that overleaps the commonest barriers to sharing information with remote places.

But in nonformal instruction, as in all the other kinds of instruction we have mentioned, there is really no one medium. The patterns of media use are as varied as the education itself. At one end of the spectrum is the kind of nonformal education we shall refer to in the following pages as "localizing the school." In that task, media are of minor importance. At the other end there is the area of development campaigns—family planning, agriculture, health, and so forth. Here the development organizations typically use every medium they can find, from radio to print to posters to puppets, and always including personal contacts with a field staff. If radio is the "chief" medium at this end of the spectrum, it is only because it provides the most direct channels to the most people. But no country would think of depending for a development campaign upon radio alone.

Thus, in Uganda, whence came the figures we quoted from the Theroux study, the *Guide for Extension Workers in Agriculture* tells these workers that "mass-media are essential in your work," and advises them to become expert in the use, not only of radio, but also of

—publications of many kinds

—news stories

—circular letters

—exhibits

—posters

—motion pictures

—slides and filmstrips

—flip charts

—flannelgraphs

—wall newspapers

—bulletin boards

—photographs

—wall charts

—puppet shows

—local talent, drama, songs, poetry, music

One interesting feature of this list is the amount of printed material it contains, despite the low literacy rate in Uganda. The agriculture ministry feels that not only will print reach influential farmers, but also that literates will pass on the message to others. A second feature of interest is what the guidebook has to say about these media. It recommends a combination of channels. For example, it suggests that entertainment, social events, and teaching be combined with exhibits. It advises the extension representative "to supplement the motion picture with other teaching methods before or after the cinema is shown." It suggests that a village should receive not one, but *most* of the media listed (Uganda Department of Agriculture, 1968: 33 ff.).

The variety of uses of instructional media in nonformal programs is fascinating. Take, for example, the use of films and videotape in the Canadian "Challenge for Change" program. The typical pattern of use might be to present a film demonstrating some desired form of community development. This has been done many times, without spectacular results. Then the Canadian Film Board decided to go to the community for its films. It sent a film-maker to live with a poor family for three weeks. She produced a powerful and sensitive film, depicting what it means to be poor, with the intention of motivating people to want to do away with conditions like those in the picture. It was an artistic success, but a complete disaster for the family that had played host to the film-maker. They were teased and mocked by their neighbors, and their whole experience ended in bitterness.

As George Stoney, who was at that time the producer of "Challenge for Change," said:

The film should have been screened for the family in their apartment, with just a few of the crew around. All the response would be sympathetic and understanding. Then, with the family itself doing the inviting and deciding who should come, it could have been screened at the church or any group where the family had connections and where people could start from a friendly base to see that the family was doing something, was involved in something important. Gee, they're going to be on TV! All this could have been done before the film was actually finished; then, if they wanted changes, you could make them [Canadian Broadcasting Corporation, 1972: 3].

So the Film Board tried another tactic. It sent interviewers and VTR cameramen to a disaffected mining area in Alberta. The interviewers talked to customers in stores, people in a pub, and people in their homes, asking what they thought of the situation in the village, what they liked about it, what they didn't like, what they would like to see changed and what ideas they had as to how to change it. All this material was edited down to one hour and presented at a community meeting. Over half the people in the village came to see themselves and others on tape. The meeting ended in heated discussion, and formation of committees to take up the main problems that surfaced in the interviews. One old man said: "I've been playing cards with these guys for years, and we didn't know what the other guy was really thinking about the place until we had to speak out for the camera." The first meeting was followed by others, and by community action, and change began to occur: a cleanup, a public park, installation of gas and water lines, a small factory, a fire engine and a home-built "firehouse" for it, a social center for the valley, and so forth (Canadian Broadcasting Corporation, 1972: 6). So, as Canada proved, there are different and creative ways to use media in nonformal education. (For further use of this method see the reports on the Fogo project, for example, Gwyn, 1972).

In this chapter, we cannot hope to present all the variety of nonformal education that exists. Rather, we shall try to represent the variety by key ideas and patterns.

THE KEY IDEA: LOCALIZING THE PROGRAM

In a strongly stated argument to the Bellagio Conference of May, 1972, Ralph M. Miller, a Professor of Education at the University of Calgary, wrote:

If people are to find meaning in their lives, unless enlisting among the urban unemployed be accepted as meaningful, they must be encouraged and helped to find new possibilities in rural living. Education alone certainly cannot revitalize rural life, it can only be a part of the total effort. But if we accept that education can accomplish nothing in this respect and that the only education people will accept is that aimed towards modern sector jobs, then we must confess the utter irrelevance of education to current development imperatives.

It is only schooling—education carried on under the familiar ritualistic forms—which is irrelevant. What we need to turn attention to are alternative forms of education which are developed in relation to local needs and which utilize local skills. Local initiative must be emphasized, for the non-formal educational models of the developed world are often wildly inappropriate to conditions in developing countries. . . .

1. Education must become less formal.

2. Education must be freed from system restrictions and be developed through a variety of specific projects on a smaller scale.

3. Education projects must be recognized as experimental and must be monitored so that we may find out what works in specific situations.

4. Education must become more of a service within a complex of development efforts and less of an instructional program for the sake of instruction [R. M. Miller, 1972: L8-9].

Although not all educators agree on the feasibility of "ruralizing" education, the spirit of this quotation is the spirit that has moved a number of less-developed countries, particularly in Africa, toward localizing their rural schools and removing them from the formal pattern. For example, President Nyerere's influential publication of 1967, *Education for Self-Reliance,* insists on a complete reappraisal of the purpose of the school in village life. Nyerere's statement draws to a considerable extent upon his own acquaintance with the village school in Litowa, in Southern Tanzania, and this is a good example with which to begin.

The Litowa school began with a change in the community, rather than vice versa. The Tanzanian rural society is typically made up of isolated dwellings, and of farmers who move every few years to cultivate new land when their own fields wear out. However, the farmers around Litowa decided to live together in a village, give up their individual plots of land, share the work, share the profits, and create a truly cooperative society. Litowa was the first village in a group of twelve to be formed in this way, and as such became the location of the school for all twelve villages. Therefore, the question arose: what kind of school?

The traditional schools of Tanzania are highly academic, with a classical curriculum, the students aiming toward winning one of the few available secondary school places in the country, from which the successful graduates may then go on to government jobs, urban careers, and possibly higher education.

This pattern did not fit the goals of Litowa. For one thing, for almost all pupils that school would necessarily be terminal education. Almost every pupil had to look forward to a career, not in the civil service, but in subsistence agriculture. The graduates were needed in the rural regions, not in Dar es Salaam. They had very little need of an understanding of European history, and a very great need to understand the problems of their own communities. In other words, the goal of education in Litowa was seen not as entrance into a distant secondary school, but as active participation in a revolutionary community close by (see Wood, 1969: 4 ff.).

The teachers at Litowa are furnished by the Ministry of Education, but do not now teach the classical curriculum. As soon as they come to Litowa, they are brought into the village council as full members, and the whole council has a great deal to say about the curriculum. The students are taught to read, write, and calculate, of course, but their schooling has two characteristics uncommon to curriculum inherited from the colonial period. In the first place, the basic, the fundamental subject is the principle of cooperative living and work-sharing, in preparation for entrance into the adult society of Litowa or one of the other villages. This pervades the first four grades, in the form of stories, songs, drama, and discussions. In the upper three grades, the principles of growth through cooperation are studied more theoretically, along with the economic and political problems and policies of the nation.

In the second place, productive labor—farming, weaving, nursing—is a part of every child's life in school. In older schools, labor had been used as a form of punishment, but at Litowa, a new attitude toward labor is created. It is not something by which one is punished or which one had to do to keep the bush from taking over the school, but a natural and expected part of life by which one contributes to the prosperity and progress of the village. As children grow older, they are allowed themselves to supervise the work projects. Much of the administration of the school is delegated to an elected executive committee of students, which is parallel to the executive committee of the village and reports to a pupil assembly corresponding to the village council. The committee is responsible for the welfare and conduct of the students, and for the planning of the work projects. Thus, what the students are *taught* in school is no more significant than what they *do* in school, and both experiences are designed to prepare them for useful and dedicated lives in their own community.

Perhaps the most important point to note about the Litowa experience (as Wood points out in his very good account of it) is that the first steps in a reconstruction of rural society preceded the beginning of a new form of rural education. It's the same point that Chu makes in his studies of China (Chu, 1977): Change in social structure must precede really effective use of communication. Once the first step is taken, it is relatively easy for the community to voice its needs to the school, and for the school to adapt to them.

What part do media play in a localized school like Litowa? At present, very little. Media do play some part in the development and reconstruction of the village, however. The district training center, where local leaders come for guidance and instruction, is supposed to have a "library/radio/ information room." Radio, with practical instruction in agriculture and health, and talks on national policies and priorities, comes into the village. So do pamphlets and posters on development subjects. When extension people come in, they often bring films or filmstrips with them. So far as the school is concerned, however, there is no part of the instruction regularly given over to radio or films; and no television is available. But because the school is such an integral part of the village, the presence of media in the village is reflected also in the school.

If time and space were available, it would be interesting to compare this experience in Tanzania with the experience of some of the French African countries in trying to localize and ruralize their schools. The difference can at least be suggested by a few notes on the attempted reform of primary education in Chad (for a good account of this, see the paper on the "Mandoul" project, submitted to OECD by the French Delegation to the Development Assistance Committee, 1972).

In 1966, the government of Chad decreed a reform in primary education which provided for "changes in the curriculum of all primary classes for rural purposes. The purpose of this change was to adapt education to the development needs of Chad—crop and livestock farming—by preparing the children for a life in a rural environment." It provided also for exclusion of older children from primary school—to keep them from "making a career" of schooling rather than entering useful labor—and for the introduction of teaching reforms devised by the Pedagogical Research Group of the Secretariat of State for Foreign Affairs (Co-operation). These latter reforms included the teaching of French for the first time as a foreign language, so as "to dissipate the magical aura which has tended to surround the French word." They also included the introduction of simple logic to train the child's mind, and from the third year onward, the study of the environment.

This altered system was put into use in the Mandoul region of Chad in 1967, with a team of trained teaching assistants, and seemed to work rather well, given these reservations stated by the authors of the French project:

> The reform can be regarded as an effective approach to solving the school problem, but with the limitations that it involves no change in the way parents or teachers perceive the role of the school. Irrespective of what may be taught or what methods may be used, the parents still take no direct interest and regard the school as a means of socially upgrading their children. This inevitably causes parents to relinquish their educational functions to the teacher, who neither can nor should perform them. In these circumstances children attending school are irrevocably cut off from their environment, whatever teaching efforts may be made toward integration. Attempts by the school to relate to its surroundings by studying the environment come up against the failure of the parents to understand the point of it, to accept the child as a questioner, or to see how the village can have anything to offer their children, whom they destine for the civil service. This attitude on the part of the parents is also that of teachers who fail to reassess their role in the village, with the result that the child's approach is to regard his living as an object for observation, external to himself. Any every-day reality brought into the classroom through the surveys is then transformed by the alchemy of the French language and of writing to become a school subject like any other [French Delegation, 1972: 4].

Thus far the project was at best a limited success. It represented a technical improvement in the school, but did not succeed in integrating the school and the future careers of the pupils into their communities. Therefore, the Rural Development Agency set in motion a major effort to change the attitudes of the adults toward the school, the teachers toward the adults, and the children toward their roles as pupils and as members of their community. "Unless far-reaching action is taken to reorganize these relationships," wrote Jacques Mercoiret, "we hardly feel that any change inside the school alone will lead to its integration."

The major need was to get the teachers and the parents talking. This was accomplished in a series of meetings, with the community development staff acting as intermediaries. The parents were asked to define what they thought the school and the teachers were doing. The teachers were asked to describe what they were trying to do, and why. The parents were asked to describe the objectives of traditional education, so that the teachers could become aware of the ancient education going on all the time around them. Then the discussion turned to what services the school should be performing for the village—what should be preserved out of the traditional educational patterns and what was helpful in the new system. Out of a great deal of talk of this kind, so it is reported, a new relationship and a new set of understandings grew up between villagers and teachers and began to include the pupils also. This required much patience on the part of the teachers, and a long step forward on the part of the villagers. One important thing that happened about this time was the offering of classes in fundamental literacy to adults, so that they would gain some necessary technical competence and have a shared experience with their children.

The parents took a more active role in their children's schooling. They began to supervise the children's attendance and check on their progress. An arrangement was made by which, from time to time, one of the villagers would sit in on a class and then tell the other villagers what was happening. Certain of the older villagers were invited to the school to tell the children about things the old people feared were being forgotten. A cotton field was set aside for the school children to cultivate under the supervision of an adult chosen by the villagers. And thus, gradually, the school grew closer to the life of the village, and mutual understanding increased on both sides.

It is interesting to note that Tanzania and Chad began at opposite ends of the relationship. Tanzania moved to reconstruct a village society and the village then actively moved toward the kind of school it felt it needed. Chad began by decreeing educational reform, and then had to take extraordinary action to bring the village society and the school together. But they were both aiming toward the same goal—a school system of, by, and for rural society. By one or the other means, the villagers were being encouraged to take a much more active part in the operation of their own schools. And practical work combined with classroom study was one device used in both systems.

It is obvious that instructional media are not the key to success in this type of nonformal education. It is worth noting also that only six of Ahmed and Coombs' seventeen cases (1975) make any mention of mass media support, and with the exception of the Sutatenza case in Colombia, the entire book devotes less than a dozen pages to discussion of the media. But the idea of *localizing* the program, serving *local* objectives, bringing about active *local* participation, is something that goes through every project in nonformal education. A change in central curriculum or central broadcasts is, therefore, less likely to make nonformal education succeed than is a change in the community itself—a change in attitude toward what the community can do for itself, what kinds of teaching and learning are needed, active participation in bringing the instructional process into the development of the community. Once that is accomplished, then it is predictable that increasing needs will be found for media in teaching, as they have been found everywhere else.

THE GROUP AS A MEDIUM

In a stimulating discussion of radio's role in development, McAnany (1973) points out that a great deal of the use of radio for nonformal education is simply open broadcasting, and he describes an apparently successful program of this kind in Zaire:

> The voice of Dr. Massikita carries a message about feeding a new-born child or getting a vaccination for older children or choosing good kinds of vegetables for the family dinner. For 15 minutes a week in five languages he speaks to Zaire's people. He speaks to basic medical and health needs in the person of a country doctor with a down home approach adapted to each cultural group. The program draws hundreds of letters a year from its audience, asking advice, thanking Dr. Massikita, even inviting him for a visit. Most of his listeners do not know that their favorite doctor is only a creation of a group at a small production center in Kinshasa called Radio-Star. Occasionally, when an enthusiastic listener comes into Kinshasa from a village, the station gets a call to see the famous doctor. The request is politely turned aside with the excuse that the "doctor" is out on a trip to the villages [McAnany, 1973: 5].

A UNESCO survey of radio in 110 countries in 1971, as McAnany notes, estimated that about 6,500 hours of educational programs are broadcast each week. This seems large, until one realizes that it is less than 3 percent of the total radio broadcasting time. For every hour of educational broadcasting, forty times as many hours are devoted to popular music, serial drama, and news. Audience studies indicate that the audiences of open-circuit educational broadcasts are typically not large or devoted (for example, see Arana de Swadesh, 1971; Spain, 1971). The problem is (a) to make the program fit strongly felt local needs, (b) to make it possible for the listeners to do something about the advice they get from the program. The audience studies just mentioned found little apparent interest in the development information available on the radio, little overlap between felt needs and program content, and consequently little listening to educational programs as compared to drama, music, and news. Radio-Star's fifteen minutes a week were apparently tapping real audience interest, but as McAnany says, will not make much difference in people's lives unless people know they are able to obtain some rural health service. Nor will the radio soap opera in New Guinea (Halesworth, 1971) persuade people not to migrate to the cities unless people can be shown that there is "something worth staying for in the countryside."

For this reason, one component of successful nonformal education built around instructional media has typically been active local participation, usually in organized groups. The group has become so important in all such programs that it might be considered a medium in its own right. It is a channel for talking things over at the receiving end, for encouragement, for practice and mutual criticism, for active participation in the operation of one's own school, for reinforcing the effort of remote and lonely students, and for assembling social support behind local activity and social change. Without exaggerating too much, we might amend what was said a few pages back about radio being the medium of nonformal education (if there is *a* medium) by saying that the most typical pattern of nonformal education, when it uses media, is *radio plus groups.*

Three kinds of groups have been more prominent than others in nonformal education in developing countries. These are the *deciding* group (of which the best-known example is the radio rural forums of Canada, India, and elsewhere), the *study* group (some of the best-known of which have been connected with Radio Sutatenza in Colombia and the Centro di Telescuola in Italy), and the *participating* or *discussing* group (which has been used widely in French Africa, among other places). We shall look at each of these.

The Deciding Group

The pattern of the radio rural forum was developed and carried on for a number of years in Canada (Nicol et al., 1954). The pattern was adopted and tried briefly in several parts of India and then was applied in a UNESCO-sponsored pilot project in 144 villages near Poona in Maharashtra State in 1956.

In India, the radio rural forum is a group of fifteen or twenty villagers who are willing to come together twice a week to listen to a radio program dealing with agriculture, health, literacy, education, local self-government, or other aspects of economic and social development, talk over what they have heard, and, where appropriate, decide to take community action. The program is from thirty to forty-five minutes long and includes news of interest to a rural audience, a talk by or an interview with an expert in some development field, sometimes a dramatization, sometimes feedback from the listeners in response to earlier programs. There is a convenor (chairman) and a secretary who is supposed to send a report of the meeting back to the district headquarters. Often a member of the community development field staff is present also.

In the pilot project at Poona, the results were studied by Dr. Paul Neurath (1960), who was at that time a visiting staff member of the Tata Institute in Bombay. He was able to compare the forum villages with villages that had no forums, some of which had village radios, some of which did not. He and his staff interviewed every forum member before

TABLE 8.1

Learning Test Results: Forum vs. Nonforum Villages, Literates vs. Illiterates

	Literate members		Illiterate members	
	Forum	Nonforum	Forum	Nonforum
Pretest	7.1	5.3	3.1	2.1
Post-test	12.2	6.5	9.4	3.1

and after the pilot project (which lasted for ten weeks, twenty programs), and also made before-and-after interviews with samples of twenty adults from each of the control villages. During the project, each forum was visited and observed four times.

Neurath's findings, in brief, were that forum members learned a great deal more about the topics under discussion than did adults in the villages without forums; and in those nonforum villages, most of the learning gains were made in the villages with radios. His chief table is reproduced here (see Table 8.1).

It is interesting to note that the illiterate members of the forums actually gained more than the literates, but, of course, started lower.

Neurath calculated, after tabulating reports from the villages, that each forum averaged at least "six decisions for action" during the pilot project. There is no evidence as to how many of these decisions actually were followed through, but pictures and observational evidence indicate that at least a number of them were.

What did all this cost? Schramm et al, (1967) tried to reconstruct the cost figures for the pilot project. Subtracting the cost of the evaluation, they calculated the cost of organizing and maintaining each of the 144 forums for ten weeks at 416.57 rupees ($87.48). That represents about $4.38 per meeting (twice a week). If the forums did indeed take "six decisions for action," then the cost of bringing about each decision was about $14.58. If only two of the decisions actually resulted in action, then the cost per action was $43.75.

That cost-effectiveness ratio looked attractive to the government of India. They could not think of any other way by which they could realistically hope to bring about a community improvement project for that price. The expansion of the forum program began more slowly than expected. The pilot ended in April of 1956; it was the end of 1958 before the social education officers began to move into the expansion project, and November 1959 before the decision was officially taken to expand the forums throughout India. Twenty-five thousand forums to be attained by 1966 were set as a goal (for a description of this period, see Bhatt et al., 1965).

The goal proved impossible to achieve. Most of the momentum from the Poona project had been lost. Indeed, some of the radios and all of the field staff had been withdrawn as soon as the pilot was over. The expansion was less well-financed than the pilot. It had fewer field personnel assigned to it, and they had little of the good morale and enthusiasm of the pilot. For the field staff, the Poona forums were a high-priority item; the later forums, less so. There was less training for the officers, and less attention was paid to making the radio broadcasts fit the needs of a particular agricultural region. Receiver maintenance was not as good, and printed materials tended not to arrive on time. In other words, the pilot project was undertaken with dedication and in the blaze of attention. The expansion was not. The radio rural forum proved to be not a good enough idea to run itself; it still needed adequate support and adequate staff. And the problem of expanding a pilot project nationwide, especially over a nation as diverse as India, was entirely different from making a successful pilot.

The goal of 25,000 was reduced to 15,000. At the end of the set period, 1966, it was reported that over 12,000 forums had been organized, but a number of them were believed to be inactive.

There was no systematic research on the expanded forum project. Some rough estimates were made of costs, and it could be demonstrated that economies of scale operate in this case, as with many other media projects. For example, the estimated cost of organizing a forum when the number of forums had reached 2,000 was less *per year* than it cost to operate one of the Poona forums for ten weeks. But the later cost estimates discount the common belief that the radio rural forum could be introduced for very little additional money. This opinion had come to be held because (a) additional costs to the radio station are indeed small, (b) many of the field costs are hidden in other field budgets, and (c) the necessary field support had been consistently underestimated. Such costs can remain hidden if there are only a few forums, but when one talks about thousands of forums, then either the costs are revealed or the forums are inadequately supported.

Even so, the cost-effectiveness ratio of a rural deciding group supported by a radio broadcast looks favorable. If the true costs of bringing about community development projects are what they were calculated to be in Poona, then it must be asked what alternative procedures would do better. There is very little reason to believe that radio listening without a group would start much community action, or that a field staff—even if one necessarily large and well-trained could be obtained—would do as much without radio and the group. Therefore, the pattern of the radio rural forum, despite its disappointing expansion in India, still looks very promising for developing countries.

And, indeed, the forum method has been and still is in use in a number of countries. After Canada and India, it was introduced into Costa Rica, Togo, Malawi, Ghana, and Dahomey. Rather careful research was done on the results of both the Costa Rica and the Ghana experiences. We shall report briefly on the latter.

The project in Ghana was an attempt to adapt the pattern of group listening to farm radio as developed in Canada and India to the needs of an African country. Canada furnished two advisers, including Dr. Abell (1968) who conducted the field research, and UNESCO gave financial assistance. An area of about 1,250 square miles in Eastern Ghana, where most of the people speak Akan, was chosen for the experiment, and sixty experimental forums were organized in forty villages. For purposes of research, forty other villages were designated as controls. Twenty programs were broadcast, one a week, between December 1964 and April 1965. Only about one out of four programs dealt directly with agriculture; others took up problems of national policy and relationships with the government. On the day of each broadcast, each forum met and exchanged ideas on the topic, then listened to the broadcast and discussed it. A secretary reported back to headquarters the ideas and conclusions of the forum and any action its members decided to take in their communities.

Thus, the procedure was very much like India's, and so was the research design. Villages were selected as nearly as possible at random within strata—small, medium, large population. Twenty villages were assisted to organize one forum each (called a Type A village), twenty others to organize *two* forums each (Type B), twenty villages had no forums but were each supplied with a government-owned village radio, and twenty other villages had neither forums nor village radios, although some of the people in them had private radios. Less attention than in India was paid to tabulating the community development of projects brought into being through the forums, but a large sample of the forum members was interviewed before the first broadcast and after the last one on what they had learned from the broadcasts and what action, if any, they had taken or planned to take.

The results of these before-and-after interviews can be summed up in tabular form (see Table 8.2).

These interviews left little doubt that participants were learning and being encouraged to action by the forum experience. The last two questions are interesting in that they indicate the practical emphasis of the forums. Nonparticipants tended to value nonformal education more in the traditional academic pattern; participants tended to value education aimed at improving village life and opportunities close to home. The other answers, however, show quite clearly that the forums were able to bring

TABLE 8.2
Some Results of Rural Radio Forums in Ghana

| | Percentages by type of village | | | |
| | Type A | Type B | Type C | Type D |
Question	(one forum) N=89	(two forums) N=82	(radio no forum) N=84	(no radio, no forum) N=83
Action taken to increase production?	60	53	42	35
Production cooperatives planned or formed?	17	13	7	2
Action to improve marketing of crops?	25	23	21	9
Marketing through a group or a cooperative?	19	19	18	7
Action to improve harvesting, storing, transporting crops?	27	24	8	13
Joined a cooperative within six months?	16	19	5	6
Able to name cooperative started somewhere within six months?	55	43	35	28
Correct ages for introducing different protein sources to baby's diet?	51	46	41	36
Now saving on a personal basis?	70	60	57	50
Emphasized young people's needs for general education?	11	11	25	39
Emphasized need of practical training?	87	87	72	61

Source: Abell, in UNESCO, 1968: 36-40

about greater changes than the public radio without a listening group, but that a considerable amount of information was being absorbed from the radio by itself.

No economic analyses were reported for the Ghana radio rural forum project.

Jain, in a doctoral dissertation (1969), critically reviewed previous literature on the effect of radio rural forums, and then reported some research of his own in India that was intended to clear up unanswered questions concerning the use of a deciding group. He pointed out, justifiably, that the results of the Neurath study in India, the Coleman-Abell study in Ghana, and others were all subject to possible contamination. This is endemic to field studies built around ongoing and fairly lengthy projects.

Then he himself selected a number of villages in one area of India, trying to match them in size, availability of mass media, and level of development. In each of these villages, he assembled a volunteer group of adult farmers, and assigned them to different experimental conditions: group listening alone, group listening plus discussion, group listening plus group decision, group listening plus discussion plus group decision, and public and private commitment plus either group listening or group listening plus discussion. He had them listen to a twenty-five-minute tape-recorded broadcast on a topic of current rural interest, and then let the discussion go on for forty minutes or so. His measures were after-only, and made use of semantic differential scales to measure attitudes, direct questions to measure beliefs and behavioral intentions, and such tests as raising hands or volunteering one's name to measure commitment.

From this field experiment, he emerged with two clear findings and a number of inconclusive ones. The two clear results, however, are of considerable importance in understanding how the radio rural forum works.

He was able to show, for one thing, that group listening followed by group discussion is more influential in changing attitudes, beliefs, and behavioral intentions toward adopting an innovation than is group listening without discussion. This is shown in Table 8.3.

He then tested the importance of group decision. Comparing group listening with and without group decision, he got only one significant difference in three tests—in favor of group decision. Comparing group discussion plus group decision with group listening plus decision, he found

TABLE 8.3

One-Way Analysis of Variance Results for the Means of Radio Listening and Discussion Groups on the Effect Variables

| | Means of effect variables for the: | | |
Effect Variables	Radio listening group	Radio listening plus group discussion	F Value
Attitude	7.29	9.78	4.35*
Belief	7.76	9.90	4.08*
Behavioral intention	3.00	4.13	4.75*

Source: Jain, 1969: 18
*Significantly different at the 5 percent level.

TABLE 8.4
Influence of Public Commitment on Listening and Discussion Groups

| Effect Variables | Means on effect variables under public commitment condition | | F Value |
	Listening group	Discussion group	
Attitude	7.50	11.56	2.02
Belief	6.00	12.44	8.90*
Behavioral intention	2.08	4.67	6.60*

Source: Jain, 1969: 21
*Significantly different at the .05 level.

all the differences favoring discussion plus decision, but again only one *significant* difference. This was an important one, however: the measure of behavioral intention.

Finally, he tested the effects of different combinations with private and public commitment. He found that combining private commitment with either listening or discussion groups made very little difference. But when public commitment—i.e., an individual in the group openly committing himself to the innovation—it was significantly more effective when preceded by discussion than when it came only after listening. He got two significant differences out of three, as shown in Table 8.4.

The field staffs who have worked with the farm forum in half a dozen countries, and the group dynamics researchers who have been studying group processes in the tradition of Lewin, will be interested but not entirely surprised to have this confirmation from field experimentation in a developing country that the most potent elements in the radio forum are *group discussion* after the broadcast and *public commitment* to action after the discussion.

The Study Group

The study group is so important to nonformal education that it is amazing to find so little hard data on it. What the school as a social unit is to formal education, the study group is to nonformal. It is the device by which nonformal students, near their homes, can be brought together to practice, to reinforce each other, to relate the teaching to their own communities, and to benefit from whatever supervision or guidance can be provided.

Furthermore, such evidence as there is indicates that addition of a study group is exceedingly helpful. Comstock and Maccoby (1966) found that teachers, given informal training by television in the "new math," learned more when they viewed in a group than when they viewed alone, more when the group actively discussed the lesson than when it did not, and still more when the group was supervised and directed. The experience of the Italian Telescuola (Lyle et al., 1967) demonstrated to its directors that the study group was an essential part of the process. In Australia, whenever it was possible to bring together as many as five or six children, in the remote areas, to form a study group and listen to the radio lessons together, this was regarded as a cost that paid its way in effectiveness. These examples were all on the borders between formal and informal education, but the lessons are clearly applicable on the informal side.

The most useful way to examine the combination of radio and the study group may be to look at the experience of the oldest of the continuing nonformal education projects built around this combination: Radio Sutatenza in Colombia.

In 1947, Father Jose Joachim Salcedo, who was then curate at Sutatenza, a small village ninety miles from Bogota, decided to try to use the radio to bring education and inspiration to some of his people. With a homemade radio transmitter and three radio receivers, he started a nonformal radio school in the valley of the Tenza, where 100,000 people lived, 80 percent of them illiterate. He received help from the government—equipment and a method for teaching literacy. He received help from UNESCO—advisers in developing broadcasting skills and a suitable program. He received help from countless volunteers in the villages, from village priests, from outside donors and advisers. He founded an organization called Acción Cultural Popular (ACPO).

From this homemade transmitter and the three receivers has grown Colombia's largest radio network. It now serves upward of 20,000 radio schools and some hundreds of thousands of students. It has probably taught many hundreds of thousands of rural Colombians to read and taken many of them through a program of basic skills and rural education. From its headquarters in Bogota, Radio Sutatenza broadcasts nineteen hours a day, and feeds much of this to three radio stations in other parts of the country, each of which contributes about one-third of its broadcast time locally. Acción Cultural Popular publishes the most widely read weekly newspaper in Colombia, has a full-time staff of 200 in Bogota, in addition to 130 employed in the editorial and publishing office, maintains 200 field workers, and relies upon hundreds of parish representatives, some hundreds of literacy group supervisors, and 20,000 unpaid auxiliaries who work in the radio schools.

One reason why Father Salcedo was able to develop Acción Cultural Popular in this spectacular way is the lack of opportunity for education in the rural parts of Colombia. The rate of illiteracy is about three times in the country what it is in the cities. Few schools are available in the rural regions, and few of those that are available offer a full five-year primary. In 1964, the International Bank estimated that 64 percent of those schools offered only one or two years (to the students who could get in); and that only about 3 percent of rural students who entered the first grade completed the fifth. Education beyond the fifth grade hardly existed in the rural regions.

But Father Salcedo saw the function of Acción Cultural Popular as doing more than filling gaps in the rural educational system. He aimed at providing educational experiences that would let the campesino (the peasant farmer) "develop from below." He wanted to create a "new type of Latin American man" who could throw off the fatalism and paternalism resulting from poverty and from dependence upon higher authority, and substitute a new vision of what a campesino could be and do. Acción Cultural Popular therefore stated as its objectives:

(1) Motivation of campesinos for development

(2) Human promotion: creation of the "whole" man, understood in terms of physical well-being, intellect, spiritual and creative senses, and capacity to fulfill social roles

(3) Integration of the campesinos into society through an effort "to diminish social distances and seek to ensure that all citizens have access to the opportunities and services that society has to offer and participate in them"

(4) Organization and development of the community, especially through participation in local organizations

(5) Productivity: increased production through new agricultural technologies, increased sales of agricultural products, creation of capital through investments, savings, credit, better use of resources, and finally an increased sense of the value of work

(6) Spirituality of development [quoted in Brumberg, 1972; see also Acción Cultural Popular, 1969].

The curriculum covered five main content areas: health, literacy, mathematics, economy and work, and spirituality. This "fundamental integral education" is for a campesino of any age and is directly related to the problems of the improvement of rural life.

This curriculum is for a "radio school," which is neither a building nor a formal organization, but rather a group of persons who have decided to study. The average number is six to ten. They come from the same neighborhood, sometimes the same family. They are usually brought together by an *auxiliar* (auxiliary), a helper who volunteers to organize the radio school. He is not paid for it, and he has little or no special training.

He may have been through it himself, and in any case he ordinarily has a little more education than the students he brings in. He organizes the group, finds a way to obtain use of a radio and a meeting place (usually in a student's home), and then serves as a group leader until and unless other leadership emerges. He usually listens along with the students and learns with them. If a student seems to be withdrawing from the study group, he tries to find out the reason and do something about it if possible. In other words, he does what he can of what needs doing, and the group *shapes itself* and its procedure.

The procedure essentially is to meet together, listen to the lesson broadcast, then talk it over and practice it if that is called for.

The school functions at three levels. There is a *basic* course, primarily for teaching literacy, to adults. This lasts about six months, has thirty-minute daily broadcast lessons, and enrolls about 25 percent of all Acción Cultural Popular's students.

At a slightly higher level is a two-year *progressive* course which is intended for farm families who are literate but have incomplete primary education. This is the main course. It is the level at which the fivefold locally centered curriculum—health, literacy, arithmetic, economy and work, and spirituality—is taught. It has an hour-long broadcast every day, six days a week. And it enrolls 60 percent of all Sutatenza's students.

The progressive course is terminal for most of its students. It is supposed to prepare them for rural life and motivate them to improve their communities and themselves. But it need not be terminal, for ACPO has added a third course, a *complementary* course, lasting three years, and aimed at preparing students to graduate from primary school. Therefore, the content of the complementary course is the systematic curriculum of the primary schools: It must get its students ready for the school-leaving examination. Most of its students are older than those in the progressive course; some are aiming toward further education, some toward jobs that require a school certificate. But the importance of this service as compared to the less formal parts of the Acción Cultural Popular schooling is shown by the fact that only 15 percent of the students are enrolled in it. In other words, most of ACPO teaching is for students who are preparing themselves for a better life in the rural areas, not for further education.

Radio Sutatenza operates a 250Kw station at Bogota, two 120Kw stations in Cali and Barranquilla, and a 10Kw station at Medellin. These are all long-wave, and are interconnected by FM repeater stations. Short-wave transmissions are sent out from Bogota on three frequencies.

The regional stations must carry the school courses that originate in Bogota, but may substitute their own programs for any other network programming. In actuality, the regional stations provide about one-third of their own programs.

What programs are on Radio Sutatenza? About one-third of the long-wave broadcast time, one-half of the short-wave, is used for the structured study—the basic, progressive, and complementary courses. This ordinarily consists of thirty minutes a day for the basic course, one hour for the progressive course, one hour for the complementary, with each of these programs repeated once at different times. A little over one-quarter of the broadcast day is used for unstructured education, which has the same objectives as the progressive course but is not in the form of a course. About 30 percent of the day is given to entertainment, in competition with the commercial radio. About 10 percent is news. When the regional stations substitute for network programming from Bogota, they usually add entertainment material.

The structured programs, of course, present core teaching. They must do so almost necessarily, because the schools do not have trained teachers. The radio teacher therefore deals directly with the students, tries to explain things clearly to them, tries to set the stage for their own study and practice.

So much time is devoted to unstructured educational programs because ACPO recognizes that much of its potential audience will not be in the radio schools, and furthermore, that it has an obligation to the alumni of its schools, who are expected to become the "new type of Latin American man."

The entertainment and news represent recognition by Radio Sutatenza that it must compete for its audience. Many of the educational radio stations in the United States have never recognized this, but successful broadcasters in developing countries invariably have. Thus, despite its spiritual emphasis and its serious purpose, Radio Sutatenza lightened its program offerings. The Telescuola programs typically included a comedy scene. A religious radio station in the Philippines (Spain, 1971) competed with a host of commercial stations by putting on its own daily serial, and by carrying a great deal of local news from the villages and barrios.

Radio is not the only medium of ACPO. The organization publishes about 600,000 textbooks annually for the basic and progressive courses, 70,000 copies each week of a newspaper *El Campesino,* and about 300,000 copies of books for general reading. These are produced in a large and well-equipped printing shop, Editorial Andes, which is owned by ACPO.

The textbooks are in the same five areas: literacy, arithmetic, health, agriculture, and spirituality. By modern standards of textbooks for broadcast teaching, they are old-fashioned; for example, they include relatively little workbook material to help the student study and practice on his own. They are said not to be up-to-date on all the practices of modern agriculture. This has been explained as a result of the inability of ACPO, which is largely self-financing, to afford the cost of a fundamental revision of its texts. It is also noted that the textbooks are fragmented, rather than systematic and continuous presentations of a topic. This has an advantage, as well as a disadvantage, in that it permits a school group or a student to start at any point in the course, although he may receive a less well-organized picture of the subject. The straitened finances of ACPO also make it impossible to provide a set of textbooks for every student. The typical pattern is to have one set per school. These are shared.

The newspaper and the books for general reading, like the unstructured educational material on the radio, are an attempt to serve the rural population outside the courses. *El Campesino* does not depend on current news; that is more likely to be carried by Radio Sutatenza. It is essentially the counterpart of the unstructured educational material on the radio. The copy is carefully rewritten to make it fit the abilities of recent literates and thus to provide another bridge between the courses and real-life use of information. The newspaper publishes monthly supplements of eight pages, which fold into a thirty-two-page booklet, and provides a text for the complementary (third-, fourth-, and fifth-grade) classes.

The newspaper sells for approximately $.02, U.S., per copy; the books, for about $.10, U.S., each.

Data on effectiveness are not very hard. The most impressive data are the numbers themselves. The schools have increased from 300 in 1950 to 14,000 in 1960 to about 20,000 in 1970. (The high point was about 28,000 in 1965.) The number of students exceeded 100,000 in 1960, reached a peak of about 230,000 in 1965, and totalled about 167,000 in 1968 when the last summary was compiled by ACPO. The newspaper has a paid circulation of 70,000 per week. One book alone, *Mother and Child*, sold over 100,000 copies in 1970. The number of nonstudent listeners to Radio Sutatenza is not known, but is variously estimated in the millions. In a country of perhaps nine million rural people, this represents a potential impact of great size and importance.

Acción Cultural Popular provides figures on enrollments and examination results for both the basic literacy and the progressive courses. From 1960 through 1968, an average of between 80,000 and 90,000 illiterates per year were reported to enroll in the basic course. About half of these took the examination during the year. Of those who took it, somewhere near 70 percent passed. The figures for 1968 were 75,000 illiterates enrolled (40,000 males, 35,000 females); 27,500 took the exam; 20,180 passed—over 73 percent.

During the same 1960-1968 period, an average of over 100,000 per year enrolled in the progressive course. Again about half these took the examination, and about three-fourths of those passed. The figures for 1968 were

TABLE 8.5
Reported Importance of ACPO and Other Influences in the
Adoption of Innovations (in percentages)

Influencing Factors	Students of ACPO	Non-student Listeners	Others
ACPO	54.0	25.5	15.0
Other development organizations	9.0	13.5	20.0
Imitation of neighbors, etc.	33.0	53.5	58.7
Other influences cited	4.0	7.5	6.3

SOURCE: Musto, 1969: 175

92,000 enrolled (49,000 males, 43,000 females); 20,000 took the exam; 15,200 passed, or about 76 percent. All these figures are rounded. (Enrollments in ACPO have declined considerably since 1965. Musto [1969] attributed this to the failure of the organization to keep up to date with changing needs of the population and with its materials.)

A number of figures are cited for community improvement projects accomplished by students in the ACPO courses. Musto (1969), in a study rather critical of ACPO, found that radio school students scored higher than nonstudents on attitude scales of modernity, innovativeness, and integration into rural society. He found also that they had higher incomes, which leads a reader to wonder whether the students are not to some extent self-selected from among the more modern, more innovative members of the rural society.

Musto's calculation of the relative influence of ACPO and other factors in the adoption of innovations is presented in Table 8.5.

It is difficult in this as in all other non-experimentally controlled field evaluations to separate out effects and causes, and even to evaluate the quality of effects. But it can hardly be doubted that the ACPO program has had an effect. Musto, one of its severest critics, recognizes that "the institution has undeniably achieved improvements at the level of subsistence economy" (Musto, 1969: 188). A detailed evaluation, with quantitative field studies, is still worth doing. But even without that, conclusions can be drawn from the experience of ACPO and Radio Sutatenza.

One can conclude that government financing and government organization are not the only possible ways to bring education to rural regions. A dedicated private organization can also accomplish remarkable things, and at some states in the development process may have advantages over governmental organization in doing so. When one realizes that this program in Colombia is twenty-five years old and continues at impressive size, one cannot but recall the difficulties of Niger and India and other developing countries with expanding official programs for village people.

In the second place, one can conclude that the study group supported by radio teaching is an effective tool for learning, even with a minimum of trained guidance, without excellent teaching materials, and without the advantage of correspondence study.

Third, the experience of Radio Sutatenza underlines a conclusion that will sound familiar to readers who have read the other evidence in this volume: The principal medium can't do it alone. It must be built into a teaching system. The architects of Acción Cultural Popular built their radio into a learning system that included textbooks, other books, charts, a newspaper, a study group, and field representatives. McAnany (1973: 14-15) presents a table of twenty-one radio school projects in sixteen countries of Latin America, all of them related in some way to ACPO. All of them are built around radio, and all of them combine it with study groups and other media. Thus, rural radio teaching also tends to become multimedia teaching.

The Discussing Group

The pattern of a community activity we have called the "discussing" group grew out of a French tradition of group dynamics, as McAnany notes (1973: 18). It was applied in French Africa in the early 1960s, influenced some projects in Latin America, and must also have had some influence on the Canadian projects entitled "Challenge for Change." The ultimate purpose of the "discussing" group, like that of the rural radio forums, is to bring about community action; and for that purpose the participants, like the students of the radio schools, must learn. But is essentially different from either of the other patterns.

The chief actor in the discussing group is a discussion leader whom the French call an "animateur"—hence the common name of "animation" group. This leader is expected to animate the community's discussion and analysis of its own problems. However, an animator is different from the leader of a radio forum or the convenor of a study group. For one thing, the animator is expected to be an expert in nondirective guidance, inasmuch as it is believed that a local community must define and understand its own problems and arrive at its own solutions for them. The leader, therefore, must encourage problem-solving but not guide it. Ideally, he or she should be identified as closely with the local community as possible, but at the same time refrain from taking leadership. If radio or television, film or tape, is used in the process, it is to help define the problems rather than to propose solutions. Feedback from the community, and perhaps from other communities, is the chief function of media in this process so that the discussing group can understand the situation as clearly and fully as possible. The radio forums also sought feedback, but the discussing groups seek from the media neither proposed solutions (as with the radio rural forums) nor teaching (as with the study groups). See McAnany (1973: 18-19) for a summation of these assumptions.

This is an ideal pattern. In practice, there are many variations. In Brazil, for example, the MEB (basic education movement) after moving from the teaching of literacy to a nondirective social animation approach to understanding the problem of development and taking appropriate local action, found that in the volatile political climate of that country in the early 1960s it was possible to be *too* nondirective, and that more directive groups were taking over the movements toward social change. In numerous countries, the animation movement has had to struggle with the question of how much the central government should participate in the groups, and how much the groups could accomplish locally without the participation of the government. But nevertheless the idea of a local community mobilizing to understand and try to solve its own problems has been a most attractive one.

Let us look at some cases.

The Radio Club Association of Niger is now twelve years old. It was observed in 1966 by Lefranc (1967b, vol. 3: 59-78), by El Hadj Badge and Robert (1972), and by McAnany (1972). None of these observers obtained hard data on effects or made detailed economic analyses.

The bases of the Niger discussion group, as of the ideal pattern we have described, are (a) the "animateur," (b) "feedback" from the community to the broadcasting station and thence to the community again, and (c) discussion.

The animateur is an organizer and group leader, who is trained in a short course, paid an average of about $20.00 a month (in Niger), and is expected to assemble the group, lead the discussion, and take responsibility for the feedback to the station.

The feedback is obtained in a most interesting way. McAnany (1972: 6-7) describes it thus;

> Suggestions for themes of the six months of broadcasts from November to June come from government ministries and from animateurs at their year-end meeting. Themes common to both sources are automatically chosen; otherwise, the suggestions from the villages are given first consideration. Once themes are chosen, the production group works with various experts from the different ministries to create a series of interview questions to be sent the animateur. He

then carries out a kind of opinion poll in his area, interviewing a small sample of farmers and the local extension agent if the topic happens to be on cotton production, or parents and the village health worker if it is vaccination. Most animateurs are asked to send by mail about five interviews to the production center. The following week the production team listens to the interviews from the two language groups in order to compile a 30-45 minute program for each group from the material that has arrived from most of the 28 paid animateurs. About two weeks after the original interview on a Thursday evening, club members can listen to themselves and their neighbors talking about some pressing problem. If the program arouses special interest or strong reaction, the recording of the discussion at the meeting is again collected by the production center from the animateurs and forms the basis of a monthly special program called "Carrefour." In addition, the animateur fills out written reports on each meeting and mails them to Niamey at the end of the month. At the year's end there is a meeting of animateurs and a final program summing up the year's work in the radio clubs is made and broadcast. Besides feedback from the animateurs, club members and other home listeners send in letters which are answered. Thus, for the Radio Clubs program content and feedback are one and the same and the audience is both speaker and listener.

The relationship of feedback to discussion is really the essence of this type of group. It requires a timely and faithful reporting by the animateur, and most skillful editing and handling by the radio staff. Thus, it is clear that central decisions are more important than the ideal pattern would have them be. Lefranc read a number of animateurs' reports in the files and concluded that there was evidence of desirable change of attitudes toward development programs and problems. This is about as far as the available evidence goes on effect.

A 1966 case study of Radio Togo (Kahnert et al., 1967, vol. 2: 209-226) provides parallel information on a somewhat similar program.

At that time, Radio Togo was broadcasting a program called *l'heure rurale* (the rural hour) every Thursday night. More precisely, it was filling an hour with three twenty-minute programs in two native languages and French. Each program included about five minutes of news prepared especially for a rural audience, plus a ten-minute educational talk. Groups were organized by animateurs, as in Niger, and special efforts were made to get reports from these animateurs on which to base the programs that followed.

The aims of the group operation were defined thus:

The role of the listeners' clubs is to propagate government action throughout the country, to invite the views of listeners on their day-to-day problems in every sphere, such as health, agriculture, education, etc., and for this purpose to organize group listening in rural communities; to give those responsible for broadcast programmes a better knowledge of their audience, and to allow listeners under the direction of qualified leaders to express themselves and make know their ideas and suggestions about the program [Kahnert et al., 1967, vol. 2: 215-216].

Thus, although there was less emphasis on direct quotation from listeners, the basic idea in Togo as in Niger was to establish a dialogue between club and government, listeners and broadcasters, under the direction of an animateur. Central authority played a much larger part than in the ideal pattern.

This requires a great deal of the animateur, as well as the station staff. The case study team examined reports in the files in 1966 and concluded that the animateurs were somewhat less than perfectly reliable: Only about one-fourth as many reports were filed as would have been expected from the number of clubs. The study team felt, however, that a number of the reports would have been very useful to the broadcasters, in stating grievances and giving constructive information. A small proportion of the reports told of villages making a real effort to establish measures for cleanliness, public health, community improvement, and so forth. This is about the extent of our evidence of effectiveness.

Senegal has a radio club project, Radio Disso (Mills, 1972) which is described as "a government project in which radio is used to solicit rural feedback about government policies and programs for the rural areas" (McAnany, 1972: 20). And in 1965, Senegal, with the aid of UNESCO, experimented with television for animation groups of women in working-class districts in or near Dakar.

The purpose of the television project was to find out whether television could be used effectively "to impart practical knowledge that is of vital importance for society, and to determine changes in attitude and behaviour as a nation develops and decides for modernity" (Fougeyrollas, 1967: 9). In this project, feedback was less important than in either Niger or Togo; the emphasis here was on discussion. The report of the project said, "The discussions which follow the programmes are of decisive importance. It is during these discussions that the activating and stimulating functions of educational television which take them beyond the actual subjects taught becomes apparent, and brings underlying social problems to the surface."

About 500 women were organized, with the help of social service officials, into ten groups. Over three-quarters of them were illiterate, and half were between sixteen and twenty-five, about the same proportion as in the total population. The clubs received two broadcasts a week, one on hygiene and illness, the other on nutrition.

General reports on the clubs were good. Attendance had fallen off only about 10 percent after nine months. Discussions were lively; at least 85 percent of the women were reported to have spoken at least once (speaking takes a certain amount of courage in a group of fifty). The women themselves gradually took over much of the managing of discussion and the maintaining of order.

There are no economic figures available on this Dakar project. Considering that television was the medium, and that the total group membership was only 500, unit costs must have been quite high. But we have some information on how much was learned, because the Psycho-Sociological Research Centre of the University of Dakar followed the experiment throughout.

This organization conducted sample surveys among the club members in February 1965, before the teleclub project, and again in December 1965 and January 1966, at the end of the experiment. A sample of ninety-nine women was drawn, and two interviews were completed with eighty-nine of them. In addition to collecting demographic information and opinions about the programs and the clubs, a number of questions were asked about the substance of the broadcasts and actions taken as a result of the meetings.

At the time of the first survey, only 41 percent of the women knew malaria was caused by a mosquito bite; 76 percent knew it at the time of the second survey. In the first survey, no one knew that quinine and its derivatives were a treatment for malaria; 71 percent had learned it by the time of the second survey. Real causes for dysentery were known by 44 percent of the sample in the first survey; 78 percent, in the second survey. Thirty percent in the first survey knew that tuberculosis was caused by a bacillus; 59 percent, in the second. In general, the learning about child care, nutrition, and national development was greater than about other topics. The younger women seemed to learn more and to be more willing to change—particularly in food and child-rearing habits—than the older women. (We are talking about women under and over twenty-five.) And the great majority of the women reported that they had talked over the subject matter of many of the programs with their husbands, other members of their families, friends, and neighbors. Therefore, there is considerable reason to believe that the club members did learn and pass along some of their new knowledge.

Reflecting on the surveys and their observations of the experiment, the Centre at the University of Dakar came to six conclusions:

(1) Education through mass media is more effective if it is addressed to a homogeneous audience and meets specific needs.

(2) Educational television ... heightens the awareness of the new exigencies in periods of transition. Properly used and planned, it can be a potent factor in national development.

(3) Discussion groups are necessary in conjunction with mass media education in order to render the information imparted socially dynamic.

(4) Adults will learn if the subject really interests or concerns them.

(5) The educational use of the mass media can accelerate, extend, and provide a control over the modernization of man.

(6) Adult education through mass media must always keep the background in mind and adapt its teaching method to the needs of development in any specific sociopsychological situation [Fougey-rollas, 1967: 33-34].

Thus, from the ideal pattern, to Niger and Togo, to the teleclubs of Senegal, we have moved steadily farther from the hope that a community will analyze its own problems and find its own solutions. The Senegal groups were considering government development programs, and the main purpose was to "impart practical knowledge." Closer to the original ideal was Canada's "Challenge for Change" program, which we have already mentioned, and which grew out of the extraordinarily active and socially conscious Canadian Film Board and, perhaps for that reason, was built around film and videotape.

Unlike the African projects we have described, which used radio or television to impart information about government policies and programs and to gather and summarize community reactions to policies and needs, the Canadian projects made little use of broadcast media and concentrated on helping communities comprehend and address their own problems. This was done in a number of places in Northern Canada by sending in film or videotaping equipment, with or without trained operators, to record village people talking about their problems and what they might do to solve them.

One of the best known of these Canadian projects was at Fogo Island, which is forty miles north of Gander, off the coast of Newfoundland. Fogo Island had been a prosperous fishing village but had fallen on hard times. About 60 percent of its residents were receiving government welfare, and the young people were told that "there is no future for you on Fogo Island." Community leaders believed that the entire community was going to be resettled, and were prepared to resist. Through the mediation of the Memorial University Extension Service (which has told the story in a publication entitled "Fogo Process in Communication," n.d.) the National Film Board of Canada became interested and sent one of its most distinguished producers to Fogo Island in 1967. He shot twenty-eight reels of film—not to make a film for public projection but rather to reflect an island as it saw itself. The publication just mentioned described the process:

> Moving away from traditional methods of focusing on issues, the technique instead became centered around personalities whose views reflected a community feeling. Film makers remained painstakingly neutral, suggesting at most general themes. Since Fogo, though not at the first experiment, the Extension Service has ensured that always and unconditionally, the person or persons filmed had final editing power. A film was never shown to another person without the consent of the film personality. With individual approval, these films were screened at convenient times for other members of the community who in turn decide whether or not a particular film or group of films are properly representative of their attitudes before being shown outside. The community also decides whether the total number of films reflect the community as it saw itself.

> The screening sessions were deemed to be of the utmost importance. The films per se were worthless, the reactions to the screening of them an integral part of the project if the process was to achieve its true intent as dialogue. It was through viewing each other and themselves that an awareness of problems emerged, that lack of organization was realized, that mistakes were recognized and that the Fogo Island community saw itself more objectively than ever before. Constructive discussion followed mass screenings and from these discussions came action. The people of Fogo Island seemed to have grasped a better understanding of themselves and their neighbors and individual communities were able to realize their common problems crystallized through film. Something of an Island community began to emerge.

> Distribution also became an essential aspect of the process, the responsibility for which lay with the community development worker. Expedient, sensitive and perceptive distribution was required if those individuals with the resources and potential for solution of a particular problem were to be exposed. On Fogo Island this meant that opposing factions of the community were given an opportunity to appreciate the other's views without direct hostility or confrontation. It meant that group meetings allowed attendants to assess their own worth and accomplishment. Each of the Island's ten communities was able to see a sufficient number of films of other communities to gather an awareness of their common problems, their aims and their basic similarities. It means that the communities viewed themselves in balance with positive aspects visible so that a renewed affirmation of their own worth and value was possible. At the core of the process was this aim: "To develop

insight into community problems, promote greater understanding and strengthen community education and government communication."

Incidentally, the films helped the government to understand the needs and ambitions of the people of Fogo island. The result was impressive.

"For an island which was all set to be destroyed under the centralization program Fogo is very much alive and kicking," said the regional newspaper. There is no more talk of resettling the island people. The economy now seems viable. A vigorous producers' cooperative has established a shipbuilding operation and upgraded the fishing industry on the island. Relief has been reduced nearly two-thirds. A new high school has been built. Morale is quite different than it was, and young people are no longer being told there is no future for them on Fogo.

Similar success stories from local use of media and resulting community discussion have come not only from other parts of Canada, but also in Alaska (National Film Board, 1973: see esp. Kennedy); Peru (Garace et al., 1972), and Tanzania (Schulz, 1974). The Tanzania project took place in three of the well-known Ujamaa villages, where spontaneous activity was under way to combat poverty and bring about desirable social change. The original purpose was to make a historical record of this movement, and in particular to picture a very successful village so as to stimulate other villages to emulate it. What actually happened, however, was that the resulting films and videotapes provided a catalyst for change in the villages that were pictured as well as others. Schulz (1974: 14-18) reports:

> People were stimulated to talk about their problems [and this] brought about a greater awareness of the existing problems and issues. . . . Passive attitudes changed into active ones: people who had passively supported an incompetent agricultural extension officer stood up against him and requested his transfer from the government: they did not listen anymore to empty promises from outside leaders but asked concrete questions as to the possibilities of implementation; they started saying "We must not wait for government help but start work ourselves."

Even if the whole truth should prove that the project was not quite that hysterically successful, still there is enough in the record to suggest that local media, where available, may bring a community closer to the ideal of the animation group than larger-scale media like radio and television.

SOME NOTES ON DEVELOPMENT CAMPAIGNS

Most development campaigns are a combination of information and persuasion. On the informing side, they are essentially nonformal education, and it may be useful to record some of the principles learned in studies of such campaigns about the choice of instructional media.

In brief:

(1) *All media are campaign media. A well-planned campaign will use whatever media it can command that will reach the audience it wants to reach. The important variable seems to be not so much the characteristics of the media as where they go and who uses them. Thus, every kind of media from the most complex and expensive (e.g., television) to the simplest and least expensive (e.g., traditional media such as puppet shows, dances, and ballads) has been used effectively to teach about development.* It is possible to illustrate these conclusions from any field of development, but it will be convenient to do so drawing mainly on population informa-tion campaigns, of which two recent reviews are available (Schramm, 1971; Ross et al., 1972). For use of the different media see the two reviews just mentioned and also Wilder (1968, 1969) and Johnson et al. (1973).

(2) *Radio, because of its wide coverage, relatively low unit costs, and ability to reach beyond literates and beyond power mains, has proved to be the pre-eminent medium for development campaigns.* To give a few examples only, in a survey of housewives in Kaohsiung, Taiwan, 35 percent of the women interviewed said they had learned about family planning from the radio; the next most used medium was newspapers—17 percent (Cernada and Lu, 1972: 201). After three radio spots per day were broadcast in the Hyderabad District of Pakistan, more than half the women who went to clinics credited the broadcasts for the action they had taken (Karlin and Ali, 1971).

(3) *A combination of media is likely to accomplish more than any medium by itself.* Thus, Freedman and Takeshita (1969: 126) found that neighborhoods informed by all available media had significantly higher acceptance rates than neighborhoods where fewer means of communica-tion were used. Gillespie (1971: 8) compared a radio-only campaign in Iran with a campaign that combined radio with other means of informa-tion. Both were effective, but the radio campaign raised the number of acceptors by about 35 percent, the combined campaign by about 55.

(4) *However, interpersonal communication, whether from change agent to potential adaptor, from friend to friend, or within a group, is the indispensable element of development communication, regardless of the mass media used.* For example, knowledge of the first public family planning clinic in Bangkok spread by word of mouth all over Thailand before any public information campaign was conducted (Fawcett et al., 1967: 9-10). In Lulliani, Pakistan, 76 percent of all acceptors during the first thirty months of a multichannel campaign came from outside the

campaign area, and more than half of the women from outside Lulliani said they had heard of the campaign from friends, relatives, or neighbors (Cobb and Raulet, 1965: 13-14). A study of new acceptors in Hong Kong found that half of them had received their information from field workers (Lam, 1967: 82). Group meetings have proved especially useful in providing social support (Park, 1968; Lu, 1967; Kincaid et al., 1975).

(5) *Therefore, a combination of media and interpersonal communication is likely to be more effective than either alone; and information in any medium is likely to be passed along by interpersonal channels.* Thus the typical development campaign counts on interpersonal channels to extend the media, and usually formalizes the interpersonal component in the form of field workers, organized groups, or community meetings (for examples of this, in Jamaica, see Stycos and Back, 1964: 79; in India, Balakrishnan and Matthai, 1967: 7, and many others).

(6) *Regardless of the pattern of media and interpersonal communication, if a campaign aims at achieving social change, the social situation must be favorable for the desired kind of change. In some cases, it may be necessary to bring about changes in the social structure before a campaign can do what is expected of it.* Thus, the Peoples Republic of China felt that it must fundamentally change the social structure before its program of group, cadre, and media communication could do what was expected of it (Chu, 1977; Schramm, Chu, Yu, 1976). Where less than complete change is required, nevertheless it is still often necessary to provide the conditions of change before a campaign can be successful (e.g., to provide clinics before advocating population measures; fertilizer, cooperatives, markets, before change in agricultural practices can be brought about, etc).

SOME CONCLUSIONS

It is evident that the media of instruction can be helpful in most types of nonformal education, but that they are not always essential. For example, they clearly are not essential in the process of localizing the school, as in Tanzania or Chad. Even without the use of media, the news of a family planning clinic in Bangkok spread all over Thailand. On the other hand, even the most localized school will benefit from audiovisual aids, from texts, and from radio where it is available. No matter how effectively the information about a development campaign can be spread by word of mouth, it will be spread more effectively with the aid of media. And it is hard to imagine a nonformal education program like Acción Cultural Popular accomplishing what it did in Colombia without a base in instructional media, nor of a rural forum or rural discussion group operating as effectively without media, except by vastly increasing the size and expertise of field staffs.

It is tempting to say that radio is the instructional medium of non-formal education. Its relatively low cost, its availability even where rural people are not able to read and where power lines do not yet reach, certainly commend it for that purpose. And yet the statement is not strictly true, for several reasons.

For one thing, radio has no monopoly on the field. It might be more accurate to say that Little Media are the media of nonformal education. And yet that also is not strictly true, for all media have proved useful, even Big Media like television in the women's discussion group in Senegal or the rural forums around Delhi. Radio has numerous things in its favor—for example, the fact that it probably can reach the widest audience in rural regions and especially in developing countries, and can do so at the lowest unit cost. It can provide the most cost-effective compromise between attention to local needs and the sharing of expert teaching and supporting information over large areas. But the most desirable medium is one that is most readily available and fits a given need in a given place at a given time.

And if we seek still further for an accurate statement, we have to say that a combination of media can be more effective than any one medium in nonformal use. Thus, development campaigns use every channel that is available to them. Acción Cultural Popular in the highlands of Colombia does not depend solely on radio, but also circulates texts, a weekly newspaper, and outside reading books. And in the interests of still greater accuracy, we must point out that interpersonal communication is perhaps the one indispensable channel of nonformal education. Whether in the form of information passed from friend to friend, or from a change agent or tutor to a prospective adaptor or a student, or communication in a group, it is a part of every program of nonformal education, and on occasion has been known to carry on the program entirely without the aid of mass media. If we were seeking the most characteristic media combination of nonformal education, we should perhaps name the *combination* of radio and an organized group—whether for decision, for study, or for discussion.

Another way to say this, and perhaps the best way, is that nonformal education, like all other types of education, tends to evolve into a *system* of instructional media and channels, using whatever will best meet the needs within the limits of availability and cost.

CHAPTER 9

SOME CONCLUSIONS

We have already developed and tested many of the ingredients of what will be a new era in education. But the pieces of the educational revolution are lying around unassembled.

> John Gardner,
> President of Common Cause;
> formerly U.S. Secretary of Health,
> Education, Welfare (Conversation quoted in Report of
> U.S. Commission on Instructional
> Technology, 1970: 40)

L et us look back over the road we have come.

We began in Chapter 1 by posing some problems and setting the stage for trying to solve them. In Chapter 2, we reviewed representative samples of many hundreds of laboratory-type experiments on learning from different media. These experiments showed an impressive amount of learning, but the better the design and control the more likely they were to show no significant or consistent differences when learning from media was compared with something else, such as learning from face-to-face teaching or from other media. Thus, although these experiments were intended to build theory, they contributed little to the theory of selecting one medium over another.

Then in Chapter 3 we turned to pedagogical theory. Here we found important taxonomy-making and analysis of learning goals and learning behavior, but no taxonomies of learning that interlock very obviously with media use. The contribution of this kind of theory, in its present state, is to the art and science of instruction in general, to the content of media rather than their selection. Despite the brilliance of the analysis, the matching of media to instruction nevertheless rests mostly on practical, commonsense questions at a fairly superficial level of analysis: What kind of stimulus is needed at a given point in the instructional sequence? Is a picture needed? Motion? Sound? Interactive practice? What? And selection of media, even on this basis, is going to be limited by what is readily available to the teacher or the school system, and by the amount of darting from medium to medium that is possible. Consequently, even if "ideal" media were to be identified for different learning tasks, it would probably be infeasible to use them all, and necessary rather to meet only *some* needs for media, or to meet a broad spectrum of needs with a medium that is less than ideal for most of them.

In Chapter 4, we turned to economic questions and found wide variation in cost among media—as much as two orders of magnitude in production cost and unit cost, still more than that in capital investment. Of course, these variations are controlled to some extent by economies of scale and decisions on level of quality. Thus, Big Media might on the average cost five times as much as Little, but wide-scale use (for example, using instructional television to serve several hundreds of thousands of students) would bring unit costs down to levels comparable to those of Little Media for small audiences. Similarly, if a school system is willing to relax qualitative demands (for example, if it is willing to eliminate most production expense by merely photographing a teacher lecturing in a classroom as Ramkhanghaeng University in Bangkok and some American universities have experimented with doing), it is possible to use Big Media at acceptable unit costs for as few as 300 to 500 students. But studies of cost-effectiveness of media use are few and thin, and the economics chapter therefore gives us general guidance, but less help than we should like in deciding how much learning can be bought for a given investment, using different media for different purposes.

Finally, we examined in Chapters 5 through 8 a series of field studies of actual projects where different media had played key parts—in national educational reform, in supplementing classroom teaching, in extending learning opportunities beyond the classroom and the campus, and in nonformal education. Here we did, indeed, find types of projects in which particular media or combinations of media had proved especially effective in practice, although the research on these, too, was less than we might have wished.

We had hoped that eight chapter of this kind might provide more specific guidelines than have been found. Obviously not everything has been tested, and what has been tested has not always been tested well enough. Hard evidence from the field is in short supply. Cost-effectiveness studies are few. Studies of the least complex and least expensive media hardly exist; the lion's share of research funds has gone to the larger and more glamorous media. Most pedagogical theory is specific to the task rather than to the media. In some respects, the first eight chapters of this book tell us less about what *has* been learned than about what *needs* to be learned. Yet there is a great deal of evidence at hand, and our task now is to draw such conclusions from it as we can.

THE PROCESS OF SELECTION

How do educators and planners, schools and governments, go about choosing media of instruction?

For one thing, the decision is necessarily *local,* whether it is made in the classroom or the Ministry of Education. There is no cookbook of recipes for media selection that can be applied automatically in every educational system. It is necessary to carefully consider local needs, situations, and resources, and then interpret such guidelines as exist.

At least that is the logical way to do it. Unfortunately there is reason to believe that the choice is not always completely professional or scientific. It depends sometimes, as we have said, on what is most easily available, or on the media system for which a donor wants to give money.

It depends sometimes on noneducational reasons such as political incentives, prestige considerations, or the attraction of providing mass entertainment, for introducing a mass medium that may become available part-time for educational use. To cite one example, it is clear that none of the four spectacular uses of television for national educational reform described in Chapter 5 could have come about if a donor country or agency had not been willing to pay most of the cost.

The situation just referred to applies to very large projects, involving entire nations or territories. There is, of course, a great difference in the complexity and weight of such a decision when a planner or a minister makes it for a nation-state and when a teacher makes it in the classroom. Yet the elements in the decision are the same: Deciding to spend the entire media budget of a classroom on making a set of slides is comparable to a nation deciding to spend some hundreds of thousands of dollars on television or films. In the classroom, the considerations are close at hand; in the larger situation, they are wider. For example if trained teachers are in short supply in a developing nation, the time and cost of training them must be weighed against the possibility of substituting another medium requiring less well-trained teachers; or perhaps the money would be better invested in teacher training than in any media whatsoever. Suppose that little technical infrastructure exists in the country; then the effort of supplying power and providing maintenance for the more sophisticated media must be considered against the use of smaller, less-sophisticated media, and the probable effectiveness of the alternative media choices must be estimated. On the other hand, the cost of introducing the larger media must be considered along with the possible advantage of using the necessary technical infrastructure (power lines, roads, technical training, and so forth) also to speed industrial development. In comparison to that order of decision, the choice facing a teacher who can spend $50.00 for media and must decide whether to subscribe to a magazine, rent a film, make a set of slides, purchase maps or charts, or some combination of these, is, to say the least, less fraught with responsibility.

It would be reassuring to think that such a decision is always made carefully and logically, and even though we know that is not the case it may be useful to consider what such a process might be.

One can think of such a decision as a resultant of three decision vectors, a Task Vector, a Media Vector, and a Cost Vector. That is to say, at whatever level the decision is made it is necessary to specify the task to be done, and to estimate the probable effectiveness of different media for doing them and the probable cost of using those different media for the objectives named. Thus the decision requires information from three different sources—pedagogy, economics, and media research and experience. But this may make it seem simpler than it is.

The Task Vector, which has its roots in pedagogy, really requires a threefold analysis: the relative needs and probable benefits of the educational tasks to be accomplished, and the psychological steps needed to accomplish them; the needs and abilities of the pupils who are to learn; and finally a set of priorities for action, including a tentative decision on scale, quality, and amount of desirable local control. Thus, graphically:

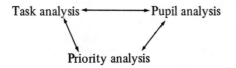

Task analysis ⟷ Pupil analysis

Priority analysis

At one level, this may result simply in a teacher deciding that his or her pupils need more than anything else in a given study unit to learn how an internal combustion engine works and at their stage of development are better able to learn this from pictures than from a verbal description. At the national level, a nation may decide that top priority should go to training more technicians, but to accomplish this will require first an emphasis on preliminary technical training. In either case, there will be a certain amount of interaction among the several analyses: The list of tasks may have to be revised in terms of what the pupils already know, the pupils analyzed in terms of what tasks they need to accomplish, and the priorities juggled in light of the way the task fits the pupils.

The Media Vector also is an interactive process, which might be graphically described this way:

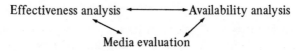

Effectiveness analysis ⟷ Availability analysis

Media evaluation

Effectiveness is estimated from experience, from reports of research and of field projects. Suppose, however, that the teacher who wants help in teaching how an internal combustion engine works and decides that a slow-motion film would be most effective, has no film projector or is unable to rent or borrow a suitable film when needed. Obviously, then, the choice of most effective *available* media will not include a slow-motion film. Perhaps a chart or a filmstrip will do the job. Suppose a nation decides its top priority is to upgrade and expand its middle school and feels the best way to do it would be the way El Salvador did, with the aid of television. If it does not have television and sees no chance to have it, the first choice would not be possible.

For a nation or large system, most media will be available or can be acquired. Therefore it is necessary to consider some of the requirements of using different media. Table 9.1 contains some of the requirements of three Big versus three Little Media. Obviously the difficulty of meeting such needs will enter into the calculation of "availability."

TABLE 9.1
What Will the Media System Require?

	ITV	CAI	Radio	Films*	PI	Simple Visuals
Widespread electrical mains	Yes	Yes	No	Yes	No	Probably No
Sophisticated machinery	Yes	Yes	Not very	Not very	No	No
Difficult maintenance	Yes	Yes	Less so	Not very	No	No
Highly trained operators	Yes	Yes	Less so	No	No	No

* If purchased or rented, rather than locally made.

The Cost Vector must take into consideration both resources and costs, in each case in terms of money, technology, and manpower. Looking at these cost-resource data and at the priority lists prepared for tasks and media, some educator or planner must cost out a series of alternate packages corresponding to higher priorities in the other lists. Thus:

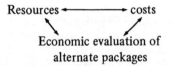

Resources ←——→ costs

Economic evaluation of
alternate packages

Each of these three major activities, if done separately, ought to result in a list of priorities—for tasks that need doing, for media to do them, for alternate media packages in terms of economic desirability, thus:

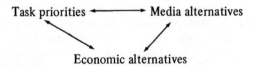

Task priorities ←——→ Media alternatives

Economic alternatives

In practice, however, all this is likely to go on together. Media analysis will take its cue from the task analysis, and cost analysis from the media analysis. But cost data may change the thinking about media priorities, and nonfeasibility of given media may revise task priorities. The overall product would in theory be a kind of Need-Cost-Effectiveness estimate that would enable the teacher or planner to conclude that for a given priority task a certain available medium is likely to be the "best buy" in terms of cost and effectiveness.

We were careful to say, "in theory." All of us know that such a careful analysis is not often likely to occur. A teacher draws a picture of cylinder positions on the chalkboard rather than look around for a slow-motion film. A country or large school system decides to employ television because donor money is available, or because two daytime hours can be used free of charge.

Yet it would be salutary if more such analyses were made. And in that perhaps vain hope let us remind ourselves of some conclusions that emerge from the preceding chapters.

Tasks and Media

Perhaps the central conclusion about media effectiveness to be drawn from the preceding pages of this book is the extremely broad band relation of media to learning tasks.

Students learn from *any* medium, in school or out, whether they intend to or not, whether it is intended or not that they should learn (as millions of parents will testify), providing that the content of the medium leads them to pay attention to it. Many teachers argue that learning from media is not the problem; it is hard to prevent a student *from* learning from media, and the real problem is to get him to learn what he is *intended* to learn. This is why the series of experiments on emphasis, contrast, repetition, subjective camera angle, attention-directing arrows, and the like have been so interesting: they represent ways to get the viewer to look at what he should be learning. But most impressive are the long list of experiments in Chapter 2 that show comparable subject matter being learned effectively from different media, and the studies in Chapter 5 through 8 that show different media, contributing effectively to much the same kind of education in different places. Television works in a mountain village of Japan or a county in Maryland. Films work anywhere they can be shown. Radio works in a technical school in Germany or the high country of Thailand. Programmed instruction has proved effective in the laboratory schools of the United States, and the veldt and forests of south central Africa. Therefore, a teacher can feel a great deal of confidence that motivated students will learn from any medium if it is competently used and adapted to their needs. The existing evidence contributes to our confidence more in the media of instruction than in our ability to discriminate among them.

Furthermore, we find the media able to carry out a wide variety of instructional tasks. It is mildly surprising to hear Gagne saying that "most instructional tasks can be performed by most.media" (1965: 364), but both research and field experience back him up. Television can teach the English language adequately in Samoa, radio can teach it in Thailand, in each case carrying the bulk of the instruction comprising many different teaching and learning acts. Students have learned foreign languages from broadcasts, computers, programmed texts, audiotapes, records, books, and cards. They have learned mathematics from at least as many different media. For any given task in any given situation, one medium is likely to perform better than others. However, the rather more important conclusion is that most media of instruction have a wider spectrum of usefulness than is sometimes appreciated. If the medium that seems ideal for a specific purpose is not available, an alternate medium is likely to do almost as well. Since no system, no classroom teacher is likely to be able to leap back and forth during any class period from "ideal" medium to "ideal" medium, it becomes therefore important to consider how second- and third-"best" media choices can be most effectively used to program a combination of tasks.

In any case, choosing media usually means choosing combinations of media. We remarked earlier in the book that most teaching is multimedia, and has been so since stone-age man used bow and axe as media of demonstration and practice. In Chapter 7, we described how the University of Delhi began with something approximating a single-medium system to relieve the demands upon it for entrance into its undergraduate program, but soon moved to a system that included correspondence study, texts, radio, class meetings, and finally a bit of television. In Chapter 8, we described Acción Cultural Popular, a private agency that teaches several hundred thousand campesinos in Colombia with a program built around radio, but also using textbooks, correspondence, a newspaper, study groups, and group leaders. As a matter of fact, most of the projects throughout the world that are designed to extend the school quickly become multimedia projects. The British Open University is one of the best examples of this. Some of its sponsors originally called it the "University of the Air," but it might more appropriately be called the "University of the Post Office" because it spends the bulk of its funds on correspondence study and texts, and, in addition to radio, television, and text, it uses study kits, study groups, tutorial consultation, and summer classrooms. One of the reasons for the unreality of some classroom experiments is that they have tried to study a single medium within classes where the instruction is clearly multimedia and no medium is ever used in isolation. This has a significant implication for the choice of media because it suggests that in practice one must learn to *combine* media as well as to choose media for more than one task, rather than to think simplistically of a single medium for a single task.

Thus, the task of selecting media is neither easy nor sharply defined, and we are perhaps unrealistic, at the present stage of the science, to think in the *micro* terms of choosing the right medium for each act of learning that we identify. Yet from the field studies described in Chapters 5 through 8 certain *macro* patterns emerge in which one medium of instruction has shown a special ability to contribute to a large educational task. Among these are:

(a) National Educational Reform (Chapter 5). This is the kind of project in which the Republic of Niger, American Samoa, El Salvador, and the Ivory Coast have each tried to make major changes in their educational systems, either expanding or upgrading the instruction or both, and to make the changes, with the aid of a massive use of media, much more quickly than they could otherwise hope to do. The Republic of Korea is now undertaking the same kind of task with a sophisticated program built on a multimedia concept, but the four countries we mentioned first above built their programs around television. In each case, television demonstrated its ability to catalyze change in a change-resistant system, and to enforce a schedule on that change. We have remarked that none of the four could have used television for that purpose unless a donor country or agency had been willing to pay much of the cost; nevertheless, they did find donors, and the results have been as described. No one has tried radio for the same purpose, and the Korean multimedia project is not yet far enough along to evaluate. But the supervisors of the four television projects feel they could not have accomplished what they did without ITV.

(b) For Supplementing Classroom Teaching (Chapter 6). This is the most common use of media, and the evidence we have presented seems to indicate that any medium can be useful for the purpose if well used and if wanted by the classroom teacher. However, films and the smaller audio-visual, visual, and audio media seem especially fitted for the task because they are subject to local control. They can be scheduled, started, stopped, repeated, when the classroom teacher or the student thinks they should be. This is not the case with television or radio, which are not under classroom control unless recorded.

(c) For Extending the School (Chapter 7). Either radio or television plus correspondence study are the favorite media for distant teaching. These projects, however, even if they begin with one basic medium, or two basic media, almost inevitably become *multimedia,* and the teachers use as many instructional devices as possible.

(d) For Nonformal Education (Chapter 8). Radio plus study or discussion groups have proved the favorite combination for this task. However, television is sometimes used in place of radio, and print is usually added to the combination where possible. Radio is the favorite distant teaching medium because its costs are lower, and many of the projects studied have been in developing countries. The group is obviously useful because it provides the social reinforcement so important to students remote from

schools. It should be noted, however, that many nonformal education projects make no use of media whatsoever, and depend only on interpersonal communication and local organization.

One more respect in which tasks and media relate is the interaction between the needs for local control and for large-scale operation. For tasks in which it is necessary to deliver instruction over a large area and for many students, the broadcast media, with or without print or an organized group of users, are the media chiefly called for. They can deliver the same content simultaneously to very large audiences at favorable unit costs. Just the opposite are the tasks which require control of the media to rest within the local classroom. The best example of these is the task of bringing special teaching or learning experiences to supplement the local teacher. Radio and television are not especially well geared to be scheduled locally, stopped for questioning or discussion, or repeated when the local teacher sees the need. Furthermore, they are much more likely to threaten the classroom teacher, either with replacement or with being outshown before his or her own pupils by the radio or television teacher. Consequently, the broadcast media are much more likely to arouse teacher resistance.

A rule of practice is that, if a given educational task requires instruction on a wide scale, one looks first at the broadcast media; if it requires local control, one looks first at films and the smaller audiovisual media. But these are better talked about in connection with the economics of the media.

Costs and Media

One of the managerial advantages of books as instructional media is that they can be delivered in a single package and for a single payment. Behind the scenes is a great deal of sophisticated typesetting, printing, and bookmaking machinery, and large editorial and merchandising staffs, but they are not usually the responsibility of the school system. On the other hand, the electronic and photographic media require reception equipment in the classroom—projectors, receivers, sound players, phonographs, and so forth—and also, for the recorded media, a supply of content materials differing with the media used. These may be films, filmstrips, slides, tapes, transparencies, discs, or other such articles. Additionally, if these materials are made locally, they will require production equipment, ranging in expense from a 35mm camera for slides to a complex of television or film studios for those media. Radio or television will also require transmitting facilities.

Any of these media of instruction will therefore require production, distribution, and reception facilities and expense. The difference in using printed texts is that no special equipment is required for the classroom. The difference between the broadcast media and the recorded media is that the broadcast content is delivered to the classroom, and the teacher need only turn on the receiver (see Table 9.2).

Whatever the medium, all three columns in the table necessarily enter into the costs. There is a notable difference between the total costs of a Big Medium like sound films and television, and of a Little Medium like filmstrips or radio. But both total costs and unit costs are affected by decisions on quality, and unit costs are very strongly affected in the broadcast media by decisions on scale of operation. These are educational

TABLE 9.2

	Production	Distribution	Reception

Books	Educators
	Writers
	Editors
	Printers
	
	plus
	
	Printing
	  machinery
		Merchandising
		  staff
		
		plus
		
		shipping
			Books
			(no machinery,
			no maintenance)

Radio and Television	Educators Writers Producers Technicians plus Studios Cameras Recorders etc.	Technicians plus Transmitting Facilities	Receivers (plus maintenance)

Recorded
Audio-visual
	Educators
	Writers
	Producers
	Technicians
	etc.
	
	plus
	
	Studios
	Cameras
	Editing
	  equipment,
	etc.
		Merchandising and
		  distributing staff
		  (if no local)
		
		plus
		
		Duplication
		
		plus
		
		Shipping
			Playback
			  equipment
			
			plus
			
			Recorded materials
			
			(plus maintenance)

decisions, but they affect economic decisions, and the interaction of these two will affect, and sometimes cause a reconsideration of, decisions on choice of media.

In Chapter 4, we mentioned one national system that reported it could produce instructional television for less than $500 per student hour. A very common figure is between $1,000 and $2,000 per student hour. But the British Open University, insisting on BBC quality standards, pays $20,000 per student hour; and *Sesame Street,* competing with commercial TV production for viewers out of school, cost $42,000 per hour. Similarly, an instructional film can be home-made for a few thousand dollars; professionally, for as much as $100,000. A filmstrip or set of slides can be made locally for less than $100; professionally, for $5,000, more or less.

The decision on quality interacts with the decision on scale. For example, if one is going to use television or film for a few key purposes in a curriculum, requiring a comparatively few programs or films, one can afford to insist on high quality. Similarly if one is going to compete in the open market for listeners, as *Sesame Street* did, he can hardly afford *not* to insist on high quality. On the other hand, if one simply wants to share teaching, classroom to classroom, over an entire course (as Hagerstown did), there is less reason to insist on expensive production.

It is production and distribution costs in the broadcast media that are most responsive to economies of scale. The cost of making and broadcasting programs can be shared equally over very large areas, and consequently the unit costs are greatly reduced by serving large audiences. The production costs of films and other recorded media can also be shared, but the effect of these is largely absorbed by the costs of duplicating and distributing audiovisual and audio materials. They are expensive to reproduce, awkward to distribute in large numbers. Looking back at Chapter 4, it will be seen that American Samoa, limited by its own geography and population to serving only 8,000 public school students, had to budget about $1.00 an hour for doing so; whereas El Salvador could serve about 40,000 for only $.14 an hour; and economists estimated that if El Salvador could expand its services to about 1 million students, as it hoped to do, the cost would be only a few cents per student per hour. On the other hand, the General Learning Corporation study estimates very little difference in unit costs between the expense of providing instructional films for a few thousand and for a million students. The costs of duplicating and distributing the films largely offsets the economies of scale in production.

In other words, if one opts for high quality and wants to distribute a large quantity of audiovisual material to a large audience (as, for instance, the British Open University does with one program per week per basic course), the economic realities suggest the use of television or radio; if one wants only to distribute a small amount, meeting special needs of students at special times, then film or another of the recorded media seems better adapted economically to the purpose. Budgetary resources will to an extent limit the decision on both quality and scale. However, there is one situation in which both education and economics might agree on being satisfied with less than professional production and small-scale distribution. That is in the making of a set of slides, filmstrips, transparencies, or tapes *locally* for the special local needs of a class or a school. In such a case, the fit of material to needs and the motivation of local involvement would seem to be more important than professional production.

LEARNING AND MEDIA

A common report among experimenters is that they find more variance *within* than *between* media—meaning that learning seems to be affected more by what is delivered than by the delivery system. How a medium is used may therefore be more important than the choice of media, if the scale of use or the need of pictorial or auditory material does not dictate the need of one certain family of media rather than another.

Studies of instruction, such as we have represented in Chapter 3, and studies of media along the lines presented in other chapters may well converge on trying to understand better the effective use of a particular medium or symbol system. At present, the educational theorists who have analyzed instruction in such detail can give us no more detailed guidance on choice of media than to ask what kinds of stimuli different acts of learning require: Pictures? Motion pictures? Pictures with sound? Print? And so forth. At the moment, therefore, we are caught up between a micro theory of instruction which is specific to instruction in general rather than to the use of media for instruction, and can only offer the most general guidance for the media; and a macro theory of media which can give only general and incomplete guidance as to how to match media most effectively to learning tasks.

The situation calls for studies of the *content* of instructional media. Typically, most experiments on learning from the media have measured how much has been learned and have given minor attention, if any, to *how* it has been learned, or what aspects of the media have been responsible for its learning. For example, the studies by Ball and Bogatz (1970, 1971) measured the amount of learning that took place from *Sesame Street*, as related to the amount of viewing and to the kind of viewer. In Israel, however, Salomon (1972) was in position to examine the learning from that series in more detail. He found evidence that much of the learning that differentiates *Sesame Street* from comparable experiences relates to the *iconic* material presented in *Sesame Street*, and some of it to the most detailed circumstances of the presentation—for example, a camera angle or a zoom effect or the size of a figure as related to ground. The studies in El Salvador of effect of television on general ability to learn also produced some evidence that it was the iconic material in the television programs that contributed most to the increase in general ability scores. These effects would never have been picked up if only the usual criterion tests had been used. It is reasonable to think that if there are micro differences that affect learning from the media they must relate in some way to the symbolic coding systems of the media: McLuhan's distinction about the difference between linear and simultaneous decoding was an insight that preceded the necessary hypothesis construction and research. We are only now beginning to understand some of the differences between iconic, digital, and analogue coding, and a comprehensive theory for the most effective use of these different coding system has yet to emerge.

Nevertheless, if we are ever able to relate media to learning effectiveness for a particular task in any except the most general way (picture? print?), it will probably come about through understanding the unique strengths and capabilities of the different symbolic coding systems. That is the window we presently stand looking through.

BIG MEDIA VERSUS LITTLE MEDIA

The preceding chapters should have satisfied us that there is no such thing as a *super* medium.

The textbook, during the last century, has come into use more widely and has proved itself more broadly useful than any other medium. Of all the learning aids available to the teacher today, it is likely to be considered most indispensable and most nearly perfected. Yet it is not a super medium. It lacks liveness; its pictures lack motion; it lacks sound; it is hard to keep up to date. It can do well whatever the linear code of print and the printing press can do, but less than the audiovisual media can do with the iconic and digital codes.

In recent decades some educators and most outsiders have looked upon television as a potential super medium. Certainly it is the most glamorous of the newer media, although some of its glamour rubs off from entertainment and news. It can probably perform more learning acts, with greater liveness, than any other channel of instruction except the teacher. Yet television is at a disadvantage compared even to the simplest media, like slides, filmstrips, or phonograph records, when instruction calls for local classroom control of scheduling, stopping, repetition. It is at a disadvantage compared to CAI, programmed texts, audio language tapes, and tape loops, in leading a student through a practice exercise.

CAI has some qualities of a potential super medium, if its unit costs can be brought down to acceptable levels. It is potentially better able than any other medium to accomplish the interactive sort of learning that occurs at times between a very good teacher and a pupil. Like the other media, it can do some things better even than a teacher: It can be endlessly patient, for example, and more consistent than a live teacher in conducting practice.

Textbook, television, CAI, films, all can contribute spectacularly to learning and to the effectiveness of a learning system, but none is really *most* effective for all kinds of learning and teaching. (Neither is the teacher, without the aid of certain media at certain times.) Gagne summed it up with scholarly caution when he said that "no single medium is likely to have properties that make it best for all purposes" (1965: 363). Note that this conclusion does not say that in any given situation, one medium may not be more effective than another, but not in *every* situation or even in *most* situations.

As this point of view has permeated educational technology, some of the glamour has rubbed off the Big Media. They are not super media. They are spectacular. They attract attention. They can do more things than smaller media, because (for instance) television and film command sight, sound, motion, and, if necessary, print, whereas the smaller ones do not command all those; in fact, one of the reasons they are smaller and less expensive is that they have fewer channels and less capacity. Similarly, CAI commands interaction in a way that no other medium does so well. But it is very hard to show from existing evidence that the Little Media are greatly inferior to the Big in any given project which they have the physical properties to carry out; or that a combination of small and inexpensive media cannot do as well as a Big Medium on a task that requires more than one Little Medium to handle. Would the Australian radio-correspondence schools have been notable more effective with television? Are there not times when classroom control of pictorial materials or sound tapes may not be a desirable tradeoff for the qualities of instructional radio or television?

A cool, hard look at media economics raises additional questions of Big versus Little Media. Are the Big Media always worth five times as much as Little Media? Sometimes they are, if a school system or a country can pay for them; and, as we have seen, their unit costs are especially attractive in situations where economies of scale apply. But one of the principal reasons why radio (plus groups) has turned out to be the favorite medium of nonformal education is precisely this matter of cost-effectiveness. Television might do the job better; that is arguable, without real evidence to prove or disprove it. But radio does the job very well. It does the job at something like one-fifth the cost of television, covers just as large an area, requires less sophisticated infrastructure and backup. One can see why the nations of Southern Asia and Africa, and such nonformal schools as ACPO in Latin America, have preferred radio to its more expensive competition. It is a fair question whether a skillful use of radio rather than television might better have been recommended to the developing nations and states for their programs of national educational reform. We cannot answer that question, because there is no comparable experience with media like radio. But some of the experience with ITV for national educational reform is likely to be re-evaluated in the next decades, and the questions will undoubtedly come up. With radio instead of television, would Niger have had to wait ten years to expand its program? With radio instead of television, would American Samoa have had to cease live broadcasting in the eleventh year of the project because of financial stringencies? Only in the large national reform projects has television so monopolized the field. Kenya can teach its teachers with radio; Purdue University can extend its courses by radio. Distant teaching by radio (the Funkkolleg) and by television (The Telekolleg) exist side by side in Germany.

As more and more teaching becomes multimedia, Big Media tend to be looked at in a different way than they were twenty years ago. At that time, educators and prophets were thinking in terms of *the* medium, rather than a combination of media. The trend now is to think of a combination of media, able to do different things and contribute to learning in different ways. In no effective distant-teaching projects is one medium given sole responsibility; and it is correspondence study that comes nearest to carrying that kind of responsibility, *not* television, films, or CAI. In classroom teaching, the trend is not to supply the core of instruction from the outside (unless textbooks can be thought of as carrying that responsibility), but rather to use different media for specific needs—a map for geography, a chart for government, filmstrips for science, programmed instruction for drill, tapes or radio for music or foreign language, films or television for a special task requiring very high-quality presentation of an audiovisual experience. Increasingly educators and planners are ceasing to rest their hopes on any "great medium," but rather to ask which *media* will do what the system needs doing, and what the teacher or planner can do best with what he has. Fit and quality are becoming more important than Bigness and Littleness.

LOOKING FORWARD

We have been mentioning some trends. It may be well to conclude by projecting a few of them into the future. Let us start with the one we have just been talking about. It seems to us likely that the increasing concern with cost-effectiveness, multimedia teaching, and local participation and control in instruction will make the Little Media look more attractive than they have sometimes looked in the past. Before deciding to invest in Big Media, educators will first take stock of the essential needs they have for media help and estimate how many of them could be met at more acceptable cost and with no great loss of learning by *Little* Media. By the same token, Big Media will more often come into the planning or teaching process in terms of what they can contribute especially or *uniquely* rather than as general carriers.

It seems to us that research and theory are likely to turn toward deeper studies of media differences, and in particular toward better understanding of how people learn from the different symbolic coding systems of instructional materials. This is not to say that much other research is not needed—for example, into the cost-effectiveness of media instruction and into the less-obvious and less-immediate effects of learning from the media. There is no doubt that we are in a period of changing communication experience, and that it is important for other reasons as well as educational ones to understanding the psychological and social effects of receiving so much information from the iconic symbols. Until we understand this better than we do, however, we shall not be in a position to use the newer media of instruction as effectively as we might nor to construct a media taxonomy that has any chance of interlocking with the sophisticated taxonomies of learning.

By the same token, it seems to us that research and experimentation is going to emphasize in greater degree the *content* of instructional media. We have said much about the wide band of instructional effectiveness common to most media, and have mentioned that the effectiveness of media seems to depend as much on how a medium is used as on its delivery system; and also that most media teaching is really *multi*media teaching anyway, and the skill of combining media experiences is little understood. What if a substantial amount of research effort were transferred from the relatively futile media-comparison experiments to the production end of the media process? What if at least a few selected projects or combinations were helped to try to maximize learning effectiveness, by the same method of test and remake and retest that is used in making programmed instruction or CAI? I dare say that a considerable number of theoretical insights would emerge from this kind of experience, and that the resulting series of models would raise the whole level of media instruction.

A visitor from another small planet, unfamiliar with the atmosphere in which educational development takes place here, might be astonished to see how much of the effort and resources of a typical project go into procuring and operating expensive hardware rather than into producing more effective software (preferably for less-expensive hardware). A change in policy of this kind, of course, would make a considerable difference in the effectiveness of the Little Media. We are not denying the importance of the Big Media. It may well be that television, optimally used, may be the most encompassing teaching tool we have today, and that Big and expensive media like CAI are likely to bulk larger on the horizon of education during the next two decades. But the point is that such a concentration on improving the effectiveness of the media would help the Big as well as the Little. A concentration on the most effective *use* of the media of instruction, rather than on the *best media,* would be good for all media, Big or Little, and consequently good for all of us.

BIBLIOGRAPHY

BIBLIOGRAPHY

Abel, F. P. Use of closed-circuit television in teacher education: Relation to achievement and subject matter understanding. *Dissertation Abstracts*, 21, 1961, 2999-3000.

Abell, H. C. Radio forum in Ghana: Assessment of the project. In UNESCO, *An African experiment in radio forums for rural development, Reports and Papers on Mass Communication, No. 51*. Paris: UNESCO, 1968, 22-71.

Acción Cultural Popular, Department of Sociology. *Conclusions of Some Studies on the Effectiveness of the Radiophonic Schools of Accion Cultural Popular*. Bogota, Colombia: ACPO, 1972.

――― *Programmacion*. Bogota, Colombia: ACPO, 1969.

Adams, E. Field evaluation of the German CAI Lab. In Atkinson, R. C. and Wilson, H. (eds.) *Computer-assisted instruction: A book of readings*. New York: Academic Press, 1969.

Ahmed, M. and Coombs, P. H., eds. *Education for Rural Development: Case Studies for Planners*. New York: Praeger, 1975.

Allander, B., with others. *Seen But Also Heard*. Stockholm: Sveriges Radio, Staff Training Department, 1974.

Allen, D. and Ryan, K. *Microteaching*. Reading, Mass.: Addison-Wesley, 1969.

Allen, W. H. Media stimulus and types of learning. *Audio-Visual Instruction*, 12, 1967, 1, 27-31.

Allison, S. G. and Ash, P. *Relationship of anxiety to learning from films*. (Instructional Film Research Reports.) Port Washington, N.Y.: U.S. Naval Special Devices Center, 1951.

Almstead, F. E. and Graf, R. W. Talkback: The missing ingredient. *Audio-Visual Instruction*, 5, April 1960, 110-112.

Andersson, G. and Bohlin, E. Sweden: Adult education by radio and TV (TRU). In ·Internationales Zentralinstitut. *Multi-media systems in adult education: Twelve project description in inine countries*. Munich: Internationales Zentralinstitut fur das Jugend-und Bildungfernsehen, 1971.

Andrus, A.M.G. Satellite techonology: State of the art for the decade and its meaning for education. Paper for the Fourth Annual Educational Technology Conference, San Francisco, California, March 12-15, 1974.

Antioch College. Experiment in French language instruction: Second report, 1959-1960. Yellow Springs, Ohio: Antioch College, 1960.

Arana de Swadesh, E. Inform sobre la influencia que la radio ejerce en una communidad indigena: Xoxcotla, Morelos. Paper for the Friedrich Ebert Stiftung seminar on rural radio, Mexico, December 1971. (mimeo)

Ash, P. and Carlson, B. J. *The value of note-taking film learning*. (Instructional Film Reports on SDC 269-7-21.) Port Washington, N.Y.: U.S. Naval Special Devices Center, 1961.

Ashford, T. H. Some long-range effects of programmed instruction in music. *Journal of Research in Music Education*, 16, 1968, 339-344.

Atkinson, C. *Public school broadcasting to the classroom*. Boston: Meador, 1942.

Atkinson, R. C. Computerized instruction and the learning process. *American Psychologist*, 23, 1968, 255-239.

Attiyeh, R., Bach, G., and Lumsden, K. The efficiency of programmed learning in teaching economics: The results of a nationwide experiment. *American Economic Review*, 1969, 217-224.

AUDECAM. *La Television scolaire du Niger, 1964-1971*. General Report. Paris: Audecam, 1975.

Avercj, H. Carroll, S., Donaldson, T., Kiesling, H., and Pincus, J. *How effective is schooling? A critical review and synthesis of research findings.* Santa Monica, Calif. RAND, 1972.

Axeen, M. E. *Teaching the use of the library to undergraduates: An experimental comparison of computer-based instruction and the conventional lecture method.* Report No. R-361. Urbana: University of Illinois, Coordinated Science Laboratory, 1967.

Balakrishnan, T. R. and Matthai, R. J. India: Evaluation of publicity program on family planning. *Studies in Family Planning,* I, 1967, 21, 5-8.

Ball, S. and Bogatz, G. A. *The first year of Sesame Street: An evaluation.* Princeton: Educational Testing Service, 1971.

Balin, H. B. et al. *Cross-media evaluation of color TV, black and white TV, and color photography in the teaching of endoscopy.* Philadelphia: Pennsylvania Hospital, September 1968.

Bedall, F. K. Federal Republic of Germany: The Telekolleg. In Internationales Zentralinstitut. *Multi-media systems in adult education: Twelve project description in inine countries.* Munich: Internationales Zentralinstitut fur das Jugend-und Bildungfernsehen, 1971, 39-58.

Beech, R. P., McClelland, S. D., Horotwitz, G. R., and Forlano, G. *Final Report: An evaluation of the Dial-a-Drill program.* New York: State Education Department, 1970.

Berelson, B. and Freedman, R. A study in fertility control. *Scientific American,* 210, 1964, 29-37.

Berger, E. J. An investigation of the effectiveness of televised presentations of self-contained television-adapted lessons on enrichment topics in mathematics. *Dissertation Abstracts,* 23, 1962, 1552.

Berman, A. I. *Learning media and selection criteria in science education.* Copenhagen: Institute for Studies in Higher Education, University of Copenhagen, 1972.

Bhatia, B., Dubey, D. C., and Devgan, A. K. A study in family planning communication: direct mailing. *Demography,* 3, 1966, 343-351.

Bhatt, B., Krishnamoorthy, P. V., Marathey, R., and Bourgeois, M. *Radio Broadcasting Serves Rural Development.* Reports and Papers on Mass Communication, 40. Paris: UNESCO, 1965.

Bitzer, D. and Skaperdas, D. *The design of an economically viable large-scale computer-based education system.* Urbana, Ill: Computer-based Education Research Laboratory, 1969.

Bitzer, M. and Boudreaux, M. Using a computer to teach nursing. *Nursing Forum,* 1969, 8, 291-296.

Bloom, B. S. (ed.), Engelhart, M. D., Furst, E. J., Will, W. H., and Krathwohl, D. R. *Taxonomy of education objectives. Handbook I: Cognitive domain.* New York: McKay, 1956.

––– et al. *Taxonomy of educational objectives; the classification of educational goals.* Handbook I: *Cognitive doman* (by Bloom et al.) Handbook II: *Affective domain* (by Krathwohl et al.) New York: McKay, 1956.

Bobier, D. T. The effectiveness of the independent use of programmed textbooks in aiding students to overcome skill weakness in English, mechanics, and arithmetic. (Doctoral dissertation, University of Michigan.) *Dissertation Abstracts,* 25, 1965, 3424.

Bretz, R. *The selection of appropriate communication media for instruction: A guide for designers of Air Force technical training programs.* Santa Monica, Calif.: RAND, 1971.

––– *Three Models for Home-Based Instructional Systems using Television.* Santa Monica, Calif.: RAND, October 1972.

Briggs, L. J. *Handbook of Procedures for the Design of Instruction.* Pittsburgh, Pa.: American Institutes for Research, 1970.

––– Campeau, P. L., Gagne, R. M., and May, M. A. *Instructional Media.* Pittsburgh, Pa.: American Institutes for Research, 1967.

Broadbent, D. E. *Perception and Communication.* New York: Pergamon Press, 1958.

Brophy, J. E. and Evertson, C. M. Low-inference observational coding measures and teacher effectiveness. Unpublished technical report, Research and Development Center for Teacher Education, University of Texas, Austin, 1973. ERIC document ED 077879.

Brumberg, S. *Radio Sutatenza. Draft report.* New York: International Council for Educational Development, 1972.

Bruner, J. S. and Olson, D. R. Learning through experience and learning through media. In Gerbner G., Gross, L. P., and Melody, W. H., eds. *Communications Technology and Social Policy.* New York: John Wiley, 1973. 209-227.

Bruner, J. S., Goodnow, J. J., and Austin, G. A. *A Study of Thinking.* New York: John Wiley, 1956.

Bryan, E. F. *A comparative study in the teaching of high school chemistry and physics.* Oklahoma City: Oklahoma State Department of Education, 1961.

Buckler, W. R. A college English teacher looks at television: Composition. *Journal of Educational Sociology,* 1958, 31, 9, 346-52.

Butman, R. C., Rathjens, G. W., and Warren, C. J. *Technical-Economic Considerations in Public Service Broadcast Communications for Developing Countries.* Washington: Academy for Educational Development, 1973.

Callaway, A. *Planning out-of-school education for development.* Paris: International Institute for Educational Planning, 1971.

Campeau, P. L. *Level of anxiety and presence or absence of feedback in programmed instruction.* San Mateo, Calif.: American Institutes for Research, February, 1965.

――― Selective review of the results of research on the use of audio-visual media to teach adults. *AV Communication Review:* 22, 1, Spring, 1974, 5-40.

Canadian Broadcasting Corporation. *Challenge for Change.* Toronto: CBC, 1972.

Carpenter, C. R. Instructional film research: A brief review. *British Journal of Educational Technology,* 3, 2, October 1971, 299-246.

――― Television or something else. In Schramm, W. (ed.) *Quality in instructional television.* Honolulu: University Press of Hawaii, 1972.

――― and Greenhill, L. P. *Comparative Research on Methods and Media for Presenting Programmed Courses in Mathematics and English.* University Park, Pa.: Pennsylvania State University, 1963.

――― *Instructional Television Research. Report No. 2.* University Park, Pennsylvania State University, 1958.

Carpenter, H. A. Teaching science by radio. *Junior-Senior High School Clearing House,* 1934.

Carpenter, M. B., Chesler, L. G., Dordick, H. S., and Haggart, S. A. *Analyzing the use of technology to upgrade education in a developing country.* Santa Monica, Cailf.: RAND, March 1970.

Cartwright, C. A., Cartwright, G. P., and Robin, G. G. CAI course in the early identification of handicapped children. *Exceptional Children,* 38, 1972, 453-459.

Castle, C. H. Open-circuit television in postgraduate medical education. *Journal of Medical Education,* 38, 1963, 254-260.

Castleberry, S. and Lagowski, J. J. Individualized instruction using computer techniques. *Journal of Chemical Education,* 47, 1970, 91-96.

Cernada, G. P. and Lu, L. P. The Kaohsiung study. *Studies in Family Planning,* 3, 1972, 8, 198-203.

Chance, C. W. *Experimentation in the adaptation of the overhead projector utilizing 200 transparancies and 800 overlays in teaching descriptive geometry curricula.* Austin: The University of Texas, 1960.

Chu, G. C. *Communication and Development in the People's Republic of China.* Honolulu: East-West Communication Institute, 1977.

――― and Schramm, W. *Learning from television.* Washington: National Association of Educational Broadcasters, 1967.

Clergerie, B. *A Regional Satellite for Education, Communication, and Culture in the Service of Development.* (For the Arab States.) Paris: UNESCO, 1973.

Cobb, J. C. and Raulet, P. Pakistan: The medical social research project at Lulliani. Studies in project at Lulliani. *Studies in Family Planning,* 1, 8, 1965, 11-16.

Coleman, J. S. et al. *Equality of Educational Opportunity.* Washington: U.S. Department of Health, Education, and Welfare, Office of Education, 1966.

Comenius, John Amos. *Selections.* Introduction by Jean Piaget. Paris: UNESCO, 1957.

Committee for Economic Development. *The Schools and the Challenge of Innovation.* Supplementary Paper No. 28. New York: CED, 1969.

Comstock, G. and Maccoby, N. *Instructional Television for the In-Service Training of the Colombian Teacher.* Research report 6. Stanford, Calif.: Institute for Communication Research, Stanford University, 1966.

Constantine, Sister Mary. Radio in the elementary school. *Science Education,* 48, 1964, 2, 121-132.

Cook, D. C. and Nemzek, C. L. The effectiveness of teaching by radio. *Journal of Educational Research,* 1939, 33, 105-109.

Coombs, P. H. and Hallak, J. *Managing Educational Costs.* New York: Oxford, 1972.

Corle, C. C. *Mathematics teaching behavior changes made by intermediate grade teachers during a 15-week period of instruction by educational television.* University Park, Pa.: Pennsylvania State University, 1967.

Craig, G. Q. A comparison between sound and silent films in teaching. *British Journal of Educational Psychology,* 26, 1956, 202-206.

Cronbach, L. J. Beyond the two disciplines of scientific psychology. *American Psychologist,* February, 1975, 116-127.

――― and Snow, R. E. *Aptitudes and instructional methods.* New York: Irvington, 1976.

Curry, R. P. *Report of three experiments in the use of television in instruction.* Cincinnati, Ohio: Cincinnati Public Schools, 1959.

Dale, E. *Audiovisual Methods in Teaching.* Third edition. New York: Holt, Rinehart & Winston, 1969.

Day, W. F. and Beach, B. R. *A Survey of the Research Literature Comparing the Visual and Auditory Presentation of Information.* Charlottesville, Va.: University of Virginia, November 1950.

Dick, W. and Latta, R. Comparative effects of ability and presentation mode in computer assisted instruction. *Audio-Visual Communication Review,* 18, Spring 1970, 1, 33.

Dietmeyer, H. J. The effect of the integration of science teaching by television on the development of scientific reasoning in the fifth-grade student. *Dissertation Abstracts,* 22 1962, 3517-3518.

Domino, G. Interactive effects of achievement orientation and teaching style on academic achievement. *Journal of Educational Psychology,* 62, 1971, 427-431.

Dordick, H. S. *The Bavarian Telekolleg: a case study.* Report for the Stanford University Institute for Communication Research. Stanford, Calif., 1972.

Doty, B. A. and Doty, L. A. Programmed instructional effectiveness in relation to certain characteristics. *Journal of Educational Philosophy,* 1964, 55, 334-338.

Dreher, R. E. and Beatty, W. H. *Instructional television research project No. One: An experimental study of college instruction using broadcast television.* San Francisco: San Francisco State College, April, 1958.

Driscoll, J. P. *The effects of mental retardation on film learning.* Los Angeles: University of California, n.d.

Dubin, R. and Hedley, R. A. *The medium may be related to the message: College Instruction by TV.* Eugene, Ore.: University of Oregon Press, 1969.

Dubin, R. and Taveggia, T. C. *The Teaching-Learning Paradox: A comparative analysis of college teaching methods.* Eugene, Ore.: Center for the Advanced Study of Educational Administration, University of Oregon, 1968.

Dworkin, S. and Holden, A. An experimental evaluation of sound filmstrips vs. classroom lectures. Abstracted in *Audio-Visual Communication Review,* 8, 1960, 3, 157.

Edwards, R. K., Williams, M. L., and Roderick, W. W. *An experiment pilot study to explore the use of an audio-visual-tutorial laboratory in the secretarial offerings at the community college level in Michigan.* Lansing, Mich.: Lansing Community College, 1968.

Egly, M. *Etude de la Reception Transnationale d'Emissions de Television Educative.* Paris: Agence de Cooperation Culturelle et Technique and Unesco, n.d.

El Hadj Badge, M. and Robert, J. *Dix ans d'animation radiophonique en milieu rural.* Niamey, Niger: Association des Radio-Clubs du Niger, 1972.

Elliott, R. W. *A study of taped lessons in geography instruction.* Westfield, Mass.:: The Abner Gibbs Schools, 1965.

Erickson, C. G. and Chausow, H. M. *Chicago's TV College: final report of a three year experiement.* Chicago: Chicago City Junior College, 1960.

――― and Zigerell, J. J. *Eight Years of TV College: A fourth report.* Chicago: Chicago City College, 1964.

Erickson, E. H. *Childhood and society.* New York: W. W. Norton, 1963.

Extension Service, Memorial University of Newfoundland. *Fogo Process in Communication.* St. Johns, Newfoundland, n.d.)

Fawcett, J. T., Soomboonsuk, A., and Khaisang, S. Thailand: An analysis of time and distance factors at an IUD clinic in Bangkok. *Studies in Family Planning,* 1, 1967, 19, 16-19.

Filep, R. and Schramm, W. *The Impact of Research on Utilization of Media for Educational Purposes.* El Segundo, Calif.: Institute for Educational Development, 1970.

Fincher, G. E. and Fillmer, H. T. Programmed instruction in elementary arthmetic. *Arthmetic Teacher,* 12, 1965, 9-23.

Fleishman, E. A. On the relation between abilities, learning, and human performance. *American Psychologist,* 2⁷, November 1972, 11, 1017-1032.

Fordham University. *Training by television: The comparative effectiveness of instruction by television, television recordings, and conventional classroom practices.* Port Washington, N.Y.: U.S. Navy Special Devices Center, 1953.

Forsythe, R. O. Purdue: An open university via radio. In *National educational radio: Radio's role in instruction.* Washington: National Association of Educational Broadcasters, September, 1972. Supplementary paper, vi-x.

Fougeyrollas, P. *Television and the social education of women. Reports and Papers on Mass Communication, No. 50.* Paris: UNESCO, 1967.

Freedman, R. and Takeshita, J. Y. *Family planning in Taiwan.* Princeton: Princeton University Press, 1969.

French Delegation to the Development Assistance Committee. Family homes. Paper for the committee meeting, Paris, October 10-11, 1972.

——— The "Mandoul" Project: A rural education experiment in Chad. Paper for the committee meeting, Paris, October 10-11, 1972.

Gagne, R. M. *The conditions of learning.* New York: Holt, Rinehart & Winston, 1965. Second edition, 1970.

——— and Briggs, L. J. *Principles of instructional design.* New York: Holt, Rinehart, and Winston, 1974.

Gagne, R. M. and Gropper, G. L. *Studies in filmed instruction: 1. Individual differences in learning. 2. The use of Visual examples in review.* Pittsburg, Pa.: American Institutes for Research, December, 1965.

Garace, F. Lazaro, H., and Mayuri, F. *Communication Dialogica a Traves de la Video Grabadora Portatil.* Lima: Accion Communitaria del Peru, June 1972.

Garnier, R. France: RTS-Promotion. In Internationales Zentralinstitut, *Multi-media systems in adult education: Twelve project description in inine countries.* Munich: Internationales Zentralinstitut fur das Jugend-und Bildungfernsehen, 1971, 105-123.

Gates, A. I. Recitation as a factor in memorizing. *Archives of Psychology,* 7, 1917, p. 40.

General Learning Corporation. *Cost study of educational media systems and their components.* 3 vols. Washington: General Learning Corporation, 1968.

Gilbert, T. F. Mathetics: The technology of education. *Journal of Mathetics,* 1962, 1, 7-73.

Gillespie, R. *Progress report: Isfahan project.* Isfahan, Iran: Population Council, 1971.

Glaser, R. G. et al. *Studies of the use of programmed instructions in the classroom.* Pittsburgh, Pa.: Learning Research and Development Center, University of Pittsburgh, and the Baldwin-Whitehall Public Schools, May, 1966.

Glasgow, M. W. *A study of the relative effectiveness of selected approaches to the inservice education of teachers in the utilization of in-school radio and television broadcasts.* Norman, Okla.: University of Oklahoma, n.d.

Goodman, L. S. Computer-based instruction: Today and tomorrow. *Data Processing for Education,* 3, 1964, 2-5.

Gordon, O. J., Nordquist, E. C. and Engar, K. M. *Teaching the use of the slide rule via television.* Salt Lake City: KUED, University of Utah, July, 1959.

Goto, K. *Up-to-date estimates on cost of radio-television-correspondence Gakuen.* Tokyo, 1972.

Grant, S. *A Report on Television in The Ivory Coast.* Washington, D.C.: Academy for Educational Development, 1974.

Grilliches, Z. Notes on the role of education in production functions, and growth accounting. In Hansen, W. L., ed., *Education, Income, and Income Capital.* New York: Columbia University Press, 1970.

Gropper, G. L. and Lumsdaine, A.A. *An experimental comparison of a conventional TV lesson requiring active student response.* Studies in Televised Instruction, Report No. 2. USOE Project No. 336. Pittsburgh, Pa.: Metropolitan Pittsburgh Educational Television Stations WQED-WQEX and American Institutes for Research, March, 1961.

Grosslight, J. H. and McIntyre, C. J. *Exploratory studies in the use of pictures and sound in teaching foreign language vocabulary.* (Technical Report SDC 269-7-53). Instructional Film Research Reports. Port Washington, N. Y.: U.S. Naval Special Devices Center, 1955.

Grubb, R. E. and Selfridge, L. D. Computer tutoring in statistics. *Computers and Automation,* 13, 1964, 20-26.

Guilford, J. P. Three faces of intellect. *American Psychologist,* 14, 1959, 469-479.

Guthrie, E. R. *The Psychology of Learning.* New York: Harper, 1935.

Gwyn, S. *Cinema as Catalyst: Film, Videotape and Social Change, a Report on a Seminar.* St. Johns, Newfoundland: Memorial University of Newfoundland, 1972.

Haleworth, B. Radio, the Cinderella medium. *Educational Broadcasting International,* 5, September 1971, 189-191.

Hancock, A. The changing role of educational media. *Educational Television International,* 3, July 1969, 2.

— — — *Planning for ETV.* London: Longmans, 1971.

Hansen, D. N., Dick, W., and Lippert, H. T. *Research and implementation of collegiate instruction of physics via computer-assisted instruction,* vol. 1. Technical Report No. 3. Tallahassee: Florida State University, Computer-Assisted Instruction Center, 1968.

Harry S. F. *Evaluation of a procedure for using daylight projection film loops in teaching skills.* (Technical Report SDC 269-7-25). Port Washington, N.Y.: U.S. Naval Special Devices Center, 1952.

Hartman, F. R. Investigation of recognition learning under multiple channel presentation and testing conditions. In *Research on the Communication Process: A Report Covering the Period September 1958-September 1960.* University Park, Pa.: Pennsylvania State University, 1960, 5/1-5/26.

Hawkridge, D. G. *Media Taxonomies and Media Selection.* Milton Keynes, England, n.d. (mimeo)

— — — *Programmed Learning in Central African Contexts.* Faculty of Education, University College of Rhodesia, Occasional Paper No. 7. Salisbury: The University College, 1966.

Hayman, R. W. and Levin, H. Economic analysis and historical summary of educational technology costs. Appendix C of Melmed, A., ed., *Productivity and Efficiency in Education.* Washington: Federal Council on Science and Technology, 1973.

Herminghaus, E. G. Large group instruction by television: An experiment. *School Review,* 65, 1957, 119-133.

Heron, W. T., and Ziebarth, E. W. A preliminary experimental comparison of radio and classroom lectures. *Speech Monographs,* 13, 1946, 54-57.

Heidgerken, L. An experimental study to measure the contribution of motion pictures and slide films to learning certain units in the course introduction to nursing arts. *Journal of Experimental Education,* 17, 1957, 2, 261-293.

Hilgard, E. R. Evolution stages in the evolution of learning. *Contemporary Psychology,* 17, October 1972, 10, 513-515.

Hill, S. A. *A comparative study: Two methods of teaching reading—conventional and programmed.* (Doctoral dissertation, Mississippi State University.) 1968.

Hirschman, A. O. *Development projects observed.* Washington, D.C.: The Brookings Institution, 1967.

Hoffbauer, H. Federal Republic of Germany—the Quadriga-Funkkolleg in Pedagogy. In Internationales Zentralinstitut, *Multi-media systems in adult education: Twelve project description in inine countries.* Munich: Internationales Zentralinstitut fur das Jugend-und Bildungfernsehen, 1971, 82-104.

Hoban, C. F., Jr. and Van Ormer, E. B. *Instructional Film Research, 1918-1950.* Port Washington, N.Y.: U.S. Navy Special Devices Center, 1950.

Hollister, W. G. and Bower, E. M. *Behavioral science frontiers in education.* New York: John Wiley, 1966.

Homeyer, F. C. *Development and evaluation of an automated assembly language teacher.* Technical Report No. 3. Austin: University of Texas, Computer-Assisted Instruction Laboratory, 1970.

Hornik, R., Mayo, J., McAnany, E. *Television and Educational Reform in El Salvador.* Stanford, California: Stanford University Press, 1976.

Hovland, C. I., Lumsdaine, A. A., and Sheffield, F. D. *Experiments on Mass Communication.* Princeton: Princeton University Press, 1949.

Hughes, J. L. and McNamara, W. J. A comparative study of programmed and conventional instruction in industry. *Journal of Applied Psychology,* 45, 1961, 225-231.

Hull, C. L. *Principles of behavior.* New York: Appleton-Century-Crofts, 1943.

Ingle, Henry T. *Communication Media and Technology: A Look at Their Role in Non-Formal Educational Programs.* Information Bulletin No. 5. Information Center for Instructional Technology, Washington, D. C. August, 1974.

Instructional Film Research Program. *Evaluation of the film: Military police support in emergencies.* (Technical Report SDC 269-7-52). Instructional Film Research Reports. Port Washington, N.Y.:" U.S. Naval Special Devices Center, 1954.

Internationales Zentralinstitut. *Multi-media systems in adult education: Twelve project description in nine countries.* Munich: Internationales Zentralinstitut fur das Jugend-und Bildungfernsehen, 1971. (Also German edition, 1971: *Medien-* systeme in der Erwachsenenbildung: *Zwolf projektanalysen aus neun Landern*).

International Research Associates. *Attitudes toward Instructional Television.* Report to the Ford Foundation. New York: International Research Associates, 1965.

Jacobs, J. N. and Bollenbacher, J. K. Teaching ninth grade biology by television. *Audio-Visual Communication Review,* 8, 1960, 176-191.

Jain, N. C. The influence of group radio listening, discussion, decision, and commitment on attitude change in radio forums. Paper (summarizing a doctoral dissertation) for International Communication Division, Association for Education in Journalism, Berkeley, Calif., August 22-25, 1969.

Jamison, D. *Notes on cost-effectiveness evaluation of schooling in developing countries.* Stanford, California: Stanford University, 1972. (mimeo)

––– The effectiveness of alternate instructional media: A survey. *Reviews of Educational Research,* 1974, 44, 1-67.

––– with Klees, S. *The Cost of Instructional Radio and Television for Developing Countries.* Stanford, Calif.:" Institutes for Communication Research, 1973.

Jamison, D. and Suppes, P. *Alternatives for Improving Productivity and Efficiency in Education.* Stanford, Calif., 1971. (mimeo)

––– and Wells, S. *The Effectiveness of Alternative Instructional Media: A Survey.* Stanford, Calif.: Institute for Communication Research, 1973.

Jamison, M., with Bett, S. T. *Satellite Educational System Costs for Three Model Developing Countries.* A Report for the U.S. Office of Telecommunications Policy. Washington, D.C.: August, 1973.

Jenkins, J. J. Mediated associations: paradigms and situations. In Cofer, C. N., and Musgrave, B. A. (eds.), *Verbal behavior and learning.* New York: McGraw Hill. 1963.

Johnson, W. B., Wilder, F., and Bogue, D. J. (eds.) *Information, Education and Communication in Population Family Planning Programs: A Guide for National Action.* Chicago: Community and Family Study Center, University of Chicago, 1973.

Kahnert, F. et al. Radio Togo's educational programme. In UNESCO, *New educational media in action–Case studies,* 2, 209-226. Paris: UNESCO, 1967.

Kale, S. V. *Learning and retention of English-Russian Vocabulary under different conditions of motion picture presentation.* State College: Pennsylvania State College, 1953.

Karlin, B. and Ali, J. M. The use of the radio in support of family planning program in the Hyderabad District of West Pakistan. In Schramm, W. *Communication in family planning,* 1971, 34.

Keislar, E. R. *Abilities of first grade pupils to learn mathematics in terms of algebraic structures by means of teaching machines.* Los Angeles: University of California at Los Angeles, 1961.

Kelley, E. C. The Fully functioning self, In Combs, A. W. (ed.) *Perceiving, behaving, becoming.* Washington, D. C.: Association for Supervision and Curriculum Development, 1962.

Kelley, T. D. *Utilization of filmstrips as an aid in teaching beginning reading.* (Doctoral dissertation, Indiana University) 1961.

Kendler, H. H. The concept. In Melton, A. W. (ed.) *Categories of human learning.* New York: Academic Press, 1964.

Kimble, G. A. *Hilgard and Marquis' "Conditioning and Learning."* New York: Appleton-Century-Crofts, 1961.

––– and Wulff, J. J. The effects of response guidance on the value of audience participation in training film instruction. *AV Communication Review,* 1, 1961, 292-293.

Kimmel, P. Educational radio and television in Australia. In Kimmel, P., Kies, N., and Lyle, J. *ITV and education of children: Cross-cultural comparison of international uses of media,* Vol. II–case studies, 7-44. Washington: The American University, January, 1971.

Kinane, K. Australia's correspondence schools, with supporting broadcast programmes, and Radio University. In UNESCO, *New educational media in action–Case Studies,* 1, 169-203. Paris: UNESCO, 1967.

Kincaid, L., Park, H. J., Chung, K. K., and Lee, C. C. *Mothers' Clubs and Family Planning in Rural Korea: The Case of Oryu Li.* Honolulu: East-West Communication Institute, 1975.

Klees, S. and Jamison, D. The Cost *of Educational Television in the Ivory Coast.* Report for the Ministry of Education, The Ivory Coast. April, 1973. (mimeo)

Komoski, P. K. An imbalance of product quantity and instructional quality. *AV Communication Review,* 22, 4 (Winter 1974), 357-386.

Koran, M., Snow, R. E., and McDonald, F. J. Teacher aptitude and observational learning of a teaching skill. *Journal of Educational Psychology,* 1971, 62. 3, 219-228.

Korean Educational Development Institute. *Research Report Series.* Seoul, Korea: KEDI, 1973-.

Krathwohl, D. R. et al. *Taxonomy of educational objectives, Handbook II: Affective domain.* New York: David McKay, 1964.

Krival, A. A. et al. *Project report: Radio/correspondence education project No. 615-11-650-129. USAID/UWEX (Kenya).* Part I: Administration (Krival); Part II: Evaluation (Thiede). Madison: University of Wisconsin, Extension Division, 1970-1971.

Laidlaw, B., and Layard, R. *Traditional vs. Open University Teaching Methods: A Comparison.* Report of a Joint Project undertaken by the London School of Economics and the Open University, 1973. (mimeo)

Lam, P. Experiences in the use of communication methods in promoting family planning in Hong Kong. Pp. 82 ff. in *Communications in Family Planning: Report of a Working group.* Bangkok: United Nations Economic Commission for Asia and the Far East, 1968.

Lefranc, R. Educational television in Niger. In UNESCO, *New education media in action–Case studies,* 2, 11-48. Paris: UNESCO, 1967.

––– Radio clubs in Niger. In UNESCO, *New educational media in action–Case studies,* 3, 59-78. Paris: UNESCO, 1967.

––– Radiovision as an aid to literacy in Niger. In UNESCO, *New educational media in action–Case studies,* 3, 41-58. Paris: UNESCO, 1967.

––– *The Combined Use of Radio and Television and Correspondence Courses in Higher Education.* Strasbourg, France: Council for Cultural Cooperation, Council of Europe, 1973.

Lu, L. P. An experimental study of the effect of group meetings on the acceptance of family planning in Taiwan. *Journal of Social Issues,* 23, 4, 1967, 171-177.

Lumley, F. J. Rates of speech in radio speaking. *Quarterly Journal of Speech,* June 1933.

Lumsdaine, A. A. and Gladstone, A. I. Overt practice and audiovisual embellishments. In May, M. A. and Lumsdaine, A. A. *Learning from Film.* New Haven, Conn.: Yale University Press, 1958, 58-71.

Lumsdaine, A. A., May, M. A., and Hadsell, R. S. Questions spliced into a film for motivation and pupil participation. In May, M. A., and Lumsdaine, A. A. *Learning from Film.* New Haven, Conn.: Yale University Press, 1958, 72-83.

Lumsdaine, A. A., Sulzer, R. L., and Kopstein, F. F. The influence of simple animation techniques on the value of a training film. *AV Communication Review,* 1, 1953, 140-141.

Lumsden, K. The Open University: A survey and economic analysis. Stanford, Calif.: Stanford University, 1973. (mimeo)

Lyle, J. Columbia's national programme for primary-level instruction. In UNESCO, *New educational media in action—Case studies,* 1, 49-76. Paris: UNESCO, 1967.

––– The NHK Gakuen of Japan. In Kimmel, P., Kies, N. E., and Lyle, J. *ITV and education of children: Cross-cultural comparisons of international uses of media,* Vol. II—case studies, 127-160. Washington, D.C.: The American University, January, 1971.

––– et al. The Centro di Telescuola of Italy, In UNESCO, *New educational media in action—case studies,* 3, 11-40. Paris: UNESCO, 1967.

Mager, R. *Preparing objectives for programmed instruction.* Palo Alto, Calif.: Frearon, 1962.

Majasan, J. K. College students' achievement as a function of the congruence between their beliefs and their instructor's beliefs. (Doctoral dissertation, Stanford University) 1972.

Margolin, J. B. Strategies for *the use of mass communications media in the technological developing nations.* Report to the Academy for Educational Development. Washington, 1971. (mimeo)

Markle, D. G. *The development of the Bell System first aid and personal safety course: An exercise in the application of empirical methods to instructional system design.* Palo Alto, Calif.: American Institutues for Research, April 1967.

Marsh, L. A. and Pierce-Jones, J. *Programmed instruction as an adjunct to a course in adolescent psychology.* Paper for the annual meeting of the American Educational Research Association, Chicago, February 1967.

Martini, H. R. *Development of filmstrip sequence photographs and sound reproduction of educational television presentations.* Coatesville, Pa.: North Brandywine Junior High Schools, February 1967.

Maslow, A. H. Some basic propositions of the growth self-actualizing psychology. In Combs, A. W. (ed.) *Perceiving, behaving, becoming.* Washington, D.C.: Association for Supervision and Curriculum Development, 1962.

Mathur, J. C. and Neurath, P. *An Indian experiment in farm radio forums,* Paris: UNESCO, 1959.

May, M. A. and Lumsdaine, A. A. *Learning from Films.* New Haven, Conn.: Yale University Press, 1958.

Mayo, J. K., Hornik, R. C., and McAnany, E. G. *Educational Reform with Television: The El Salvador Experience.* Stanford, Calif.: Stanford University Press, 1976.

Mayo, J. K., McAnany, E. G., and Klees, S. J. *The Mexican Telesecundaria: A cost-effective analysis.* Stanford, Calif.: Institute for Communication Research, 1973.

McAnany, E. *Radio clubs of Niger: September, 1972.* Stanford, Calif.: Institute for Communication Research, 1972. (mimeo)

––– *Radio's Role in Development: Five Strategies of Use.* Information Bulletin No. 4. Information Center on Instructional Technology, Washington D.C., September 1973.

McCombs, M. Chicago's Television College. In UNESCO, *New educational media in action: Case studies for planners,* 2, 99-128. Paris: UNESCO, 1967.

McIntyre, C. J. *Training film evaluation: FB 254—Cold weather uniforms.* Technical Report SDC 269-7-51. Port Washington, N.Y.: U.S. Naval Special Devices Center, 1954.

––– *An application of the principles of programmed instruction to a televised course in college economics.* Urbana, Ill.: University of Illinois, 1966.

McKeachie, W. J. The decline and fall of the laws of learning. *Educational Researcher*, 3, 3, 1974, 7-11.

McLuhan, Marshall. *The McLuhan DEW-LINE*, vol. 1, no. 6, December 1968.

——— *The Gutenberg galaxy*. Toronto: University of Toronto Press, 1962.

——— *Understanding Media: The Extensions of Man*. New York: McGraw-Hill, 1964.

MacKenzie, N., Postage, R., and Scupham, J. *Open Learning: Systems and Problems in Post-secondary Education*. Paris: UNESCO, 1975.

McNeil, J. D. Programmed instruction as a research tool in reading: An annotated case. *Journal of Programmed Instruction*, 1, 1962, 1, 37-42.

Menne, J. W., Klingenschmidt, J. E., and Nord, D. L. *The feasibility of using taped lectures to replace class attendance*. Paper for the American Educational Research Association, Los Angeles meeting, 1969.

Mercer, J. *The relationship of optical effects and film literacy to learning from instructional films*. Port Washington, N. Y.: U.S. Navy Special Devices Center, 1952.

Merrill, M. D. and Goodman, R. I. *Selecting Instructional Strategies and Media: A place to begin*. Provo, Utah: National Special Media Institutes, 1971.

Miller, J. G. *Deciding whether and how to use educational technology in the light of cost-effective evaluation*. Cleveland, Ohio: Cleveland State University, n.d.

——— Deciding whether and how to use educational technology in light of cost-effectiveness evaluation. In U.S. Commission on Instructional Technology, *To Improve Learning*. New York: Bowker, 1970. Vol. 2, 1007-1027.

——— The range of instructional technologies and priority research areas relating to their potential contribution in less-developed countries. In *Research and Development Priorities for the Less Developed Countries*, a report by the Academy for Educational Development for the U.S. Agency for International Development. Washington: Academy for Educational Development, 1973.

Miller, R. M. *Alternatives for educational development: Case studies of practical applications*. Paper for annual meeting of the Comparative and International Education Society of Canada. Montreal, May 29-30, 1972. (mimeo)

——— *The meaning of development and its educational implications*. In Agricultural Development Council reprint, October, 1972, 5-10. New York: Agricultural Development Council, Inc.

Mills, A. Senegal: Radio Disso. Unpublished report. Stanford University, 1972.

Ministry of National Education, The Ivory Coast. *Reports of the Secretary of State in Charge of Primary Teaching and Educational Television*. Abidjan: Government of the Ivory Coast. 1968- .

Moldstad, J. A. Selective review of research studies showing media effectiveness: A primer for media directors. *AV Communication Review*, 22, 4, Winter 1974, 387-407.

Monahan, P. E. et al. *Multimedia instruction programs in mathematics–demonstration and experimentation*. Whitewater, Wisc.: Wisconsin Heights Schools System and University of Wisconsin, 1966.

Monsivais, Carlos. Y todo mundo digo "Gulp"! *Cuadernos de Communicacion*, 1975, 1, 4, 13-17.

Mowrer, O. H. *Learning theory and behavior*. New York: John Wiley, 1960.

Murphy, F. E. The relative effectiveness of filmed introductions to a general science motion picture. *Dissertation Abstracts*, 22, 1962, 3121.

Musto, S. A. *Massenmedien als Instrumente der landlichen Entwicklungsforderung: Wirkingsanalyse von "Accion Cultural Popular–Radio Sutatenza" (Kolumbien)*. Berlin: Verlag Bruno Hessling, 1969. (Republished in Spanish with ACPO comments, 1971.)

National Association of Educational Broadcasters. *Television in Instruction: What is possible*. Washington: NAEB, 1970.

National Film Board of Canada. *Challenge for Change*. Toronto: National Film Board, 1973.

Nelson, H. E. *The relative contribution to learning of video and audio elements in film*. State College: Pennsylvania State College, 1951.

Neu, D. M. The effects of attention-gaining devices on film-mediated learning. *Abstracts of Doctoral Dissertations*, Pennsylvania State College, vol. 13. State College: Pennsylvania State College, 1951, 414-417. And *Journal of Educational Psychology*, 42, 1951, 479-490.

Neurath, P. *School television in Delhi.* New Delhi, India: All-India Radio, 1968.
——— *The Radio Rural Forum—Report on the pilot project.* New Delhi: Government of India, 1960.
NKH Radio-Television Cultural Research Institute. *The effects of educational radio music classroom, April-December 1956.* Tokyo: NHK, 1957.
———*The listening effect of radio English classroom.* April 1954-March 1955. Tokyo: NHK, 1956.
Nicol, J., Shea, A., Simmins, G., and Sim, R., eds. *Canada's Radio Farm Forum.* Paris: UNESCO, 1954.
Nyerere, J. K. Education for Self-Reliance. In *Freedom and Unity.* Dar es Salaam: Government of Tanzania, 1967.

Open University of Great Britain. *Second submission of the Open University to the Committee on the Future of Broadcasting.* Milton Keynes, England: April 1975. (mimeo)
——— *Report of the Vice-Chancellor, 1973.* Milton Keynes, England: Open University Press, 1973.

Pant, N. K. Correspondence education in India. *Bulletin of the UNESCO Regional Office for Education in Asia,* VI, September 1971, 1, 19-24.
Patrick, R. B. *The measurement of the effectiveness of the documentary sound-film as a supplement in the teaching of methods to college students being prepared to teach in the secondary schools.* University Park, Pa.: Pennsylvania State University, 1958.
Paulu, B. Europe's second chance universities. *Educational Broadcasting Review,* 3, June 1969, 3, 60-82.
Pavlov, I. P. *Conditioned reflexes.* London: Oxford, 1927.
Peerson, N. *An experiment, with evaluation, in the eradication of adult literacy by use of television instruction over a state educational television network supplemented by supervised group viewing and by the related use of project-supplied materials of instruction.* Florence, Ala.: Florence State College, August, 1961.
Piaget, J. *Six psychological studies.* New York: Random House, 1967.
Pickrel, G., Neidt, C., and Gibson, R. Tape recordings are used to teach seventh grade students in Westside Junior-Senior High School. *National Association of Secondary School Principals Bulletin,* 42, 1958, 234, 81-93.
Plowright, P. Towards a school TV service in the Sudan. *Education Television International,* 2, 1968, 1, 17-23.
Popham, W. J. Tape recorded lectures in the college classroom—II. *Audio-Visual Communication Review,* 10, 1961, 94-101.
Porter, D. A. *An application of reinforcement principles to classroom teaching.* Cambridge: Laboratory for Research in Instruction, Graduate School of Education, Harvard University, 1961.
——— Some effects of year long teaching machine instruction. In Galanter, E., ed. *Automatic Teaching: The State of the Art.* New York: John Wiley, 1959, 85-90.
Postman, L. The present status of interference theory. In Cofer, C. N. (ed.) *Verbal learning and verbal behavior.* New York: McGraw-Hill, 1961.
Psacharoupoulos, G. *Returns to Education: An international comparison.* Amsterdam: Elsevier, 1972.

Raina, B. L., Blake, R. R., and Weiss, E. M. India: A study in family planning communication, Meerut District. *Studies in Family Planning,* 1, 1967, 21, 1-5.
Ratanamungala, B. *Instructional radio: A decade of Thai experience.* Bangkok: Ministry of Education, 1972.
Razran, G. *Mind in evolution: An East-West synthesis of learned behavior and cognition.* Boston: Houghton-Mifflin, 1971.
Reid, J. S. and MacLennan, D. W. *Research in instructional television and film.* Washington: U.S. Department of Health, Education, and Welfare, Office of Education. 1967.
Roid, G. H. *Covariates of learning in computer-assisted instruction.* Montreal: McGill University, n.d.
Romano, L. *The role of sixteen millimeter motion pictures and projected still in science unit vocabulary learnings at grades five, six, and seven.* (Doctoral dissertation, University of Wisconsin) 1955.

Roshal, S. M. *Effects of Learner Representation in Film-Mediated Perceptual-Motor Learning.* Port Washington, N.Y.: U.S. Navy Special Devices Center, 1949.

Ross, J. A. Cost analysis of the Taichung experiment. *Studies in Family Planning,* 1, 1966, 10, 6-15.

Ross, J. A., Germain, A., Forrest, J. E., and van Ginneken, J. Findings from family planning research. *Reports on Population/Family Planning,* 12, October 1972, 1-47.

Rosselot, L. *Evaluation of the Otterbein College Film-text method of teaching French, at five Ohio institutions.* Westerville, Ohio: Otterbein College, September 30, 1961.

Rothkopf, E. Z. Two scientific approaches to the management of instruction. In Gagne, R. M. and Gephart, W. R., eds. *Learning Research and School Subjects.* Itasca. Ill.: Peacock. 1968.

Roy, P., Waisanen, E., and Rogers, E. *The impact of communication on rural development: An investigation in Costa Rica and India.* Paris: UNESCO, 1969.

Rulon, P. J. *The sound motion picture in science teaching.* Cambridge: Harvard University Press, 1933.

Rural Development Division. *Establishing district training centres.* Dar es Salaam: Ministry of Local Government and Rural Development, 1968.

Saettler, P. Design and selection factors. *Review of Educational Research,* 38 (1968), 115-128.

Salomon, G. *Educational Effects of Entertaining TV: The case of Sesame Street in Israel.* Final report. Jerusalem: Hebrew University, 1972.

––– What is learned and how it is taught: The interaction between media, message, task, and learner. *Seventy-third yearbook of the National Society for the Study of Education.* Chicago: NSSE, L974, 383-406.

––– and Sieber, J. E. Relevant subjective response uncertainty as a function of stimulus-task interaction. *American Educational Research Journal,* 7, 1970, 337-350.

Samuels, S. J. Effects of pictures on learning to read, comprehension, and attitudes. *Review of Educational Research,* 40, 3, June 1970, 397-408.

Scanland, F. W. *An investigation of the relative effectiveness of two methods of instruction, including computer-assisted instruction, as techniques for changing the parental attitudes of Negro adults.* Tallahassee: Florida State University, July 15, 1970.

Schalock. H. D. Learner outcomes, learner processes, and the conditions of learning. In Edling, J. et al. *The contributions of behavioral science to instructional technology.* Monmouth, Ore.: Teaching Research–Adivision of the Oregon State System of Higher Education, 1970.

Schiefele, H. and Schardt, A. *Telekolleg im Studienprogram des Bayerischen Rundfunks.* Wissenschaftliche Begleit-untersuchung. Heft 1. Munich: Tleekolleg, 1971.

Schramm, W. Communication in family planning. *Reports on Population/Family Planning,* 7, 1971, 1-43.

––– Japan's broadcast-correspondence high school. In UNESCO, New educational media in action–case studies, 1, 135-169. Paris: UNESCO, 1967.

––– Ten years of the radio rural forum in India. In UNESCO, *New Educational Media in Action–case studies,* 1, 105-134. Paris: UNESCO, 1967.

––– *ITV in American Samoa–after Nine Years.* Stanford, Calif.: Institute for Communication Research, Stanford University, 1973.

––– ed. *Quality in Instructional Television.* Honolulu: University Press of Hawaii, 1972.

––– *Report on Chicago's "TV College."* Stanford, Calif.: Institute for Communication Research, 1970.

––– and Oberholtzer, K.E. *The context of instructional television: Summary report of research findings.* Denver, Colo.: Denver Public Schools, 1960.

Schramm, W., Chu, G. C., and Yu, F. T. C. China's use of communication–how transferrable is it? In Schramm, W., and Lerner, D., eds. *Communication and Change: The Last Ten Years–and the Next.* Honolulu: University Press of Hawaii, 1976.

Schramm, W., Coombs, P. H. Kahnert, F., and Lyle, J. *The new media: Memo to educational planners.* Paris: UNESCO, 1967.

Schramm, W. et al. Educational radio in Thailand. In UNESCO, *New educational media in action—case studies,* 11-58. Paris: UNESCO, 1967.

Schultz, P. *Communication and Social Change: Video-tape recording as a tool for development.* Rome: Food and Agricultural Agency, 1974. (mimeo)

Schurdak, J. J. *An approach to the use of computers in the instructional process and an evaluation.* Research report. Yorktown Heights, N.Y.: IBM Watson Research Center, 1965.

Searle, B., Friend, J., and Suppes, P. *Application of Radio to Teaching Elementary Mathematics in a Developing Country.* Stanford, Calif.: Institute for Mathematical Studies in the Social Sciences, 1975.

Simmons, A. B. and Stycos, J. M. *Information campaigns and the growth of family planning in Colombia.* Ithaca: International Population Program, Cornell University, 1970.

Sjogren, D. D. *Programmed materials in high school correspondence courses.* Lincoln: University of Nebraska, n.d.

Skinner, B. F. *The behavior of organisms: an experimental analysis.* New York: Appleton-Century-Crofts, 1968.

Slattery, Sister M. J. *An appraisal of the effectiveness of selected instructional sound motion pictures and silent filmstrips in elementary school instruction.* Catholic University, 1953.

Smith, D. D. *Satellite Applications for Education, Culture, and Development.* Paris: UNESCO, n.d.

Smith, K. U. and Smith, M. F. *Cybernetic principles of learning and education design.* New York: Holt, Rinehard & Winston, 1966.

Spain, P. *A Study of the System of Radio Primaria in the State of San Luis Potosi, Mexico.* Stanford, Calif.: Institute for Communication Research, Stanford University, 1973.

––– *A Survey of Radio Listenership in the Davao Province of Mindenao, the Philippines.* Stanford, Calif.: Institute for Communication Research, Stanford University, 1971. (mimeo)

Speagle, R. E. *Educational reform and instructional television in El Salvador: Costs, benefits, and payoffs.* Washington, D.C.: Academy for Educational Development, 1972.

Spector, P., Torres, A., Lichtenstein, S., and Preston, H. O. *Communication and motivation in community development: An experiment.* Report to the U.S. Agency for International Development, November, 1963. (mimeo)

Spencer, R. E. Comparisons of televised with teaching machine and televised with instructor presentations of English grammar. In Carpenter, C. R. and Greenhill, L. P. (eds.) *Comparative research on methods and media for presenting programmed courses in mathematics and English.* University Park, Pa.: Pennsylvania State University, March 1963.

Stanford University, Institute for Communication Research. *Learning in American Samoa.* Reports to the Government of American Samoa by W. Schramm: Quick reference tables of scores, 1972. Some key questions concerning standardized testing and improvement in the schools of American Samoa, 1972. The locally-made tests, 1972. Attitudes toward instructional television, 1973. Effect of the new program on oral English, 1973.

Stein, S. C. An experimental study of the use of motion picture film loops in the instruction of beginning typewriting. *Dissertation Abstracts,* 19, 1959, 3253.

Stickell, D. W. *A critical review of the methodology and results of research comparing televised and face-to-face instruction.* (Doctoral dissertation, Pennsylvania State University) 1963.

Stolurow, L. M. and Beberman, M. *Comparative studies of principles for programming mathematics in automated instruction.* Urbana, Ill.: Training Research Laboratory, University of Illinois, July, 1964.

Stycos, J. M. and Back, K. W. *The control of human fertility in Jamaica.* Ithaca: Cornell University Press, 1964.

Suppes, P. *Computer-assisted instruction at Stanford.* Stanford: Institute for Mathematical Studies in the Social Sciences, May 19, 1971.

––– and Morningstar, M. *Computer-assisted instruction at Stanford, 1966-69: Data, models, and evaluation of the arithmetic program.* New York: Academic Press, 1969.

Sveriges Radio. *The Day the Rainbow Wept: Articles by Bergstrom, S., Frey, C., and Allander, B.* Stockholm: Sveriges Radio, 1974.

Taba, H., Levine, S., and Elzey, F. F. *Thinking in elementary school children.* San Francisco: San Francisco State College, 1964.

Takeshita, J. Lessons learned from family planning studies in Taiwan and Korea. In Berelson, B. et al. (eds.) *Family Planning and Population Programs.* Chicago: University of Chicago Press, 1966.

Tannenbaum, P. H. *Instruction through television: A comparative study.* Urbana: Institute of Communication Research, University of Illinois, June 1956.

Tanner, G. L. *A comparative study of the efficacy of programmed instruction with seventh grade low achievers in arithmetic.* Doctoral dissertation, University of Michigan, 1966.

Television Scolaire du Niger. *Report of the project.* Paris: French Ministry of Cultural Cooperation, 1965.

Tendam, D. J. et al. *Preparation and evaluation in use of selected demonstrations from the introductory college physics course.* West Lafayette, Ind.: Purdue Research Foundation, August 31, 1961.

Theroux, P. *Education by radio: An experiment in rural group listening for adults in Uganda.* Kampapa, Uganda: Makerere College, Makerere Adult Studies Centre, Occasional Paper No. 6, n.d.

Thorndike, E. L. Animal intelligency: An experimental study of the associative processes in animals. *Psychological Review Monograph Supplement,* 2, 1898, No. 8.

––– *Education.* New York: Macmillan, 1912.

Tickton, S. G., ed. *To improve learning: An evaluation of instructional technology.* Report by the Commission on Instructional Technology. New York: Bowker, 1970.

Tiffin, J., and Combes, P. The media selection process. *Educational Broadcasting International,* December 1974, 201-207.

Toffel, G. M. *Effectiveness of instruction by television in teaching high school chemistry in Alabama schools.* University, Ala.: University of Alabama, August, 1961.

Tolman, E. C. There is more than one kind of learning. *Psychological Review,* 56, 1949, 144-155.

Torfs, J., Timmers, A. G. W., Coleman, W.F.K., and von Rundstedt, M. *Preliminary Study of an African Regional Satellite System for Education, Culture, and Development.* Paris: UNESCO, 1973.

Traversm R.M.W. *Research and Theory Related to Audio-Visual Information Transmission.* Salt Lake City, Utah: Bureau of Educational Research, University of Utah, 1964, 1966.

Tsuji, I. *The effect of TV school broadcasts on children in isolated villages.* Tokyo: NHK Radio and TV Culture Research Institute, 1964.

Twyford, L. C., Jr. Implementing the standards established for school media programs. In U.S. Commission on Instructional Technology. *To improve learning.* Bowker: 1960. Vol. 2, 353-356.

Tymowsky, J. Poland–Politechnika Telewizjna. In Internationales Zentralinstitut, *Multi-media systems in adult education: Twelve project description in inine countries.* Munich: Internationales Zentralinstitut fur das Jugend-und Bildungfernsehen, 1971, 152-166.

––– et al. *Television for higher technical education of the unemployed: A first report on a pilot project in Poland. Reports and Papers on Mass Communication,* No. 55. Paris: UNESCO, 1969.

Uganda Department of Agriculture. *A guide for extension workers.* Entebbe, Uganda: Ministry of Agriculture, Forestry and Cooperatives, 1968.

U. K. Commonwealty Secretariat. *The Use of New Media for Educational Purposes in the Commonwealth. Phase I: A survey.* London: Commonwealth Secretariat, 1973.

Underwood, B. J. The representativeness of rote verbal learning. In Melton, A. W. (ed.) *Categories of human learning*. New York: Academic Press, 1960.

UNESCO. *Mass Media in an African Context: An evaluation, of Senegal's pilot project*. Reports and Papers on Mass Communication. No. 69. Paris: Unesco, 1973.

——— *Television for Higher Technical Education of Workers*. Reports and Papers on Mass Communication, No. 67. Paris: Unesco, 1973.

——— *John Amos Comenius, 1592-1670: Selections*. Introduction by Jean Piaget. Paris: Unesco, 1957.

——— Regional Office for Education in Asia. Exploring New Approaches and Methods in Education in Asia. *Bulletin of the Unesco Regional Office*, Bangkok, Vi, 1, September, 1971.

University of Illinois. *Report of progress for the field test of the University of Illinois' PLATO System of CAI, sponsored by the National Science Foundation*. Urbana, Illinois, University of Illinois, 1975.

U.S. Commission on Instructional Technology. *To improve learning*. (Report of the Commission). New York: Bowker, 1970.

VanderMeer, A. W. Relative effectiveness of instruction by: *films exclusively, films plus study guides, and standard lecture methods*. Port Washington, N.Y.: U.S. Naval Special Devices Center, 1950.

——— The economy of time in industrial training: An experimental study of the use of sound films in the training of engine lathe operators. *Journal of Educational Psychology*, 36, 1945, 65-90.

——— Training Film Evaluation: *Comparison between two films of personal hygiene*. Port Washington, N.Y.: U.S. Navy Special Devices Center, 1953.

Vernon, P. E. An experiment on the value of the film and filmstrip in the instruction of adults. *British Journal of Educational Psychology* 16, 1946, 3, 149-162.

Vestal, D. A. *The relative effectiveness in the teaching of high school physics of the photographic techniques utilized by the sound motion pictures*. Lincoln, Nebraska: University of Nebraska doctoral dissertation, 1952.

Von Mondfrans, A. P., and Houser, R. L. *Toward a paradigm for selecting media to present basic concepts*. Paper presented to annual meeting of the American Educational Research Association, March, 1970. West Lafayette, Ind.: Purdue University, 1970.

Wade, Serena. Hagerstown: a pioneer in closed-circuit television instruction. In UNESCO, *New Educational Media in Action*, 1, 59-82. Paris: UNESCO, 1967.

Wagner, G. Austria—The radio course "Lebendige Wirtschaft." In Internationes Zentralinstitut. *Multi-media systems in adult education: Twelve project description in inine countries*. Munich: Internationales Zentralinstitut fur das Jugend-und Bildungfernsehen, 1971, 26-38.

Wagner, R. V., Lybrand, W. A., Reznick, W. M. *A Study of Systemic Resistances to Utilization of ITV in Public School Systems*. Report to U.S. Department of Health, Education, and Welfare. Washington: February, 1969.

Wells, R. F. A study to determine whether general concepts which are usually taught by motion pictures can be learned as effectively by sequential still photography during traditional versus self pace study periods. (Doctoral dissertation, Purdue University) 1969. Available from University Microfilms, Ann Arbor, Michigan, 1970, No. 23674.

Wendt, P. R., and Butts, G. K. *A report of an experiment in the acceleration of teaching tenth grade world history with the help of an integrated series of films*. Carbondale, Ill.: General Publications, 1960.

Wermer, F. E. Netherlands—TELEAC (Stichting Televisie Academie). In Internationales Zentralinstitut. *Multi-media systems in adult education: Twelve project description in nine countries*. Munich: Internationales Zentralinstitut fur das Jugend-und Bildungfernsehen, 1971, 138-151.

Westley, B. H., and Barrow, L. C., Jr. *Exploring the news: A comparative study of the teaching effectiveness of radio and television*. Research Bulletin No. 12. Madison, Wisc.: University of Wisconsin Television Laboratory, 1959.

Whitted, J. H., Jr. et al. *Development and experimental evaluation of an automated multi-media course on transitors*. Camden, N.J.: RCA Service Company, September, 1966.

Wilder, F. *Suggestions for finding the best media and messages in family planning mass communications.* Paper for Bangkok workshop on family planning programs, December 1968. (mimeo)

––– *What do we know about promoting family planning through the mass media?* Paper for Pakistan International Family Planning Conference, January-February, 1969. (mimeo)

Williams, D. C., Paul, J., and Ogilvie, J. C. Mass media, learning, and retention. *Canadian Journal of Psychology,* 11, 1957, 157-163.

Wisconsin Research Project in School Broadcasting. *Radio in the Classroom.* Madison, Wisc.: University of Wisconsin Press, 1942.

Wise, H. A. *Motion pictures as an aid in American history.* New Haven: Yale University Press, 1939.

Wittich, W. A., et al. *The Wisconsin physics film evaluation project.* Madison: University of Wisconsin, 1959.

––– and Schuller, C. F. *Instructional Technology: Its nature and use.* Fifth edition. New York: Harper & Row, 1972.

Wood, A. W. The community school in Tanzania–The experience at Litowa. *Teacher Education in New Countries.* 14, 1969, 4-12.

Woodworth, R. S. *Dynamics of behavior.* New York: Holt, Rinehart & Winston, 1958.

Wrightstone, J. W. Radio education. *In Encyclopedia of Educational Research,* New York: Macmillan, 1950, 953-61.

Xoomsai, T. and Ratanamangala, B. *School broadcast: Its evaluation.* Bangkok: Ministry of Education, 1962.

Young, J. P. and Stolurow, L. M. *A CAI study of learning geologic time and evolution.* Cambridge: Harvard University, Computer-Aided Instruction Library, September, 1969.

SUBJECT INDEX

Ability, related to learning from media, 39-40, 58
Acción Cultural Popular. See: ACPO
ACPO (Acción Cultural Popular), 18, 135, 226, 235, 237, 244-250, 259-260, 276, 279
Adult education. See: Extending the school; Nonformal education
Agency for International Development (U.S.), 9, 134, 144, 150
Agriculture teaching by media: programmed instruction, 190-191; radio, 56, 135-136, 233, 237-242; smaller audio media, 56; smaller visual media, 56
Alaska media project, 257
American Samoa, educational television in, 18, 21, 110, 127-128, 136, 139, 142-146, 149-153, 160-164, 171-174, 226, 269, 272, 276
Animateurs, 250 ff.
Antioch College, 279
Audiodiscs, teaching by, 13, 80-82, 84-85, 91
Audiotape, teaching by, 13, 22; experiments on, 32, 51-52, 55; pedagogical treatment of, 57, 62, 80-82, 84-85, 88, 91, 101; economics of, 111, 121, 126-127
Australia, instructional media in: radio-correspondence schools, 18, 132-133, 137, 198, 200, 208, 210, 222, 223; "flying doctors' radio," 132, 200; open university, 205
Austria, instructional media in, 201, 208, 213, 214, 221

Brazil, instructional media in, 251
Big media, little media, definition, 16

British Open University, 14, 19, 20, 85, 95-98, 120, 129, 131-132, 137, 204, 207, 208, 210, 211, 213, 214, 222, 223, 272, 289

Canada, instructional media in. See: Challenge for Change, Fogo project; Radio rural forum
CAI. See: computer-assisted instruction
Cassettes, teaching by, 13, 85, 88, 91. See also: Audiotape
Central African Republic, instructional media in, 189
Challenge for Change (Canadian media project), 229-230, 250
Chicago TV College, 129, 201, 206, 208, 211, 213, 214, 216-219, 222
China, use of instructional communication in, 233, 259
Classroom teaching. See: Face-to-face teaching
Coding systems of media: analogue, 88-91; digital, 87-88, 91; direct vs mediated experience, 91-92; iconic, 87-88, 91; McLuhan on, 87; Salomon on, 87; summary, 102-103
"Coleman Report": (Equality of Educational Opportunity), 19
Colombia, instructional media in: ACPO, 18, 135, 226, 235, 237, 244-250, 259-260, 276, 279; school television, 110, 127, 129-130, 185-186
Commercial skills—teaching, by media: CAI, 56; film, 41, 42, 46, 53, 54, 55; programmed instruction, 56; smaller audio media, 52, 54, 55; smaller visual media, 52, 53, 54, 55; television, 41

Commitment in group discussion, effect of, 242-243

Committee for Economic Development, 281

Communication satellite, teaching by, 21, 114

Computer-assisted instruction (CAI), 16, 22, 24; experiments on, 30-32, 36, 47-49; pedagogical treatment of, 83, 84-85; economics of, 122-124, 126-127

"Cone of Experience" (Dale), 77

Correspondence study, 18; experiments, 57; pedagogical treatment of, 88; economics of, 132-135; for extending the school, 199-204

Cost-benefit analysis, 108-109, and Chapter 4 (Economic Evidence), throughout.

Cost-effectiveness analysis, 108-109, and Chapter 4 (Economic Evidence), throughout.

Costs of instructional media; big vs little media, 110-111, and throughout; CAI costs, 122-124; capital costs, 106; comparative costs of different media, 126-127, and throughout; cost-benefit analysis, 108-109; cost-effectiveness analysis, 108-109; depreciation of capital expenditures, how figured, 106-107; distribution costs, 114, 121; economies of scale, 110-116, 137-139; extended school costs, 131-135; fixed and variable costs, 107; General Learning Corporation study, 109-122, 272, 283; "notional" interest, 106; production costs, 120-121; programmed instruction costs, 122-123; high-quality programming, costs of, 120-121, 137; radio vs television production costs, 120-121, 129; radio group costs, 135-136; reception costs, 116ff.; recurrent costs, 107; smaller media costs, 125-126; cost figures for ACPO, 135; Australia radio-correspondence, 132-133; American Samoa, 128-130, 136; British Open University, 131-132; Chicago TV College, 129; Colombia ETV, 130; El Salvador, 128-130; German Tele-

kolleg, 133; Hagerstown, 128-129; Ivory Coast, 127-128; Kenya, 134-135; Mexico, 129-131; NHK Gakuen, 133-134; Niger radio clubs, 136; "Sesame Street," 120-121; Togo radio clubs, 136; Thai radio, 136

Côte d'Ivoire educational television. See: Ivory Coast

Deciding groups, 237-243

Design of instruction: big vs little media, 103; Briggs' outline of, 75-76; British Open University outline, 95-99; control limitations, 80-83; cost considerations, 86 (and Chapter 4); delivery capabilities, 83-86; Gagne on, 76-77, 100; judgment vs theory, 77-79; managerial questions, 79ff.; media capabilities (Allen), 101; relating media to tasks, 75ff.; selection, 75-79, and throughout; symbol and coding questions, 86-93; taxonomies of, 63-77, 79-95

Development, use of media for, 256-259, and throughout.

Dial access, teaching by, 111, 121, 126

Discussion and commitment, effect of, 242-243

Discussion groups, 250-257

East-West Center (Honolulu), 9

Economies of scale, 110-122, 137-139

Educational games, teaching by, 13

"Electric Company," 28, 120

El Salvador, instructional media in: school television, 18, 110, 120-121, 127-138, 142-144, 146-147, 149-153, 164-168, 171-174, 226, 269, 272

Encyclopedia of Educational Research, 32

Economic and social development. See: Development

Economics of instructional media. See: Costs of instructional media

Experiments on instructional media: ability as a variable, 39-40, 58; big vs little media, 33-34, 53-56; conclusions from experiments, 34-36; content and style questions, 43; films, 30, 46-47; instructional radio,

30, 50-51; instructional television, 27-30, 44-47; multi-media combinations, 34, 56-57; programmed instruction, 30, 47-49; reliability and realism of media experiments, 56-57; smaller media, 30, 51-53; summary by Gagne, 59-60

Extending the school, use of media for: audience composition, 212-214; choice of media for, 205-207; completion rates, 214-216; correspondence study in, 198-199, 210-211, 216-224; effectiveness of, 208-224; enrollments and audiences, 209-214; learning from, 216-222; need for, 198-199; outline of, 199-204; print as basic medium for, 205-206; radio for, 199-201, 203-205, 209-211, 214-216, 219, 224; television for, 201-205, 209-211, 214-224; trends, 206-208; use and results in Australia, 200-208, 210, 213, 222; Austria, 201, 208, 214, 221; East Germany, 201, 208-209; France, 200, 202-203, 208-209; India, 199, 206, 208, 210-211, 221; Israel, 205, 212; Japan, 203, 208, 211, 212-213, 215-216; Kenya, 201, 208, 211, 221, 222; Mexico, 202, 208, 211, 216, 219-220, 222; Netherlands, 202, 208-210; Poland, 202, 208, 213, 221-222; Sweden, 203-204, 208, 210; Thailand, 204, 208, 211; United Kingdom, 204, 207, 208, 211, 212, 213, 214, 222-223; United States, 199-200, 201, 206, 208, 211, 214, 216-219; West Germany, 201, 204, 208, 210-212, 213, 215, 221, 222

Face-to-face teaching, compared with media. For estimated cost, see 126-127. Also, many of experiments reported in Chapter 2 compare face-to-face with media instruction, and face-to-face teaching is an important part of most of the field projects reported in Chapters 5-8

Family planning, media research on, 257-259

Films, teaching by, 13, 16, 22; experiments on, 30, 36-39, 41-42, 46-47, 53-58; pedagogical treatment of, 63-64, 80-83, 84-85, 88, 91, 101, 103; economics of, 111-122, 126-127; in nonformal education, 229-230, 255-257

Filmstrips and loops, teaching by, 13, 20, 24; experiments 32, 52-57; pedagogical treatment, 80-82, 84-85, 88, 91

Fogo (Newfoundland) media project, 255-257

Ford Foundation, The, 9, 177, 179, 181

Fordham University, 41, 283

France, instructional media in, 18, 189, 200, 202, 208, 209

Friedrich Ebert Stiftung, 279

F-Scale (California), 40

Fund for Advancement of Education, 26. See also: Ford Foundation

Gaston Berger Resolution (UNESCO), 144

General Learning Corporation study, 109-122, 272, 283

Germany, East, instructional media in, 201, 208, 209

Germany, West, instructional media in, 22; Telekolleg, 18, 129, 133, 137, 202, 208, 210-211, 213, 215, 221, 222, 276; Funkolleg, 194, 201, 208, 210, 215, 223, 276; open university, 205

Ghana, radio rural forums in, 240-241

Great Britain, instructional media in. See: British Open University

Hagerstown (Washington County, Maryland) use of educational television, 110, 128, 177-181, 194

Health and family planning—teaching, by media: film, 32; radio, 56, 57, 233, 237-242; smaller audio media, 56-57; smaller visual media, 56-57; television, 254, 255

"Hiding hand, the," (Hirschman), 170-171

Hong Kong, media for campaigns in, 259

Humanities—teaching, by media: programmed instruction, 49; radio, 51, 187-189; television, 218, 219

Illinois, University of. See: "Plato" system

India, instructional media in: communication satellite, 20, 21; correspondence teaching, 199, 206, 210-211, 221; radio teaching, 22-23; radio rural forum, 56, 135-136, 237-239, 241-243, 260; school television, 184-185, 208; campaigns, 258-259

Indonesia, instructional media in, 21, 127, 128

Internationales Zentralinstitut (Munich), 285

International Research Associates, 179, 285

Iran, instructional media in, 21, 57

Israel, instructional media in, 28, 205

Italy, instructional media in. See: Telescuola

Ivory Coast, educational television in, 18, 110, 127-138, 139, 142-144, 147, 150-152, 168, 171-174, 269

Jamaica, use of media for campaigns, 259

Japan, instructional media in, 18: NHK Gakuen, 129, 133-134, 203, 208, 211, 212, 213, 216, 222, 223; school television, 51, 181-194; radio teaching, 129; correspondence study, 198

Kenya, instructional media in: radio-correspondence teaching 134-135, 137, 201, 208, 211, 221, 222, 226, 276

Korea, instructional media in: multimedia educational reform, 21, 110, 142-144, 147-149, 156-158, 168-171, 269; media for campaigns, 259

Korean Educational Development Institute (KEDI), 143, 148-149, 156-157, 169, 286

Language laboratories, 121. See also: Audiotape

Language teaching by media: CAI, 30-31, 47, 48; films, 53; programmed instruction, 50; radio, 51, 187-189; smaller visual media, 53; television, 45, 57, 160-163, 182, 217, 218, 219, 220

Litowa villages (Tanzania), 231-233, 235

Malawi, instructional media in, 189, 240

Mandoul Project (in Chad), 233-235

Mathematics teaching by media: CAI, 47, 48, 49; print, 210; programmed instruction, 49, 50, 56, 190-191, 193; smaller visual media, 52; television, 45, 56, 57, 160-163, 182, 210, 218, 219, 220, 222

Media of instruction. See also: names of individual media (e.g., audiodiscs, audiotape, computer-assisted instruction, cassettes, correspondence study, dial access, educational games, face-to-face teaching, films, filmstrips, overhead projectors, programmed instruction, radio, radiovision, textbooks, videotape), subjects taught by media (e.g., mathematics, language, science, etc.), countries using instructional media, media projects (e.g., Hagerstown, El Salvador, radio rural forum, etc.),·and large topic headings related to media (e.g., economics, experiments, nonformal education, etc.). Also, relation to other media, 12; origins, 12; print, first modern medium of instruction, 12; electronic and photographic media, 12-13; as extension of teacher, 13; size of instructional media system, 13-14; can they teach? 14; is one better than others? 14; importance of being able to select them, 15; big media, little media, 15-16; productivity of, 16-18; in developing countries, 18-19; some conclusions, 261-278

Mexico, instructional media in: radio-primaria, 127-131, 137, 201, 208, 216-217, 219-220; telesecondaria, 127-131, 137, 202, 208, 211, 216-217, 219-220, 223

Miami University, instructional television, 116

Military skills teaching by media: CAI, 56; film, 41, 42, 46, 53, 54, 55; programmed instruction, 56; smaller audio media, 52, 54, 55; smaller visual media, 52, 53, 54, 55; television, 41

National Association of Educational Broadcasters (NAEB), 288
National education reform projects, differences in, 142-158 (table, 142, 150-151); financing of, 143-144; monitors in classrooms, 153; origins of, 144-149; pace of development, 149-155; planning in Korea, 156-158; reasons for media selection, 144-149; results: Niger, 158-160; Samoa, 160-164; El Salvador, 164-168; Ivory Coast, 168; Korea, 168-169; some conclusions, 171-173; teacher training in, 150-153; television, why important in these projects, 170-172
National Film Board of Canada, 229-230, 250, 288
Nebraska, University of, open university program, 21, 205
Netherlands, instructional media in, 129, 202, 208, 209, 210-211
New Zealand, instructional media in, 198
NHK (Nippon Hoso Kyokai—Japan Broadcasting Corporation), 51, 129, 203, 211, 212, 289
Niger, instructional media in: educational television, 18, 110, 142-145, 149-153, 158-160, 171-174, 226, 269, 276; radio clubs, 251-252; radiovision, 18, 189-190
Nonformal education, use of media for: big vs little media in, 260; costs 238-239; definition of the concept, 226-228; development campaigns and nonformal education, 257-259; group, importance of, 236-257 (deciding group, 237-243; study group, 243-250; discussing group, 250-257); importance of, at present time, 227; interpersonal communication in, 228; local activity, the key idea, 230-235; mass media not the key, 235; multi-media nature of, 222-230; radio as basic medium, if any, 228; radio rural forums, 237-243; some conclusions, 259-260; use and results in: ACPO, 243-250; Canada, 229-230, 237; "Challenge for Change," 229-230; China, 233; Colombia, 243-250; Fogo project, 255-257; Ghana, 240-242; India, 237-240; Litowa schools, 231-232; Mandoul project, 233-235; Senegal, 253-255; Tanzania, 231-232; 257; Togo, 252-253; Zaire, 236

Office of Education (U.S.), 26
Overhead projectors and transparencies, teaching by, 13, 16, 32, 52

Pakistan, use of media for campaigns, 258-259
Papua New Guinea, use of radio serials, 236
"Paris University III," radio and correspondence programs in, 201
Penn State studies, 27, 44, 116
Perception of instructional media, 33
Phonograph, teaching by. See: Audiodiscs
"Plato" system of computerized instruction (University of Illinois), 21, 123-124
Poland, instructional media in, 202, 208, 213, 221-222
Programmed instruction, teaching by, 16; experiments on, 30-32, 49-50, 55-58; pedagogical treatment of, 101; economics of, 122-124, 126-127; to supplement classroom teaching, 190-194
Programmed texts (See: Programmed instruction)
Purdue University, teaching by radio, 199-200, 206, 208, 211, 276

Radio rural forum: in Canada, 237; Costa Rica, 240; Dahomey, 240; Ghana, 240-241; India, 56, 135-136, 237-239, 241-243; Malawi, 240; Togo, 240
Radio Sutatenza. See: ACPO
Radio, teaching by, 16, 18, 20, 22; experiments on, 32, 36, 38, 50-51, 54, 56; pedagogical treatment of, 80-83,

84-85, 88, 91, 95-102; economics of, 111-122, 126-127, 127-130, 132, 135-136; in educational reform, 171; in supplementing classroom teaching, 186-190; in extending the school, 199-204, 219-223; in non-formal education, 236-250, 251, 253, 258-260

Radiovision, teaching by, 18, 84, 91, 190-191

Ramkhamhaeng University. See: Thailand

Reading taught by media: print, 38; radio, 135; smaller visual media, 38, 53; television, 45, 244

Research on instructional media. See especially: Experiments on instructional media, Design of instruction, Tests of instructional media, National educational reform projects, Supplementary use of instructional media, Extending the school, Nonformal education

Rhodesia, programmed instruction in, 190-194

RTS-Promotion (France), extension programs in, 202

Samoa, educational television in. See: American Samoa

Satellite. See: Communication satellite

Sarvodoya Movement (Sri Lanka), 227

School curriculum (in general) taught by media: correspondence study, 133-135, 211-212, 221; films, 56, 57, 62; print, 56, 62, 131-133, 222, 248-250; radio, 211-212, 221, 248-250; smaller audio media, 57, 62; smaller visual media, 57, 62; television, 38, 62, 127-130, 131-133, 158-169, 177-186, 211-212, 221, 222

Science teaching by media: CAI, 47; correspondence, 57; films, 46, 53, 54; print, 210; radio, 50; smaller visual media, 52, 53, 54; television, 44, 45, 57, 58, 182, 210, 212, 213, 217, 218, 220

Selecting media: act of selection, 19-23; attraction of technology, 19; big vs little media, 274-278; program capabilities of media, 267-269; cost considerations, 270-273; importance of selection, 16-19; importance to developing countries, 18-19; "leapfrogging" into new media, 22-23; logical vs actual process, 263-264; media for different tasks, 269-270; process of selection, 263-267; questions of content, 273-274; reasons for selection, 22; selective media means selecting systems, 267-269; tasks media can do, 267-270; unrealism of trying to choose "ideal" medium, 268-269

Senegal, instructional media in: teleclubs, 171, 253-255, 260; radio clubs, 253

"Sesame Street," 28-30, 45, 120, 272, 273-274

Silent films in teaching. See: Films

Slides, teaching by, 14, 18, 22; experiments, 32, 53-54, 57; pedagogical treatment of, 80-82, 84-85, 88, 91

Slide films. See: Filmstrips

Social science and psychology teaching by media: films, 46; programmed instruction, 49, 50, 55; radio, 51, 54, 55, 57, 182, 210, 212, 217, 218, 219, 221

Sound films in teaching. See: Films

Soviet Union, 20

Spain, instructional media in, 22

Stanford University, teaching by television, 21, 205, 206

Study groups, 243-253

Supplementary use of instructional media: active classes, effect of, 185-186; effective television teachers, characteristics of, 178; financing of, 177; how are media chosen, 177, 181-182; opinions of, 179; programmed instruction as supplement, 190-194; radio as supplement, 186-189; radiovision as supplement, 189-190; results of, 179-189; some conclusions, 194-195; supplement vs enrichment, 176; television for supplement, 177-186; use and results in Colombia, 185-186; Hagerstown,

177-181; India, 184-185; Japan, 181-184; Rhodesia, 190-194; Thailand, 186-189

Sveriges Radio (Swedish Broadcasting Corporation), 292

Sweden, instructional media in, 18, 203-204, 207, 208, 210

Taiwan, use of media for family planning campaigns, 258

Talkback (in television teaching), 27-28

Tanzania, use of instructional media, 21; Litowa schools, 231-233, 235; Ujamaa villages, 257

Taxonomies: Bloom's taxonomy of the cognitive domain, 63-65; Dale's cone of experience, 77; events of instruction (Gagne), 74-75; Gagne's types of learning, 62-73; Krathwohl and affective domain, 63-65; media taxonomy, steps toward, 79-95

Teachers for television. See: Television teachers

TELEAC. See: Netherlands

Telekolleg (in West Germany), 18

Telescuola (Italy), 237, 244

Television teachers, qualities of effectiveness, 178

Television, teaching by, 16, 18, 20-22, 24; experiments on, 26-29, 36-38, 41-42, 44-45, 54-58; pedagogical treatment of, 62, 80-83, 84-85, 88, 91, 95-103; economics of, 111-122, 126-127, 127-130; in educational reform, 142-173; in supplementing classroom teaching, 176-186; in extending the school, 199-204, 210-223; in nonformal education, 253-255

Textbooks (printed texts or workbooks are a part of most of the instructional systems reported on in this book, but their presence is usually assumed rather than studied), 13-14, 56, 80-82, 84-85, 88, 91, 101, 126-127, 199-204

Thailand, instructional media in: open university, 203, 208, 211, 213, 223; school radio, 18, 110, 127, 186-189, 194

Togo, instructional media in: radio forums, 240, 253

Traditional media, teaching by, 20

TRU. See: Sweden

Uganda, rural radio in, 228-229

United Kingdom, instructional media in. See: British Open University

UNESCO (United Nations Educational, Scientific, and Cultural Organization) 16, 144, 147, 150, 171, 185-186, 293

United States, instructional media in (most of the experiments reported in Chapters 2 and 3, the theoretical work in Chapter 3, and the economic studies in Chapter 4, were done in the United States. See those chapters especially, and also Hagerstown; Chicago TV College; *Sesame Street;* Stanford University television; and throughout.)

University curriculum (in general) taught by media: correspondence study, 133-135, 211-213, 216-217, 221; print, 131-132, 222; radio, 133-135, 214; television, 116-117, 131-135, 215

Upper Volta, instructional media in, 226; radiovision, 18

Videocassettes, teaching by. See: Videotape

Videotape, teaching by, 13, 22, 80-83, 84, 88, 91, 114, 121, 126. See also: Television

Zaire, instructional media in: radio teaching, 236

NAME INDEX

NAME INDEX

Abel, F.P., 279
Abell, H.C., 240-241, 279
Adams, E., 48, 279
Ahmed, M., 226-227, 235, 279
Ali, J.M., 258, 286
Allander, B., 89, 279
Allen, D., 279
Allen, W.H., 99-101, 279
Allison, S.G., 279
Almstead, F.E., 45, 279
Andersson, G., 210, 279
Andrus, A.M.G., 279
Arana de Swadesh, E., 236, 279
Ash, P., 46, 279
Ashby, Sir Eric Lord, 11, 16
Ashford, T.H., 49, 279
Atkinson, C., 279
Atkinson, R.C., 47, 279
Attiyeh, R., 49, 279
Austin, G.A., 281
Averch, H., 19, 280
Axeen, M.E., 280

Bach, G., 49, 279
Back, K.W., 259, 291
Balakrishnan, T.R., 259, 280
Balin, H.B., 280
Ball, S., 29, 45, 273, 280
Barrow, L.C., Jr., 38, 54, 58, 293
Beach, B.R., 33, 282
Beatty, W.H., 58, 282
Beberman, M., 291
Bedall, F.K., 280
Beech, R.P., 280
Beneke, Walter, 146
Berelson, B., 280, 292
Berger, E.J., 280
Berman, A.I., 280
Bett, S.T., 285

Bhatia, B., 280
Bhatt, B., 235, 280
Bitzer, M., 48, 123, 280
Blake, R.R., 289
Bloom, B.S., 62-65, 280
Bobier, D.T., 49, 280
Bogatz, G.A., 29, 45, 273, 280
Bogue, D. J., 285
Bohlin, E., 210, 279
Bollenbacher, J.K., 58, 285
Boudreaux, M., 48, 280
Bourgeois, M., 280
Bower, E.M., 65, 285
Bretz, R., 80-83, 176, 280
Briggs, L.J., 61-62, 65, 72-79, 102, 280, 283
Broadbent, D.E., 33, 280
Bronson, Vernon, 145
Brophy, J.E., 95, 280
Brumberg, S., 245, 281
Bruner, J.S., 72, 91-92, 281
Bryan, E.F., 57, 281
Buckler, W.R., 58, 281
Butman, R.C., 25, 281
Butts, G.K., 47, 293

Callaway, A., 281
Campeau, P.L., 61-63, 65, 77, 95, 280, 281
Carlson, B.J., 46, 279
Carpenter, C.R., 22-23, 31, 41, 43, 44, 281, 291
Carpenter, H.A., 281
Carpenter, M.B., 281
Carroll, S., 280
Cartwright, C.A., 48, 281
Cartwright, G.P., 48, 281
Castle, C.H., 45, 281
Castleberry, S., 281

Cernada, G.P., 258, 281
Chance, C.W., 52, 281
Chausow, H.M., 217-219, 282
Chester, L.G., 281
Chu, G.C., 27, 233, 259, 281, 290
Chung, K.K., 286
Clergerie, B.A., 281
Cobb, J.C., 259, 281
Cofer, C.N., 285, 289
Coleman, J.S., 19, 162-163, 281
Coleman, W.F.K., 241, 292
Combs, A.W., 286, 287
Comenius, J.A., 13, 16, 42, 281
Comstock, G., 186, 243-244, 281
Constantine, Sister M., 50, 282
Cook, D.C., 282
Coombes, P., 84, 88, 292
Coombs, P.H., 109, 226-227, 235, 279, 282
Corle, C.C., 45, 282
Craig, G.Q., 55, 282
Cronbach, L.J., 39-40, 42, 94-95, 282
Curry, R.P., 58, 282

Dale, E., 77, 282
Day, W.F., 33, 282
Devgan, A.K., 280
Dick, W., 48, 95, 282, 284
Dietmeyer, H.J., 282
Domino, G., 95, 282
Donaldson, T., 280
Dordick, H.S., 129, 133, 210-213, 221, 281, 282
Doty, L.A., 49, 282
Dreher, R.E., 58, 282
Driscoll, J.P., 282
Dubey, D.C., 280
Dubin, R., 27, 282
Dworkin, S., 52, 282

Edling, J., 290
Edwards, R.K., 57, 282
Egly, M., 282
Einstein, A., 69
El Hadj Badge, M., 251, 282
Elliott, R.W., 52, 282
Elzey, F.F., 292
Engar, K.M., 58, 283
Engelhart, M.D., 62-65, 280
Erickson, C.G., 217-219, 282
Erickson, E.H., 63, 283
Evertson, C.M., 95, 280

Fawcett, J.T., 258, 283
Filep, R., 26, 283
Fillmer, H.T., 50, 283
Fincher, G.E., 50, 283
Fleishman, E.A., 283
Forlano, G., 280
Forrest, J.E., 290
Forsythe, R.O., 211, 283
Fougeyrollas, P., 253-255, 283
Freedman, R., 258, 280, 283
Friend, J., 291
Furst, E.J., 62-65, 280

Gagne, R.M., 46, 59-62, 65-77, 100, 102, 103, 275, 280, 283, 290
Galanter, E., 289
Garace, F., 257, 283
Gardner, John, 261
Garnier, R., 209, 283
Gates, A.I., 41-42, 283
Gephart, W.R., 290
Germain, A., 290
Gibbon, E., 89
Gibson, R., 289
Gilbert, T.F., 66, 283
Gillespie, R., 57, 258, 283
Gladstone, A.J., 41-42, 287
Glaser, R.G., 65, 283
Glasgow, M.W., 283
Goodman, L.S., 283
Goodman, R.I., 48, 92-93, 288
Goodnow, J.J., 281
Gordon, O.J., 58, 283
Goto, K., 211, 212, 283
Graf, R.W., 45, 279
Grant, S., 152, 284
Greenhill, L.P., 41, 44, 281, 291
Grilliches, Z., 109, 284
Gropper, G.L., 31, 46, 58, 283, 284
Grosslight, J.H., 53, 284
Grubb, R.E., 48, 284
Guilford, J.P., 284
Guthrie, E.R., 65, 67, 284
Gwyn, S., 230, 284

Hadsell, R.S., 42, 287
Haggart, S.A., 281
Haleworth, B., 236, 284
Hallak, J., 109, 282
Hancock, A., 284
Hansen, D.N., 48, 284
Hansen, W.L., 122, 284

Harry, S.F., 284
Hartman, F.R., 33, 284
Hawkridge, D.G., 14, 25-26, 65, 75, 190-194, 284
Hayman, R.W., 111, 120-121, 284
Hedley, R.A., 27, 282
Heidgerken, L., 53, 284
Herminghaus, E.G., 45, 284
Heron, W.T., 51, 284
Hilgard, E.R., 284
Hill, S.A., 284
Hirschman, A.O., 170-171, 284
Hoban, C.F., Jr., 42, 285
Hoffbauer, H., 210, 215, 284
Holden, A., 52, 282
Hollister, W.G., 65, 285
Homeyer, F.C., 48, 285
Hornik, R., 143, 167, 285, 287
Horstwitz, G.R., 280
Houser, R.L., 293
Hovland, C.I., 42, 46, 54, 285
Hughes, J.L., 50, 285
Hull, C.L., 65, 285

Illich, I., 225
Ingle, H.T., 285

Jacobs, J.N., 58, 285
Jain, N.C., 241-243, 285
Jamison, D., 106-109, 123, 127-130, 138-139, 285
Jenkins, J.J., 42, 68, 285
Johnson, W.B., 258, 285

Kahnert, F., 136, 252-253, 285, 290
Kale, S.V., 53, 285
Karlin, B., 258, 286
Keislar, E.R., 286
Kelley, T.D., 53, 65, 286
Kendler, H.H., 66, 286
Khaisang, S., 283
Kies, N., 286
Kiesling, H., 280
Kimble, G.A., 42, 286
Kimmel, P., 210, 286
Kinane, K., 132, 286
Kincaid, L., 259, 286
Klees, S., 106-109, 123, 127-130, 138-139, 211, 219-220, 285, 286, 287
Klingenschmidt, J.E., 52, 288
Komoski, P.K., 13, 286

Kopstein, F.F., 41, 287
Koran, M., 43, 286
Krathwohl, D.R., 62-65, 280, 286
Krishnamoorthy, P.V., 280
Krival, A.A., 211, 221, 286

Lagowski, J.J., 281
Laidlaw, B., 286
Lam, P., 259, 286
Latta, R., 95, 282
Layard, R., 286
Lazaro, H., 283
Lee, C.C., 286
Lee, Rex M., 145, 172
Lefranc, R., 136, 143, 189-190, 251, 286
Levin, H., 111, 120-121, 284
Levine, S., 292
Lewin, K., 40-43
Lichtenstein, S., 56, 291
Lippert, H.T., 48, 284
Lu, L.P., 258, 259, 281, 286
Lumley, F.J., 51, 287
Lumsdaine, A.A., 31, 41-43, 46, 54, 58, 65, 284, 285, 287
Lumsden, K., 49, 129, 279, 287
Lybrand, W.A., 293
Lyle, J., 185, 244, 286, 287, 290

McAnany, E., 129, 136, 143, 211, 219-220, 236, 250-251, 253, 285, 287
McClelland, S.D., 280
Maccoby, N., 186, 243-244, 281
McCombs, M., 129, 211, 214, 287
McDonald, F.J., 43, 286
McIntyre, C.J., 41, 53, 55, 284, 287
McKeachie, W.J., 95, 288
MacKenzie, N., 288
MacLennan, D.W., 289
McLuhan, M., 13, 38, 87, 197-198, 274, 288
McNamara, W.J., 50, 285
McNeil, J.D., 45, 288
Mager, R., 287
Maheu, Rene, 141
Majasan, J.K., 95, 287
Mangrove, B.A., 285
Marathey, R., 280
Margolin, J.B., 287
Markle, D.G., 32, 287

Marsh, L.A., 50, 287
Martini, H.R., 287
Maslow, A.H., 63-64, 287
Mathur, J.C., 56, 287, 289
Matthai, R.J., 259, 280
May, M.A., 42, 62, 77, 280, 287
Mayo, J., 129, 143, 211, 219-220, 285, 287
Mayuri, F., 283
Mead, Margaret, 142
Melton, A.W., 65, 286
Menne, J.W., 52, 288
Mercer, J., 41, 288
Mercoiret, Jacques, 234
Merrill, M.D., 92-93, 288
Miller, J.G., 85, 105, 288
Miller, R.M., 230-231, 288
Mills, A., 253, 288
Moldstad, J.A., 288
Monahan, P.E., 95, 288
Monsivais, C., 35, 288
Morningstar, M., 30-32, 47, 292
Mowrer, O.H., 103, 288
Musto, S., 249, 288

Neidt, C., 289
Nelson, H.E., 55, 288
Nemzek, C.L., 282
Neu, D.M., 41, 46, 288
Neurath, P., 56, 184-185, 237-238, 287, 289
Nicol, J., 237, 289
Nord, D.L., 52, 288
Nordquist, E.C., 58, 283
Nyerere, J.K., 21, 231, 289

Oberholtzer, K.E., 34, 290
Ogilvie, J.C., 54, 294
Olson, D.R., 91-92, 281

Pant, N.K., 210, 221, 289
Park, H.J., 259, 286
Patrick, R.B., 289
Paul, J., 54, 294
Paulu, B., 209, 289
Pavlov, I.P., 66, 289
Peerson, N., 45, 289
Piaget, J., 13, 63, 289
Pickrel, G., 289
Pierce-Jones, J., 50, 287
Pincus, J., 280

Plowright, P., 289
Popham, W.J., 51, 289
Porter, D.A., 50, 58, 289
Postgate, R., 288
Postman, L., 66, 289
Preston, H.O., 56, 291
Psacharoupoulos, G., 109, 289

Raina, B.L., 289
Ratanamungala, B., 51, 187-188, 289, 294
Rathjens, G.W., 125, 281
Raulet, P., 259, 281
Razran, G., 289
Reid, J.S., 289
Reznick, W.M., 293
Robert, J., 251, 282
Robin, G.G., 48, 281
Roderick, W.W., 57, 282
Rogers, E., 290
Roid, G.H., 289
Romano, L., 57, 289
Roshal, S.M., 42, 290
Ross, J.A., 258, 290
Rosselot, L., 290
Rothkopf, E.Z., 72, 290
Roy, P., 290
Rulon, P.J., 46, 290
Ryan, K., 279

Saettler, P., 63, 290
Salcedo, Father J.J., 244-245
Salomon, G., 39, 42-43, 86-87, 94, 273, 290
Samuels, S.J., 38, 290
Scanland, F.W., 290
Schalock, H.D., 75, 290
Schardt, A., 290
Schiefele, H., 290
Schramm, W., 26-27, 34, 41, 42, 133, 135, 141, 143, 211, 238-239, 258, 259, 281, 283, 290-291
Schuller, C., 90, 294
Schultz, P., 256, 291
Schurdak, J.J., 49, 291
Scuphan, J., 288
Searle, B., 291
Selfridge, L.D., 48, 284
Shea, A., 289
Sheffield, F.D., 42, 46, 54, 285
Sieber, J., 39, 290

Sim, R., 289
Simmins, G., 289
Simmons, A.B., 291
Sjogren, D.D., 291
Skaperdas, D., 123, 280
Skinner, B.F., 65, 66, 67, 72, 291
Slattery, Sister M.J., 291
Smith, D.D., 291
Smith, K.U., 24, 291
Smith, M.F., 24, 291
Snow, R.E., 39, 42, 43, 282, 286
Soomboonsuk, A., 283
Spain, P., 219-220, 236, 291
Speagle, R.E., 105, 123, 291
Spector, P., 56, 291
Spencer, R.E., 56, 291
Stein, S.C., 52, 291
Stickell, D.W., 27, 44, 291
Stolurow, L.M., 65, 291, 294
Stoney, George, 229-230
Stycos, J.M., 259, 291
Sulzer, R.L., 41, 287
Suppes, P., 30-32, 47, 285, 291, 292

Taba, H., 292
Takeshita, J.Y., 258, 283, 292
Tannenbaum, P.H., 55, 292
Tanner, G.L., 49, 58, 292
Taveggia, T.C., 282
Tendam, D.J., 292
Theroux, P., 228, 292
Thorndike, E.L., 65, 66, 175-176, 292
Tickton, S.G., 105, 125, 142, 292
Tiffin, J., 84, 88, 292
Timmers, A.G.W., 292
Toffel, G.M., 292
Tolman, E.C., 65, 292
Torfs, J., 292
Torres, A., 56, 291
Travers, R.M.W., 33, 292
Tsuji, I., 182-184, 292
Twyford, L.C., Jr., 52, 125, 292

Tymowsky, J., 213, 222, 292

Underwood, B.J., 66, 293

VanderMeer, A.W., 41, 46, 56, 292
van Ginneken, J., 290
Van Ormer, E.B., 42, 285
Vernon, P.E., 53, 293
Vestal, D.A., 41, 293
Von Mondfrans, A.P., 292
von Rundstedt, M., 292

Wade, S., 128, 177-180, 293
Wagner, G., 214, 293
Wagner, R.V., 293
Waisanen, E., 290
Warren, C.J., 125, 281
Weiss, E.M., 289
Wells, R.F., 54, 293
Wendt, P.R., 47, 293
Wermer, F.E., 129, 210, 293
Westley, B.H., 38, 54, 58, 293
Whitted, J.H., Jr., 56, 293
Wilder, F., 258, 285, 294
Will, W.H., 62-65, 280
Williams, D.C., 54, 294
Williams, M.L., 57, 282
Wilson, H., 279
Wise, H.A., 46, 58, 294
Wittich, W.A., 46, 90, 294
Wood, A.W., 232-233, 294
Woodworth, R.S., 294
Wrightstone, J.W., 294
Wulff, J.J., 42, 286

Xoomsai, T., 51, 187-188, 294

Young, J.P., 294
Yu, F.T.C., 259, 290

Ziebarth, E.W., 51, 284
Zigerell, J.J., 282

ABOUT THE AUTHOR

WILBUR SCHRAMM has for more than three decades been one of the prime creators and integrators of the emerging field of mass communications. He is presently Professor Emeritus of Communication at Stanford University and Director Emeritus of the East-West Communication Institute (of the East-West Center, Honolulu). He is the author and editor of numerous standard works in the field such as *Mass Communications* (1960, University of Illinois Press), *Men, Messages, and Media: A Look at Human Communication* (1973, Harper & Row), *Mass Media and National Development* (1964, Stanford University Press), *Quality in Instructional Television* (1973, University of Hawaii Press), *The Science of Human Communication* (1963, Basic Books), *Responsibility in Mass Communication* (with William L. Rivers; 1969, Harper & Row), *Process and Effects of Mass Communications* (with Donald F. Roberts; revised edition, 1971, University of Illinois Press), and *Television in the Lives of Our Children* (1971, Stanford University Press). His other books and articles in the field are too numerous to catalogue here.

Schramm received his B.A. from Marietta College, his M.A. from Harvard, and his Ph.D. from the State University of Iowa, where he taught English and journalism and was founder of the creative writing program in the 1930s. He then taught at the University of Illinois at Champaign-Urbana, where he founded the doctoral program in communication, was founding head of the Institute for Communication Research, and was for a time head of the University of Illinois Press. In the mid- to late 1950s, he went to Stanford University and was there founder of the Institute for Communication Research at that school. Retired from Stanford, he became Director of the East-West Communication Institute. He has been a newspaper reporter and writer (winner of the O'Henry Prize for Fiction for a short story which appeared in the *Saturday Evening Post*), and an adviser to a number of foreign governments (largely Asian and other Third World) on the role of the mass media in building educational systems and national economies.

NOTES

NOTES

NOTES

NOTES